W9-BMY-631

How can we welcome twice as many people on Earth without jeopardizing the natural resource base for later generations? This is the key question the coming century poses. The present book attempts to provide an answer. As is well known, the affluent 20 per cent among the world's population consume 80 per cent of the planet's resources. If the affluent have any intention of becoming good global neighbours, they will have to set out to build economies that retreat from overconsumption and weigh much less heavily on both the planet and its population.

This book presents a path-breaking analysis as well as highly innovative proposals for the transition of Northern countries to sustainability. Emanating from Europe's foremost environmental policy think-tank, the Wuppertal Institute, it has already stirred up a major debate on radical, but feasible, directions in which industrial societies ought to be moving. The concept of environmental space, measuring a country's global environmental impact, is combined with an emphasis on both eco-efficiency – how to do things right – and sufficiency – how to do the right things – to give this book its intellectual power and potential political impact.

As the USA, Britain and other industrial countries, North and South, are forced to grapple with the realities of environmental limits, here is a book no policy-maker, socially curious intellectual, environmental activist or concerned citizen can ignore. The mixture of pioneering policy proposals and attention to new life-styles based on moderation and mindfulness make this an important and exciting book which contributes to the shape of the civilization to come.

About the Authors

Wolfgang Sachs is a senior research fellow at the Wuppertal Institute for Climate, Environment and Energy. He has long been active in the German and Italian Green movements and is currently chairman of Greenpeace in Germany. Amongst the various posts he has held are co-editor of the Society for International Development's journal *Development* in Rome; Visiting Professor of Science, Technology and Society at Pennsylvania State University; and Fellow at the Institute for Cultural Studies in Essen. His first book, *For Love of the Automobile: Looking Back into the History of Our Desires*, was published by University of California Press in 1992. He also edited the immensely influential *Development Dictionary: A Guide to Knowledge as Power*, which was published by Zed Books in 1992 and has since been translated into numerous languages. He travels and lectures widely in Europe, the United States and the South.

Reinhard Loske is Senior Economist in the Climate Policy Division of the Wuppertal Institute for Climate, Environment and Energy and heads the Institute's study group, Sustainable Germany. Trained originally as a banker, he subsequently studied Economics, Public Administration and Political Science at the Universities of Bonn, Nottingham, Paderborn and Kassell. Before joining the Wuppertal Institute, he worked as a government official in the State Ministry for Economics and Technology in Dusseldorf and as a policy advisor to the Green Party in the Federal Parliament in Bonn. Besides his scientific work, Loske has been a co-founder of various environmental and North/South NGOs. His main fields of work are energy policy, sustainable development, international relations and ecological economics

Manfred Linz originally studied Theology, Psychology and the Social Sciences. He then spent his professional career in broadcasting as a researcher and editor, eventually becoming Head of the Department of Social Affairs at the West German Broadcasting Company. He is now also on the staff of the Wuppertal Institute, mainly responsible for North–South relations.

Greening the North

A POST-INDUSTRIAL BLUEPRINT FOR ECOLOGY AND EQUITY

Wolfgang Sachs, Reinhard Loske and Manfred Linz

with

Ralf Behrensmeier, Willy Bierter, Raimund Bleischwitz, Stefanie Böge, Stefan Bringezu, Bernhard Burdick, Manfred Fischedick, Friedrich Hinterberger, Wolfgang Jung, Kora Kristof, and Helmut Schütz

A Study by the Wuppertal Institute for Climate, Environment and Energy

Translated by Timothy Nevill

ZED BOOKS
London & New York

Greening the North: A Post-Industrial Blueprint for Ecology and Equity was first published by Zed Books Ltd, 7 Cynthia Street, London N1 9JF, UK, and Room 400, 175 Fifth Avenue, New York, NY 10010, USA in 1998

Distributed exclusively in the USA by St Martin's Press, Inc., 175 Fifth Avenue, New York, NY 10010, USA

Typeset in Monotype Garamond by Lucy Morton, London SE12
Cover designed by Andrew Corbett
Printed and bound in the United Kingdom
by Redwood Books, Trowbridge, Wiltshire

A catalogue record for this book is available from the British Library

Library of Congress Cataloging-in-Publication Data has been applied for

ISBN 1 85649 507 8 (Hb)
ISBN 1 85649 508 6 (Pb)

Contents

Preface

As the year 2000 approaches, exhortations about the future will come upon us from many quarters. Doomsdayers will point to the panorama of threats facing humanity, neo-liberals will urge the final breakthrough towards a friction-free capitalism, and born-again evangelists will call for mass conversion of sinners to the right path. The chorus at the *fin de siècle* will be made up of many and dissonant voices. And yet they will have to be measured against one key question posed by the coming century. How can we extend hospitality to all the people on the planet, expected to double in numbers, without jeopardizing the natural resource base for subsequent generations? This book has been written as an attempt at an answer. It starts with the awareness that this question must first be directed towards the world's affluent societies. History will certainly judge them in terms of the talent, imagination, and moral strength they are able to muster to confront this question.

For a number of years now activists and researchers, politicians and managers, have pursued such a search under the banner of "sustainability". This study builds upon the insights and the competence acquired during that journey. It sets out to draw a comprehensive picture of what this lofty ideal could mean for Northern countries. Taking one country as its principal example, the book outlines how a sustainable Germany might look over a period of 50 years and indicates the major avenues that need to be taken. However, at a time when "sustainability" has become an all-purpose cement gluing together the most contradictory interests and is pasted to all kinds of business-as-usual strategies, it is necessary right away to flag the major signposts guiding our search for sustainability.

First, ecology cannot be separated from equity, nor equity from ecology. The crisis of nature and the crisis of international justice are interlinked.

This intuition has existed since the days of the Brundtland Commission on "Environment *and* Development", but subsequently has often been forgotten, particularly in Northern countries. It is tempting for the well-to-do to think of the environment in terms of clean rivers, clear air, healthy food, and an adventurous outdoors for their enjoyment. But from a global perspective it is sufficiently obvious that such concerns in fact embellish islands of wealth swimming in a sea of misery. Seen against the backdrop of a divided world, the excessive use of nature and its resources in the North is a principal roadblock to greater justice in the world. In a finite world, the claim by 20% of the world's population to 80% of the world's resources makes marginalization of the majority world inevitable. A retreat of the rich from overconsumption is thus a necessary first step towards allowing space for improvement of the lives of an increasing number of people. If the affluent really want to become good global neighbours, they will have to set out to build economies which weigh much less heavily on the planet and on other nations.

Second, for the affluent countries a transition to sustainability involves reducing the overall throughput of nature by a factor of 10 within the next 50 years. Such a quantitative yardstick is indispensable in order to pin down often woolly talk of sustainability to verifiable objectives. After all, how should we recognize success or failure? There has to be some indicator by which society is able to gauge its environmental state and its performance on the path to sustainability. Conventionally, environmental policy has busied itself with combating pollution in air, water, and soil, plugging emission sources at the "end of the pipe". This study calls for a shift of attention away from the tail-end to the front-end of transformative cycles in the economy. It focuses on the tonnes of energy and materials which are continuously put into the productive process, because it assumes that the vast majority of environmental problems derive in the last analysis from the voracity of the (post-)industrial system, from the volume and the speed with which nature is consumed. As a consequence, sustainability means gradual reduction of the physical scale of the rich economies until they are no longer at odds with either nature or justice in the world.

Third, a civilizational change of this dimension calls for perspectives of both efficiency and sufficiency. Creating a nature-saving society is first of all an invitation to engineers and planners to redesign the way we do things. Technologies and organizations will have to be refashioned to allow us to produce one unit of output with ever less input of natural resources. For decades technological progress has been directed towards making production more labour-efficient; now it is time to make production more eco-efficient. However, efficiency will not be enough. More fuel-efficient cars or paper production with a higher recycling rate will save resources only as long as these efficiency gains are not eaten up by further growth in output. For this reason, this book goes to great lengths in suggesting thresholds of sufficiency for dimensions like speed, economic interdependence, paid work, and consumption. It dips into the history of our desire-boosting nature-intensive life-styles, and traces the attrition these desires have experienced in recent times, giving rise to an inclination towards moderation and mindfulness. While efficiency is about how to do things right, sufficiency is about how to do the right things. Taking this road, environmentalists will have to speak of ethics and aesthetics rather than just resources and economics. Sustainability ultimately springs from a fresh inquiry into the meaning of the good life.

The book grew out of a remarkable joint venture. BUND, the German Friends of the Earth, along with Misereor, the Catholic agency for Third World development, commissioned the Wuppertal Institute for Climate, Environment and Energy to carry out a study outlining how the Federal Republic of Germany must change in order to satisfy the demands of global sustainability. The book therefore focuses on Germany. But by implication, it addresses itself to conditions which are by and large shared by most other developed countries. For the foreign-language editions, the text has been considerably shortened and adapted for international discussion.

In January 1996 the study was published, accompanied by great interest on the part of politicians, NGOs, and the media. The response was beyond our expectations. Since then across Germany there have been almost a thousand public meetings organized by political parties, elected bodies, trade unions, consumer associations, universities, environmental organizations, development action groups, and church congregations. Nearly 40,000 copies of the book-length study have been sold, and around 100,000 copies of a popularized shorter version. A parallel television film has received several awards. In numerous German towns and regions initiatives have sprung up to put some of the study's findings into practice, giving a boost to the local Agenda 21 process. Above all, the book produced a flurry of discussions about the politics of sustainability in Germany, ranging from learned journals to children's drawings. This echo encouraged the authors to present the study to an international audience.

It goes without saying that many minds have worked together to bring a report like this to life. The study is truly a collective product; it draws its strength from the fertile soil of research and debate at the Wuppertal Institute. All fourteen contributors have participated in the design and writing of the study, while Thomas Pössinger, Martina Schmitt, and Beate Schöne have collaborated in its technical implementation. We would like to thank all of them for their assistance and expertise, just as we are grateful for the great input we received from a much larger circle of colleagues in the institute and beyond. Finally, we are indebted to those who initiated the study: to Angelika Zahrnt of BUND and Reinhard Hermle and the late Norbert Herkenrath of Misereor, and to the president of the Wuppertal Institute, Ernst Ulrich von Weizsäcker, who has created a space where creativity and companionship can flourish.

Wolfgang Sachs, Reinhard Loske, Manfred Linz
Wuppertal

1 Introduction

Seldom has there been so much discussion of the future as in today's industrial nations. In an age of globalization businesspeople, trade unionists, and politicians extol future markets and hope for profits, jobs, and worldwide status. Germany – say public spokespersons – should be well prepared in the great competition for world markets: lean, efficient, fast, flexible, modern.

Certainly this debate about the future must be pursued – in Germany and everywhere else in the world. In just the past five to ten years more has changed than in previous decades, and it is realistic to assume that the extent and speed of change are likely to increase rather than diminish for some time to come. That assumption is strengthened by even a fleeting look at the important events and major trends: the fall of the Berlin Wall and the end of a bipolar world, the economic rise of Asia and intensified competition in Europe, the co-existence of globalization and neo-nationalism, and the return of racism, violence, and war. In the years and decades ahead all affluent countries will have to make important choices. How can the further division of society into above and below, rich and poor, be prevented? How must future social security systems be designed for societies where the average age is increasing? What is necessary for achieving a healthy economy, allowing as many people as possible to provide for themselves? What role can and should the state play? How should the world of work be structured? What political changes and institutional adaptations are required?

Answers have to be found to all those questions, but remain deceptive so long as they do not accord with ecological exigencies and the demands of global justice. That is precisely what is lacking today – both in Germany and other industrial states. Debate about the future is one-sided. A restricted concept of economics predominates. Some people even idealize competition as war.[1] Then everything else – the requirements of ecology, welfare, and democracy – is subordinated to this martial logic.

In such a political climate ecology only seems to have a chance if presented in conjunction with technical innovations and promising markets. In fact much of what helps protect nature pays off over the short or long term. Great effort is thus devoted to showing the public how many jobs could be created through protection of the environment, how much money would be saved and available elsewhere, or how a country's competitiveness would benefit if only efficient use of energy and resources were made a top priority. Similar arguments will also be deployed in this study.

Such a strategy involves both opportunities and dangers. It is good if ecological concerns can be combined with powerful economic interests and technological capacity. The dangers arise if certain ecological aims also call for the virtues of prudence, sufficiency, and moderation where technology provides no answer. Preserving diversity of landscapes or animal and plant species does not require rapid innovation. The tension between those viewpoints permeates the whole of this study of "Sustainable Germany". This tension cannot be eliminated; it must be tolerated. There cannot be a conclusive answer to the question of what balance of efficiency and sufficiency, technical innovation and appropriate moderation, would characterize a sustainable Germany. Both elements will be of importance and the thesis here is that they can complement one another.

In the years since the 1992 UN Environment and Development Conference, the issue of a more equitable balance between North and South has vanished to the periphery of public discussion – to an even greater extent than the environmental debate. It is thus not surprising that results in this sphere are very sobering. The Rio conventions on protecting the earth's atmosphere and biological diversity may have come into force, but in both cases signatory states' initial follow-up conferences have achieved little. In the sphere of development and co-operation the industrial states are also far from fulfilling the promises made at Rio. Hardly any country adheres to the commitment to boost development aid to 0.7% of gross national product, originally made at the 1972 UN Stockholm conference on protection of the environment and repeated at Rio. Instead development aid is cut (supposedly because of budgetary deficits) and increasingly transformed into a means of assisting industrial states' own exports.

Low world market prices for raw materials and agricultural products virtually enforce rapacious practices in countries of the South. The poorest countries are still oppressed by an enormous burden of debt, which they are compelled to service by concentration on exports and neglect of national economies. International financial institutions still largely pursue a course that demands of the developing countries orientation towards the world market, deregulation, and policies of social austerity at almost any price. The North increasingly divides the countries of the South into anxiously viewed competitors, promising sales outlets, and apparently hopeless cases.

A good part of the developing countries' problems are certainly self-induced. The industrial states are not responsible for the corruption, nepotism, mismanagement, infringements of human rights, and lack of democracy in many parts of the South. The indifference of some political leaders towards the sufferings of their people cannot be blamed on the USA or Europe. Human rights activists and protectors of the environment in Africa, Asia, and Latin America criticize their political elites' anti-imperialist rhetoric as an attempt at distracting attention from their own failures.[2] However, the convenient conclusion that the existence of all this internal mismanagement eliminates the need for balancing relationships between North and South is wrong and could prove expensive for the world.

Without justice between industrial and developing countries it will not be possible to restrain the global environmental crisis and enter upon sustainable global development. That can be illustrated by way of a simple example. Today the oceans and the terrestrial biomass can absorb around 13 to 14 billion tonnes of carbon dioxide across the world annually. That is the volume which humanity could discharge into the atmosphere through burning wood and other sources of fossil energy if it wished to remain within the natural limits and avoid heating the earth's atmosphere. If this "budget" were equally distributed between the earth's 5.8 billion inhabitants today, each would have the right to discharge somewhat over 2.3 tonnes of carbon dioxide per year. In fact energy-linked CO_2 emissions in the South are sometimes considerably less: in India 0.8 tonnes, in China 2 tonnes, and in Egypt and Brazil 1.5 tonnes. The situation is very different in the North. A US citizen discharges 20 tonnes annually, a German just under 12 tonnes, and a Japanese 9 tonnes

If the entire global population discharged as much CO_2 as the Germans, humanity would need five planets for nature to be able to process these emissions. If complete disruption of the world's climate is to be avoided, North and South must work together. Industrial countries will have to reduce their use of raw materials, energy, and nature significantly by way of social adaptation, changed life-styles, and technological innovation, while developing countries will for a considerable time to come have to call on more resources than at present – but increases in such demands can and must be limited through autonomous forms of development and rapid stabilization of the population.

Figure 1.1 A thousand Germans consume about ten times as much as a thousand Argentinians, Filipinos, or Egyptians (*Source*: Bleischwitz and Schütz, 1993)

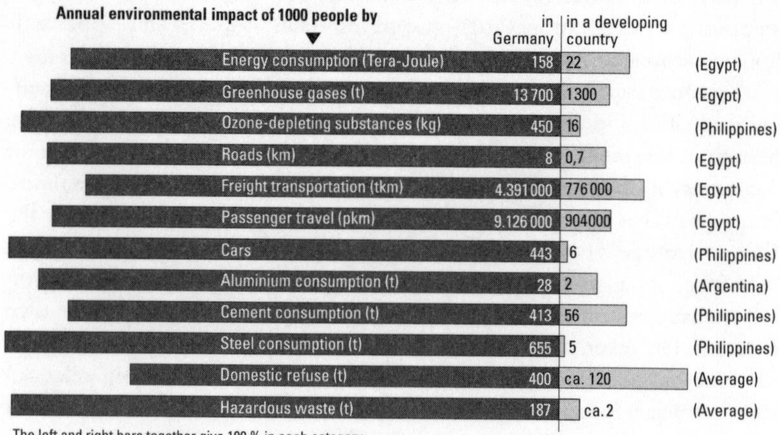

1.1 Why this Study?

First, a great civilizational and cultural challenge is involved in pointing the way towards a sustainable future. Our current affluence is deceptive since it is based on consumption of resources at the expense of ecological stability, global justice, and generations to come. However, giving politics an ecological orientation would offer our pluralist society a unique opportunity for consensus – beyond all ideological differences. In future, firms could earn money by providing elegant and resource-saving products and services rather than by throughput of ever greater amounts of goods. Technicians and engineers would enjoy unprecedented social status if they made "redundant" kilowatt-hours, tonnes of raw materials, and barrels of oil rather than human beings; if they protected resources rather than changing human genes; if they pursued solar power rather than splitting the atom. Consumers would have a clear conscience when buying something whose production, processing, and utilization accorded with ecological demands. Anyone whose legitimate striving for happiness avoided harming other people and nature would receive social acclaim. In brief, this would entail an exciting step forward, requiring active and aware human beings who take on this challenge. The number of such people is on the increase in many parts of society. New alliances are being formed across old divides. If politicians have the courage to bring about an ecological restructuring of the legal and fiscal framework, a historically unparalleled dynamism of innovation could occur.[3]

Second, the industrialized countries are already paying a high price for one-sided orientation towards growth, globalization, and acceleration in their economic and political policies. The price paid ranges from environmental degradation to all kinds of illness, from disorientation to the fragmentation of society, from meaninglessness to increased violence. Social resources are also being eroded together with nature. Researchers have shown that development of the gross national product in all the industrial states surveyed has become decoupled from increases in well-being, particularly since the mid-seventies.[4] For a long period an increasing volume of goods and services went hand in hand with improved quality of life, but beyond a certain material level growth of the same is more of a burden than a gain in quality. More goods then compete with free time, more mobility with social involvement, more gainful employment with family and personal interests, and more emphasis on career and money with leisure and imagination. In a system subject to limits – the day will continue to be restricted to 24 hours and the year to 365 days – one cannot have more and more of everything. All cultures have known that. In Ancient Greece the Delphic Oracle advocated "Nothing to Excess". That, as we know today, was not a call for asceticism, but rather the certain knowledge that happiness will only be found by the person who succeeds in balancing the material and the spiritual.

Today more and more people are weary of the status quo and are once again seeking the right balance. They would be ready to exchange income for greater self-determination, and working-hours for more time for their own needs. However, that can only happen on a large scale if the state, business, and those involved in collective bargaining create real options, ranging from a guaranteed basic income to part-time work, from a sabbatical year to grants for setting up small firms. If such objectives are seriously pursued, it should ultimately be possible to achieve a situation where different interests can be largely harmonized: workers' interest in self-determination and greater freedom in disposing of their time; employers' interest in greater flexibility; and social and ecological interest in a reduction in the grinding pressures towards growth.

Third, ecological policy in the home country makes a practical contribution towards global peace and security at a comparatively low cost and with positive side-effects. Today Germany imports virtually all its oil, three-quarters of its natural gas, and most unprocessed minerals. Such dependence is problematic. It exposes the country to the actions of despots, containing – as the Gulf War showed – the nucleus of military conflict. If the national economy uses energy and raw materials more efficiently, external dependence is reduced. Such a strategy leaves more resources for developing countries striving for progress and leads overall to conservation of stocks of natural capital. It also exerts a positive impact on the German national economy. Imports of energy and raw materials are replaced by engineering expertise, industrial productivity, and consultancy and craft skills when houses are insulated, more efficient cars manufactured, and power stations "pruned". New, more environmentally acceptable jobs can thus be created. However, a compensatory strategy must be sought together with countries in the South that export raw materials, so that the burden of our ecological reconstruction is not dumped on them unilaterally. Efficient use of energy and resources also contributes to peace since global environmental changes could spark off unprecedented migration from South to North as a result of desertification, harvest failures, local wars, famine, or the flooding of islands and coastal areas. The industrial countries are not just morally obliged to reduce the demands they make on the global envionment. Their security is involved too since an island of affluence amid a rising tide of ecological and social problems cannot be defended over the long term.

1.2 An Overview

The study can be roughly divided into five parts: methodological and quantitative aspects of sustainability (chapters 2, 3, and 4), paradigms (chapter 5), ways of transition (chapter 6), and the social context for ecological change (chapter 7). These chapters involve different ways of looking at the situation, based on different disciplines, so a mixed approach was unavoidable. Criticism of such a stylistic procedure is almost inevitable. Perhaps some may not like the sobriety of the empirical section; others may think the paradigms too imprecise. The authors are aware of such stylistic divergences but believe them to be dictated by the nature of the subject.

Chapter 2 first covers conceptual issues within sustainable development. It also presents the idea of "environmental space" which assumes equal rights for everyone in utilization of nature within the limits of its capacity. That concept was introduced into political discussion in "Sustainable Netherlands"[5] and has been further developed by the Wuppertal Institute and others.[6] Indicators are presented to demonstrate the potential impact human activities exert on the environment. Biological diversity and the general issue of risks are mainly treated qualitatively.

Chapter 3 attempts to sketch the sustainable environmental space for a country like Germany. What are the natural limits to economic development if life-opportunities for people in the South are to be improved, and the resources of nature preserved for future generations? Selected indicators are used to determine targets for the years 2010–2050.

In chapter 4 indicators are again employed in an investigation of German consumption of the environment. This raises such questions as: what sectors of the economy and what areas of demand result in specific levels of consumption of resources and toxic emissions? The outcome is an overall picture seen in terms of both production and consumption. The global consequences of our present way of running the economy are also considered. This makes clear that Germany, as a typical industrial country, uses far too much in the way of global environmental goods and resources.

Chapter 5 begins with a transition from stock-taking to a setting of qualitative goals. Restriction of analysis to investigation of quantitative objectives does not lead to any vision of the future. Various scenarios, which in the authors' views are both culturally attractive and ecologically sustainable, are thus presented. These involve appropriate dimensions of space and time, the future of the market and of production and service enterprises, the relationship between being and having, urban and rural perspectives, and neighbourly relations on a global scale with countries of the South.

Chapter 6 asks whether the previously advocated environmental objectives really are attainable and what measures will be required. Attention is focused on what can be achieved over the medium term. The global environmental objectives for energy, raw materials, and CO_2 refer to the year 2050, but this chapter is concerned with the interim stages of 2010 and 2020. However, it must be clearly stated that integrated scenarios, taking into account all recognizable environmental factors and their interaction, do not as yet exist. A considerable amount of research is still necessary.

Chapter 7 concludes the study and to some extent pre-empts anticipated objections. In discussions during preparation of this study, three arguments against the approach presented here were encountered particularly often. Our objective was said to be unviable because jobs would be lost with a decline in the volume of goods produced, ultimately endangering social security; because in our form of democracy no politician could demand retrenchment from the electorate without being rejected; and because the countries of the South are expressly interested in ongoing economic growth in industrial states as markets for raw materials and finished products.

Discussion of synchronizing ecological, political (in terms of securing liberties), social, and economic objectives must now be resolutely pursued so as to implement decisions opening up a way towards the future. Come what may, the twenty-first century will be the century of the environment – either the century of ecological catastrophes or the century of ecological transformation.

Notes

1. D'Aveni, 1994.
2. Soyinka, 1991.
3. See also Weizsäcker et al., 1997.
4. Cobb and Cobb, 1994.
5. Friends of the Earth Netherlands, 1993.
6. Friends of the Earth Europe, 1995.

2 Guidelines

2.1 Sustainable Development

Industrial production across the world seems hell-bent on relentless growth. The great majority of countries and people strive to attain Western levels of material affluence by industrializing their economies following the Western model. That model's unbroken dominance entails a danger that globalization of current patterns of production and consumption will lead to severe disruptions of ecological systems. The West's old dream has come to an end. Running economies at the expense of nature harms affluence in the West and the lives of future generations, and makes it more difficult for the countries of the South to become part of the world economy.

Initial reports and forecasts on the state of the environment in the seventies drew public attention to the finite nature of raw materials, particularly fossil fuels. The situation has changed since then. By now it is ecological systems' restricted capacity to absorb pollutants and waste of all kinds – rather than shortage of resources – that threatens to dictate limits to the economy. Confronted by global warming and other environmental problems, there can be little doubt that economies are still on collision course with the natural environment. Despite all environmental endeavours, production and consumption increasingly reduce nature to serving as a supplier of industry and recipient of industrial waste. That is the bitter situation after some twenty years of environmental politics.

Since the end of the eighties – and certainly since the 1992 Rio de Janeiro Earth Summit – a new understanding of the common good has gradually emerged internationally. "Sustainable development"[1] is the term used for development which satisfies today's needs without endangering those of future generations. This basic principle also entails recognition that environmental problems cannot be considered in isolation from economic and social development. A holistic approach is necessary since the environment and development are inextricably linked. The old developmental maxim about first achieving economic affluence and then repairing the social and ecological damage has become untenable. The new thinking demands integration of ecological, social, and economic interests.

The concept of sustainability can, to some extent, be expressed objectively by way of a system of indicators. Nevertheless it is essentially a normative concept rooted in three value judgements. First, it postulates the right of people alive in the future to the resources of our earth, making inter-generational equity a guiding principle for political action. This ruling may be intuitively reasonable but it is not compelling for everyone. So why should future generations be accorded the same claims to the earth's resources as the people of today? Of the arguments which can be put forward in favour of international equity,[2] the principle of reciprocity between generations is the most important. Awareness that a generation should not use up what it inherited – as the principle of reciprocity demands – is also accompanied by enlightened self-interest, making this rule seem plausible when thinking of one's own children and grandchildren. Advocating equality of life-opportunities for future generations is at any rate an ethical decision.

Second, another question can be derived from the sustainability debate: What environment do human beings want? Two arguments, both influenced by economics, are put forward in this discussion. The first assumes the substitutability of nature and can be called "weak sustainability". Adherents of that position argue that future generations will receive what amounts to an "affluence package", consisting of a constant or increasing sum of material and natural capital.[3] If the natural foundations of life are harmed – "diminishing natural capital" in economic jargon – sustainability would be achieved through increased production of material assets. According to this way of seeing things, even irreversible damage such as the destruction of primal forests or rare species of animals would be sustainable so long as the capital thus produced created corresponding affluence. In the extreme case a science fiction world without nature would come into being where climate, the water cycle, and important raw materials were produced artificially. This view of economic resources is narrow and cannot be maintained. By now an increasing number of economists recognize that there are only very limited possibilities of replacing nature's contributions to well-being by material capital, so that at least irreversible damage to the environment must be avoided. Adherents of this second position talk of "constant natural capital" for future generations. Consensus has largely been achieved here.[4] Just as each generation has been entrusted with the earth and its natural resources, so too is it obliged to leave future generations nature in a viable state, no matter how great the manufactured components of affluence. That is the second non-negotiable value judgement.

Third, the concept of sustainability contains another necessary dimension alongside the ecological one: the dimension of international justice. Laying claim to equal rights to unimpaired nature should not be restricted to future generations. Global equality of opportunity should also be viewed as crucial for each generation. Every human being has the same right to an intact environment. Also everyone has an equivalent right to globally accessible resources so long as the environment is not over-exploited. Alongside equality of rights for future generations and the obligation to hand down nature in an unimpaired state, this is the third value judgement within the concept of "sustainability". The dimension of international equity lays the foundation for achieving a balance of interests with the countries of the South.

2.2 The Concept of Environmental Space: Ecology and Equity

From pollution control to reduction of inputs

Environmental policy to date has primarily involved control of pollutants. There have been successes in reducing emissions of such substances as sulphur dioxide, carbohydrates, and volatile organic compounds (VOCs), and in maintaining others at almost constant levels. However, since the start of the nineties awareness is spreading that pollutant controls are by no means ecologically sufficient and also result in mounting costs. It may even be possible to conceive of a pollutant-free economy, but such environmental problems as urban sprawl, depletion of the landscape and raw materials, loss of biological diversity, soil erosion, water shortages, and mountains of refuse will persist. Global warming can hardly be regarded as a pollution problem since CO_2, the most important greenhouse gas, does not cause any direct damage but instead brings about an increase in the temperature of the earth's atmosphere when concentrated there in sufficient quantities. Alongside the specific impact of individual pollutants, the amounts of energy used and the materials moved around constitute the crucial problems within environmental policy.[5]

Every product and every service is linked with energy and material throughput from the start to the finish of its life-cycle. This involves interventions in nature, damaging biological diversity and leading to emissions, effluents, dissipative losses, and refuse. Even their beginnings involve mountainous slag heaps, the pumping of ground-water, kilometres of tunnels, and tonnes of churned-up earth. Such amounts, which are usually not put to economic use, can be characterized as "forgotten megatonnes" or additional ecological impact (known as "ecological rucksacks").[6] Reducing them would make an outstanding contribution to the protection of nature. It is also often forgotten that right at the start of a product's life great amounts of such soil-bound pollutants as sulphur are released. Throughput of energy and materials must therefore be reduced. Where that takes place, further reductions in various waste-products follow.

If preservation of the natural bases of life is a necessary precondition for a country's sustainability, there exists a natural framework for taking action. In what follows this is termed the "environmental space".[7] The basic concept was developed by Hans Opschoor from the Netherlands. Environmental space refers to the area that human beings can use in the natural environment without doing lasting harm to essential characteristics. This environmental space is a function of the carrying capacity of eco-systems, the recuperative efficiency of natural resources, and the availability of raw materials. The concept thus expressly recognizes physical "new limits to growth" (Meadows et al.), resulting from the carrying capacity of eco-systems and the finiteness of natural resources. That is the immediately obvious strength of the term "environmental space". Environmental space can, however, also be expanded when, say, polluted eco-systems are regenerated, biomass is increased through reforestation, landscapes are recultivated, or desertification is reversed.

The concept of environmental space acknowledges the diversity of possible human uses of the natural world. The functions served by nature include supplying raw materials, dealing with waste, regulation of geochemical and biological cycles, and not least the integrity and beauty of a landscape or individual species. Forests can serve as an example. For centuries they were mainly seen as sources of wood. Forestry gradually established itself as a commercial venture. By now the ecological management of forests includes recognition of their importance for climate, regional water supplies, as environment for animals, and for human recreation. The concept of environmental space essentially entails the ecological use of nature.

In this study a key factor in environmental space is that throughputs of energy and materials must be considerably reduced.

The ecological criteria for utilization of environmental space can be summarized in the following often-quoted guidelines:[8]

1. Utilization of a renewable resource should not be greater than its regeneration rate.

2. Discharge of materials should not be greater than the environment's capacity to absorb them.
3. Utilization of non-renewable resources should be kept to a minimum. Use should be dependent on creation of a physically and functionally equivalent renewable substitute.
4. The time-factor in human intervention should be in balance with that of natural processes: the decomposition of waste or the regeneration rates of renewable raw materials and eco-systems.

The demand that throughput of energy and materials must be reduced over-simplifies guideline 3, suggesting that only non-renewable resources need be replaced.

Guidelines for Use of Resources

Regeneration guidelines

- No more of a renewable resource should be utilized than can regenerate in the same period.
- Only that amount of materials should be released into the environment as can be absorbed there.

Throughput guidelines

- Throughputs of energy and materials must be reduced to a low-risk level.

In attempting to formulate objectives for environmental policy the question arises: What risks should be regarded as still acceptable, and which should no longer be tolerated? Answers always involve a broad range of pollution affecting both human beings and the environment,[9] indicating that harm is certain above a specific level and can be largely excluded below a lower level.

The above formulation, laying down a target for throughput, is based on the low-risk level as threshold value. There are three good reasons for minimizing risks.[10] The first is of a general nature. The precautionary principle is irreconcilable with high risks for generations to come. The second reason is clearly directed towards protection of the weak. Such social groups as children, old people, or the physically handicapped are more dependent on effective protection than others. In nature the vulnerability of eco-systems varies. For instance the impact of soil acidification fluctuates, depending on the land involved. Poor grass and low marshland can tolerate more toxics than heathland, rainwater ponds, and high marshland. Here too it should be possible to protect the more vulnerable areas.

The third reason for minimizing risk is of a political character. Many economists expect natural scientists to provide highly precise statements on limits and standards, enabling optimal allocation of costs. Advocates of that viewpoint believe that production-processes and even national economies can be driven right up to the limits of the optimum. Individual countries could thus ascertain what for them is "optimal warming". That will of course diverge greatly from country to country – being much lower for, say, Bangladesh than for Canada. With the egoism of nation-states expressed in a policy of optimal pollution, there will be a clear-cut increase in potential for international conflict. Minimizing risks entails reaching agreement on objectives involving few ecological or international risks and striving for a dynamism that almost inevitably leads to further reductions.

Justice as a guideline for international environmental policy

This study attempts to advocate the demand for justice without transforming it into a call for "development". That involves taking a long overdue step in North–South discussions: decoupling the idea of justice from that of development. Particularly after the second world war the hope was that international (and national) inequality could be surmounted through massive participation of the poor in economic growth. Prevalent thought viewed claims to justice as being met by acceleration of economic development. That hope came to grief when it encountered biophysical limits. In a finite biosphere the search for justice involves restriction of traditional development among the rich rather than greater economic growth for the poor. In other words, after the end of the age of development, the prime commandment for the North is to take less rather than giving more.

This book is based on the assumption that long-established structural power, leading to a drastically unequal distribution of world resources, is the prime cause of the South being deprived of justice. In this situation the venerable Aristotelian distinction between distributive and compensatory justice all of a sudden becomes topical. This does not primarily involve the redistribution of accumulated resources but rather organization of one's own behaviour so that no-one else is systematically deprived of their rightful due. The environmental space available for a society's use is thus calculated on the basis of both the ecological limits and other societies' claims to utilization. The present generation must be able to raise the same claim to intact nature as future generations. Yet it would be mistaken to want to make such a postulate into a planning guideline for planetary redistribution. Instead it is a concept for regulating one's own behaviour. In a free adaptation of Kant's categorical imperative, a society can only be called sustainable when the maxims underlying its behaviour could in principle also serve all others. For that reason in this study the postulate of equal rights of utilization for all the world's inhabitants has been integrated in the definition of targets for reduction of consumption of energy and raw materials.

As early as 1991 the South Centre demanded sufficient environmental space for the South.[11] The rule of thumb that 20% of the world's population consumes 80% of global resources is largely valid. Relaxation of international tension would be much helped by acceptance of the principle that every human being has the same right to an intact environment, and this applies equally to future generations. However, this right to equality of utilization in no way implies a collective imperative calling for constant exploitation of the environment to the limits. What is required is implementation of the principle at a level entailing the least possible risk to the environment.

People may object that real differences have not been taken into account here. For example, higher energy consumption for domestic heating is necessary in certain latitudes. That argument is not completely convincing. It is not the heating of homes that accounts for high energy consumption in states like California. Other large countries like India, Nigeria, or Brazil could argue similarly that an extensive national market makes greater demands on transportation. Ultimately rights per head are the most comprehensible and simplest criteria in the real world.[12] Certainly that increases the degree to which the industrial states must reduce utilization of environmental space. They must cut back their polluting activities to a greater extent than the global average. In the 1992 Rio declaration on environment and development they recognized that principle as a shared but different responsibility. Preservation of what one has is a bad argument in any dialogue with the countries of the South. In addition the South has sometimes demanded that the North's long history of emissions should be taken into account too. That is plausible in view of the fact that many pollutants stay in the atmosphere for decades. Above all, however, it makes clear that the industrial countries should not feel one-sidedly disadvantaged by per capita rights.

Alongside equal rights of utilization for global environmental goods this study also proposes similar rights for a number of traded primary raw materials, treated as a single unit in the final balance. That takes into account the fact that conditions vary greatly in different regions. Diversity of endowment with natural resources must be taken into account alongside differing climatic conditions. It would thus be ecologically, economically, and culturally inappropriate to specify equal rights across the world for individual raw materials.[13] The environmental space for raw materials is differently composed from region to region. Thus no identical "basket" of raw materials can be identified across the world. Instead a sustainable overall throughput has been devised for environmental space.

2.3 Environmental Indicators: Measuring Environmental Space

The introduction and discussion of the concept of environmental space have made the idea of sustainability more tangible in essential respects. Preservation of the natural foundations of life and equitable distribution of limited possibilities of utilization are the main preconditions for globally sustainable development. A first step towards formalization of those principles was taken by developing guidelines for utilization of resources and formulation of the precept of equal rights to jointly shared goods. In this section a set of quantifiable physical magnitudes will be introduced as the basis in what follows for appraisable objectives. In line with current scientific discussions we term these magnitudes environmental indicators.

Why indicators?

The necessity of establishing indicators is laid down in Agenda 21. The text of that agreement favours the most comprehensive starting-point possible:

> Commonly used indicators such as the gross national product (GNP) and measurements of individual resource or pollution flows do not provide adequate indications of sustainability.... Indicators of sustainable development need to be created to provide solid bases for decision-making at all levels and to contribute to a self-regulating sustainability of integrated environmental and developmental systems.[14]

The United Nations Commission on Sustainable Development (UNCSD), established after the Rio conference to push forward implementation of Agenda 21, recently developed proposals for indicator systems but these are still far from being as consistent and manageable as is necessary.[15] Considerable methodological problems must still be overcome in order to summarize ecological, social, economic, and institutional aspects within just a few significant magnitudes.[16] The following reflections are thus restricted to the realm of environmental indicators, which can later be integrated in a comprehensive system embracing sustainable development.

Generally speaking, an indicator is a measurement providing information about a specific phenomenon. Indicators to some extent fulfil a need that Lichtenberg summed up as "reduction", intended – unlike

Body Temperature – Indicator of the State of Health

A vivid example is provided by body temperature, which can yield information about the state of the human organism. With above-normal temperatures the assumption must be that the body is reacting to an infection or something similar. The fever-level also indicates how critical the patient's state is. That is measured by way of a thermometer which supplies (a) a measurement of body temperature and (b) approximate but sure information about the person's state of health through comparison with a scale (roughly 37 to 41°C) derived from experience. This indicator is easily manageable, but the value of the information gained somewhat limited. Only rarely is a thermometer sufficient as an indicator, so it must be combined with other more costly diagnostic methods.

"magnification" – to make increased information possible through summarization. Indicators thereby possess both analytical and synoptic value. They summarize information in order to facilitate a specific evaluation (see box).

Of special importance is the fact that value judgements have to be made alongside the selection of indicators – and not only when limits or environmental objectives have already been formulated using these indicators. The selection of magnitudes for describing the humanity–environment relationship is never solely based on nature. Martin Jänicke says that "patterns of interpretation in reporting on the environment are always subject to socio-political conditions". Even projected measurements of sustainable development are subject to such conditions and should be based on generalizable insights and circumstances "if they rightly lay claim to general recognition".[17] That insight will be taken into account in what follows.

What indicators?

The OECD Pressure–State–Response Model has become established on the international level as a framework for developing environmental indicators.[18] This model distinguishes between three levels of indicator-formation:

- Indicators of environmental pressure as criterion of the potential impact of human activities on the environment (including use of resources, discharge of waste/emissions);
- Indicators of environmental state as criterion of environmental quality (e.g. the CO_2 content of the atmosphere);

- Response indicators describing social reactions to changes in the state of the environment (e.g. reduction of energy consumption per unit of gross national product).

Construction of this model follows the classic human behaviour pattern of "see–assess–act", initially suggesting the existence of simple linear dependences along the lines of "pressure causes change of state causes reaction". Nevertheless such simple causal chains seldom occur in practice. In addition this model's basic structure entails the danger of favouring one-sided strategies for combating symptoms instead of equally promoting preventive measures.

The 1993 indicator system[19] advocated by the OECD puts the emphasis on pragmatic and political demands such as "rapid availability of data in all OECD states" – at the expense of easy comprehensibility and ease of selection of indicators. In addition this model only allows to a limited extent the deduction of objectives serving the guideline of sustainable development.

Probably the most far-reaching proposal to date is the "eco-capacity"[20] method devised by the Netherlands Council for Environmental Research.[21] Utilization criteria (following the rules formulated in section 2.1) were defined there for selected non-renewable resources, the totality of renewable resources (in the form of total biomass), and selected inputs into the environment. This procedure can also be criticized, like the OECD model, for lack of easy comprehensibility and deficiencies in manageability of selection criteria. In addition consumption of non-renewable resources is limited to the criterion of "exhaustibility", which, as already mentioned, is scientifically too restricted.

In developing an environmental indicator system a balance must be achieved between competing demands. The greater the number of indicators, the more accurate the description of reality, but the clarity and manageability of the overall system are less. If, for instance, one wants to compare products – say re-usable bottles with single-use cartons – by constructing life-cycle eco-balances, accuracy would demand a set of between 200 and 300 individual indicators. Apart from the money, personnel, and time involved, such a system is unusable by politicians and the public. For clarity's sake it will be necessary to express a broad-based summing up in an easily comprehensible number of indicators. Moving on from that dilemma, what follows contains a proposal for a practicable, prevention-oriented, and readily understandable system of environmental impact indicators. This is to be viewed as a complement – rather than an alternative – to a set of delicate, eco-systemic indicators at the level of state of the environment. The success of measures for reducing pollution (positive changes in indicators) must thus be checked by way of parameters of environmental quality. New findings in environmental research may also suggest changes in pollution indicators.

A preventive system of environmental indicators

Even though bottlenecks are to be expected in supplies of a number of important raw materials as early as the beginning of the next century, known economically exploitable reserves of many non-renewable resources are still mounting. This increase can make good or even more than compensate for rates of utilization for some time.[22] Even though humanity should already base economic activities on the prospect of future shortages of raw materials, for today's development the limiting factor is not such shortfalls but the capacity of air, water, and soil to absorb emissions from human sources.

What does that signify for measuring potential environmental impact?

In theory account must be taken of all emission rates that overburden eco-systems' buffer-capacity or directly endanger human health. Development of a system of pollution indicators involves two problems, one methodological and one practical.

The methodological problem entails the fact that the current state of knowledge is insufficient for evaluation of the environmental relevance of many of the substances we discharge today. Reliable assessment of the impact of all that is released into the environment also seems unlikely for the foreseeable future. The incalculable leaps are too great, the interactions and feedback mechanisms too complex. Not even the precise chemical composition of some substances is known. An indicator system fixated on emissions thus entails a danger of constantly lagging behind problems, describing phenomena rather than the underlying causes.[23]

By now even the list of known toxic emissions, affecting both environment and human beings, is so enormous as to be scarcely surveyable. An indicator system which incorporated that list would be too long in terms of political manageability and public comprehensibility.

The consequences are as follows:

1. The state of scientific knowledge about man-made emissions' impact on health and environment must be extended. Individual substances with comparable forms of impact should be incorporated in the broadest possible categories (such as an index of heavy metals or toxicity) so as to make dealings with them more manageable, but also in order to delineate the connections between emissions and pollution to make assignment of responsibility possible.

Figure 2.1 Complementary strategies for reducing environmental impact
Controlling pollutants for protection against known dangers and minimization of resource-use as a precautionary strategy for avoiding risks (*Source*: Wuppertal Institut)

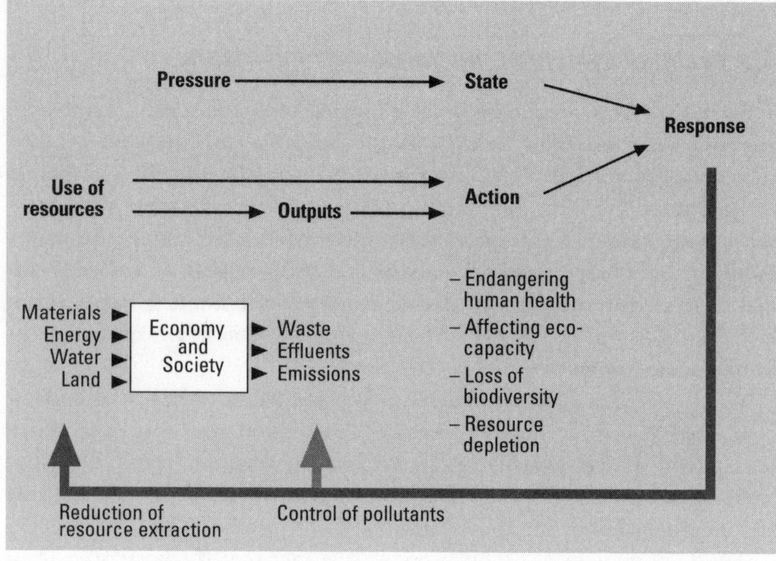

2. However, it will not be possible to solve the "complexity dilemma" even if efforts are intensified and limited to new emissions. Precautionary determination of indicators will involve orientation towards the "source" of environmental pollution, towards the withdrawal of resources from the environment (figure 2.1). This step derives directly from the guidelines underlying the environmental space concept formulated in the previous section. That entails striving for a reduction of material and energy throughputs during products' entire life-cycle, starting with taking resources out of the environment. In the categories of the Pressure (or Driving Force)–State–Response Model, that can be expressed as follows: specific emissions exert acute pressure on the environment and must be reduced.

We suggest a system of indicators of environmental impact reflecting the complementary strategies shown in figure 2.1. This consists, on the one hand, of indicators for emissions affecting health and the environment, presented so far as possible in a summarized form. On the other hand, the precautionary principle demands emphasis on use of resources, expressed in high-aggregate magnitudes for consumption of materials,

Table 2.1 A preventive system of environmental impact indicators

Resource withdrawal	Selected substance emissions	Impact index
Materials • Materials withdrawn (million t/year) • Proportion of renewable raw materials (%)	CO_2 SO_2	GWP[1] ODP[2]
Energy • Primary energy consumption (PJ/year) • Proportion of renewable energy (%)	NO_x NH_3	Acidification potential Eutrophication potential
Water • Water withdrawal (billion m^3/year) • Proportion of ground-water withdrawal (%)	VOC[3] Erosion	Toxicity index[4]
Land • Growth/reduction of use for settlement and transportation (%/year) • Growth/reduction of number of unfragmented areas of critical size (%/year)	Synthetic fertilizers Pesticides	

1 GWP: Global Warming Potential
2 ODP: Ozone Depletion Potential
3 VOC: Volatile Organic Compounds
4 Development is currently subject of research efforts

energy, water, and land. There is little point in playing off these generalized magnitudes against detailed information about individual substances or special risks. The particular gains importance by way of the general. A politically usable picture of long-term problems can only be formed against the background of overall balances.[24] A battle of ideas between "ideologists of quantity" and "toxicity-hunters" is thus more than unnecessary.

The proposed magnitudes do not initially apply to a particular sphere. Specific application can range from a firm, a community, to the national level. In section 4.1 this specification will be applied to a "national environmental balance-sheet".

We suggest the following individual magnitudes (see table 2.1), starting with the various categories of resource input:

Material input: Material input comprises all assets (except water and air) taken from nature during the relevant year. That entails all assets actively moved by human beings (i.e. employing technical means). Material input involves both assets subjected to ongoing processing (raw materials) and assets only employed for the extracting of raw materials and then returned to nature as waste (e.g. overburden in mining). The second category constitutes the former's "ecological rucksack". This way of looking at things, including the "forgotten tonnes",[25] constitutes a further development in stock-taking of resource consumption, and is now also taken into account in the German Statistics Office's overall environmental audit.[26]

It follows from the guidelines on resource utilization formulated in section 2.2 that a sustainable economy should be characterized by (among other things) a growing proportion of renewable resources. That is why no distinction is made between non-renewable (abiotic) and renewable (biotic) raw materials and the proportion of renewable raw materials in overall input is expressed as a sub-indicator.

Primary energy consumption:[27] This states the energy content of the total energy-sources in the reference year. Viewed historically, the discovery and utilization of fossil fuels (first coal and then oil and natural gas) were the starting-point and ongoing precondition for material-intensive economic development in industrial societies. Some toxic emissions (CO_2, NO_x, SO_2, and VOCs [volatile organic compounds] to diminishing degrees[28]) are more or less coupled with use of energy. For those reasons it seems necessary to state primary energy consumption as an indicator and the share of renewable energies as a sub-indicator.

Water use: The extraction and throughput of water is by far the greatest man-made mass flow, amounting in Germany in 1991 to over 90% of all moved assets. Because of this dominance and the particular ecological significance of this cycle, water, as an "elementary good", is stated separately here. A distinction is made between use of rapidly replaced surface water and of ground-water, which is only very slowly renewed – regeneration of ground-water can take up to 10,000 years – and is of great importance for assuring future supplies. The proportion of ground-water extraction is thus stated as a sub-indicator.

Land use: The character and intensity of land and soil use were long underestimated as a factor affecting the environment. That is why both the development of indicators and methods for collecting and processing land-related data are still at an early stage and the object of current research.[29] Unlike the flow-magnitudes of energy, materials, and water, land is a fixed quantity and basically cannot be "extracted" or "consumed". Nevertheless the image of consumption does apply if one form of land use excludes others.

Sealing off the soil by buildings or transportation infrastructure is one form of such utilization. It is highly revealing that other species cannot live on asphalted or built-over areas, and rain-water cannot seep through and replenish local ground-water reserves. Sealing off the soil thus massively impairs maintenance of important functions in the soil ecosystem. The proportion of areas of settlement and transportation infrastructure within the total surface area can be used as a rough measure of the overall degree of building and the associated impact.

A structural criterion should be developed alongside quantitative measurement for more accurate description of the ecological significance of human use of land. For instance, biological diversity is threatened by patterns of distribution as well as by the purely quantitative spread of settlement and the transport network. Sprawling settlement of a landscape always also entails fragmentation of nature since areas of habitation are linked by transportation infrastructure. These links constitute unpassable barriers for many species of animals and plants, and for others the remaining habitats can be too small to provide a minimum basis for existence. Along the peripheries the noise and toxic emissions accompanying the flow of traffic constitute an additional impact. The proportion of untouched areas of a certain size could thus be viewed as a criterion of this form of dismemberment.

Utilization of land for agriculture and forestry must be evaluated differently. Here the most important ecological factor is the quality or intensity of utilization rather than the extent. Environmental problems in agriculture are mainly caused by increasing use of chemicals and mechanization rather than the amount of land used. Intensity of utilization can be described in terms of quantities of fertilizers and pesticides and levels of erosion. However, since these magnitudes also involve pollutants, they are assigned to indicators of "selected emissions" in table 2.1.

Selected emissions: Selection of further emissions is based on the "list" of today's most important known environmental problems as presented by the OECD and EUROSTAT.

There exist two internationally recognized examples of aggregating emissions of individual substances as impact-indices: Global Warming Potential (GWP) is presented as the weighted sum of the most important trace-gas emissions (CO_2 + CH_4 + several CFCs + N_2O),[30] and Ozone Depletion Potential (ODP) as the sum of the substances involved (several

CFCs + N_2O + several halons…). Comparable proposals exist for acidification potential (SO_2 + NO_x + NH_3), eutrophication potential relating to airborne emissions (NO_x + NH_3),[31] a heavy-metal index, and even a general toxicity index.[32]

Can the selected set of indicators describe today's environmental problems?

Today's knowledge of the most important environmental issues[33] and their main physical causes is briefly presented in what follows – in terms of the already mentioned indicators. Also examined is the degree to which these selected magnitudes can demarcate today's observable problems.

The global warming caused by human activity occurs through emission of trace-gases (CO_2, CH_4, various CFCs, N_2O) and of similar gases exerting an indirect impact on the climate (such as NH_3). The proportion of CO_2 is globally estimated at around 50%. The "driving-force" behind CO_2 emissions is use of fossil fuels.

Around 80% of depletion of the ozone layer is due to emissions of CFCs, and to a limited extent to halons and N_2O.

Soil degradation: Over 80% of degradation (in terms of the global average) consists of loss of soil through erosion by water and wind, increasingly putting food supplies at risk. There are many man-made causes of erosion: deforestation, use of virgin land for farming, monocultures, intensive use, etc. Erosion in turn affects the environment (see below on eutrophication).

Acidification of soil and water: This is directly caused by emissions (SO_2, NO_x), and indirectly by acid-forming substances.

Eutrophication of surface waters and coastal areas: This is brought about by introduction of nutrients from industrial and private effluents (mainly nitrates and phosphates), by leaching of nutrients (nitrates – partly because of excessive use of inorganic fertilizers) and erosion of fields (phosphates), and through airborne nitrogen compounds (NO_x, NH_3).

Loss of biological diversity: This is mainly linked with homogenization of habitats (cultivation of a limited number of high-yield crops) in agriculture and forestry, introduction of man-made substances into ecosystems (particularly pesticides, inorganic fertilizers in agriculture, and airborne nitrogen [NO_x, NH_3] in nutrient-poor sites), and diminution, fragmentation, and even destruction of living-space.

Dwindling of non-renewable resources: As already mentioned several times, this is not an acute problem. An overview of the pressure exerted on such resources can be provided by description of total consumption of non-renewable materials and sources of energy. More accurate analysis would involve investigation of how long individual raw materials will still be available.

Excessive utilization of renewable resources (including deforestation and over-fishing): This can only be partially described by way of the indicator system. The need for increasing the proportion of renewable resources in overall utilization is a basic strategic element within running a sustainable economy. Nevertheless individual resources should not be used more quickly than they regenerate (see guidelines on resource utilization in section 2.2). In principle maximum utilization rates should be determined for all renewable resources and stated as aggregated magnitudes for ongoing use.

Use of water reserves: This is recorded in terms of total water withdrawal, emphasizing the share of ground-water.

Pollution of ground-water: This is mainly the outcome of introduction of agricultural residues (nitrates, pesticides), and to a lesser extent of leaching of acidified forest soils (nitrates) and deposits from industrially polluted land and areas of settlement (including heavy metals and volatile organic compounds).

Summer smog: This arises in the form of increased ozone concentrations in the troposphere as a result of the interaction of NO_x and VOC emissions during intensive sunshine.

Death of forests: This is probably caused by complex interaction between increased ozone concentrations and the introduction of acids and nitrogens into forest soils.

The problem of waste (and the general extent of emissions): This is approached by way of magnitudes of material input. Sooner or later, depending on the number of recycling-loops involved, each material input ends up as waste or discharge into the environment.

Environmental quality in urban areas: Today this is mainly affected by emissions (NO_x, VOCs, CO, preceding ozone – see above), noise from transport systems (and to a lesser extent industry), and the impact of settlement and communications.

Toxic contamination: This results from many substances (including heavy metals, CFCs such as dioxin, PCB, etc.) from a great variety of sources, and could be aggregated in an overall index still to be developed.

Notes

1. This concept was established by the World Commission on Environment and Development, often named the Brundtland Commission after its chairperson. The final report was published in 1987. On earlier developments see: Busch-Lüty, 1994; Costanza, 1991; Daly, 1990; Enquete-Kommission "Schutz des Menschen und der Umwelt", 1994; Harborth, 1991; Moll, 1991; Pearce et al., 1989; Pearce and Warford, 1993; Sachs, 1997; Turner, 1995; World Bank, 1992.
2. We cannot get involved here in the extensive debate on the rights of future generations – see Brown-Weiss, 1990.
3. Discussed in: Bergen Report, 1990, p. 233; Daly, 1990; Pearce et al., 1989, pp. 37f.
4. Internationally this consensus is represented by the people grouped around the journal *Ecological Economics*.
5. Above all Ayres and Simonis, 1992; Daly and Cobb, 1989; Ekins, 1992; Jänicke, 1993; Meadows et al., 1992; Schmidt-Bleek, 1994a; and as precursor Kneese et al., 1970.
6. Schmidt-Bleek, 1994a.
7. Developed by Opschoor, 1992 and 1994. Also see: Dutch Advisory Council for Research on Nature and Environment, 1994a; Friends of the Earth Europe, 1995; Friends of the Earth Netherlands, 1993; Weterings and Opschoor, 1992. Environmental space is sometimes differently defined there.
8. Such criteria have been popular since contemporaneous publications by Daly and Pearce and Turner: cf. Daly, 1990; Pearce and Turner, 1990, pp. 45f. They were first explicitly mentioned by Barbier, 1989, p. 188.
9. See: Dutch Advisory Council for Research on Nature and Environment, 1994, p. 42. Also cf. Schmidt-Bleek, 1994a.
10. See: Müller and Hennicke, 1994; Sachverständigenrat für Umweltfragen, 1994.
11. South Centre, 1991, pp. 4 ff.
12. Also Grubb, 1989; Kaiser et al., 1991. The Rio declaration, the climate convention, the convention on biological diversity, and the principles relating to forestry also refer to equity.
13. The present study differs here from "Sustainable Netherlands" (Friends of the Earth Netherlands, 1993).
14. Agenda 21, chapter 40.4.
15. United Nations Economic and Social Council, 1995.
16. The most important beginnings here are:
    - integration of economic and ecological aspects within an environmental + economic audit ("Green national product"): see Dieren, 1995.
    - integration of economic and social aspects in the human development index: see UNDP, 1994 (annual updating of the HDI).
    - integration of all three aspects in an overall index of sustainability: ISEW (index for sustainable economic welfare). On development and interpretation of the ISEW for various countries, see Cobb and Cobb, 1994.

17. Gethmann and Mittelstraß, 1992. Jänicke, 1995, holds similar views.

18. The PSR model is further developed in UNSTAT's driving-force–state–response (DSR) model. The United Nations Commission on Sustainable Development has recognized this model as the basis for development of ecological, economic, and social indicators within implementation of Agenda 21.

19. OECD, 1993.

20. "Eco-capacity" is used as a shorthand for "ecological carrying capacity", and signifies the environment's capacity for maintenance of its ecological functions.

21. Weterings and Opschoor, 1992.

22. BP, 1994; Dutch Advisory Council for Research on Nature and Environment, 1994b. However, it is very doubtful whether such compensation can be maintained if industrial countries' resource-intensive economic model is transferred to the countries of the South.

23. Assessment of chemicals currently on the market provides an example of this competition. At present between seven and eight thousand chemicals are traded in Germany. At the end of 1992 only 140 had been officially assessed. If resources are not increased, only about 30 more chemicals can be assessed each year when over 50 new ones are appearing annually. (Source: Umweltbundesamt.)

24. Jänicke, 1995.

25. Schmidt-Bleek, 1994a.

26. Kuhn et al., 1994.

27. Unlike matter, energy cannot be recycled but only converted into other forms, usable at a technically lower level (e.g. fossil energy into heat). The extraction and conversion of primary energy can thus be termed "consumption".

28. Lack of filtering techniques to date means that CO_2 emissions are directly linked with use of fossil fuels. With NO_x, SO_2, and VOC emissions the degree of coupling depends on the efficiency of end-of-pipe technologies.

29. Hoffmann-Kroll and Wirthmann, 1993, provide an overview.

30. Even though NO_x emissions contribute 7% to global warming by way of formation of tropospheric ozone, they have hitherto been left out of account because of scientific uncertainty about their Greenhouse Warming Potential (GWP) value.

31. Sachverständigenrat für Umweltfragen, 1994, p. 108.

32. Walz, 1995.

33. Selection of environmental issues after OECD, 1993.

3 Targets

After ascertaining criteria for the most important influences on the environment, the next issue is the setting of targets. Guidelines are provided by the objectives involved in preservation of the natural foundations of life and global justice (section 2.1). Expressed in terms of environmental space: what are the natural limits to the economic and social development of an industrial country like Germany if life-opportunities for people in the countries of the South are to be improved and the sources of life preserved for future generations? What changes are necessary for industrial countries, at present living beyond their means, to fit once again into this natural framework?

The following considerations and calculations refer to Germany, but are fundamentally applicable to other industrial countries.

Environmental research endeavours to elucidate the connection between human activities and their impact on the environment – so far as possible numerically, and ideally through establishing a clear-cut, functional relationship, i.e. in a graph showing the links between the rise in average global temperatures and emissions of gases affecting the climate. Thanks to great efforts in recent years and decades, knowledge has been considerably improved in some spheres and the connections between causes and effects better explained. However, even when a cause and effect graph can be produced, this is not yet sufficient for determining what level of environmental impact is sustainable. Even in well-investigated cases a normative decision about the degree of environmental damage society will accept is unavoidable. The question of where the "limits" of sustainability lie is thus directly coupled with the question of what environmental risks society is ready to tolerate.

If the existence of an environmental space – in terms of a frame of reference limiting economic and social development – is accepted, then that should not be based on maximum risks, allowing the overall system to just about survive. Measurement of environmental space – and thus formulation of objectives in terms of minimization of risk – should be concerned with the most vulnerable parts of the system (ozone-sensitive asthmatics and children as much as acid-sensitive forest soils). The precautionary principle also lays down that targets must be set for both reducing existing pollution and avoiding future impact.

3.1 Targets for Risk Containment: Cutting Pollution

Ecological sustainability is at present endangered more by the damage human activities cause to eco-systems than by shortage of raw materials. Targets for reducing the emissions which generate the previously described environmental problems are presented in what follows.

Global warming

Human activities across the world release considerable quantities of gases (CO_2, N_2O, CFCs) that influence the greenhouse effect. Carbon dioxide, which is responsible for at least half of global warming, mainly derives from the combustion of fossil fuels (around 23 billion tonnes) and clearing forests by burning (around 6 billion tonnes).[1] In Germany carbon dioxide accounts for as much as three-quarters of the national greenhouse potential.[2] Natural sinks (oceans, terrestrial biosphere) have only limited capacity for absorbing the carbon created through human activities. The atmosphere's carbon content is thus mounting all the time. During the eighties CO_2 concentration in the atmosphere rose by an average of 1.5 ppmV[3] annually to a total of 355 ppmV in 1992.[4]

The increased concentration of greenhouse gases in the earth's atmosphere is causing global warming, which in turn leads to further climatic change. Climate models predict average global warming of between 1 and 3.5°C over the next hundred years if current emission patterns continue.[5] The accompanying displacement of climate and vegetation zones would occur at a rate exceeding vegetation's capacity to adapt. Extensive destabilization and even possibly the breakdown of many natural eco-systems might be expected. The frequency of extreme forms of weather (droughts, floods, storms) would increase, and the sea-level rise by around 70 cm over the next century. There would be permanent flooding and frequent swamping. Tropical and sub-tropical arid regions and deserts would continue to spread, especially in the already afflicted developing countries. Water supplies would be endangered too and agriculture threatened with harvest failures and loss of crops across the world. Food shortages and starvation would increase, leading to swarms of refugees and conflicts over distribution of resources.

In order to head off or at least limit such threats, countries at Rio de Janeiro in 1992 concluded an agreement binding in international law. Article 2 of the Framework Convention on Climate Change contains a commitment to reduce worldwide emissions of trace-gases affecting the climate sufficiently so as to "achieve stabilization of greenhouse gas concentrations in the atmosphere at a level that would prevent dangerous anthropogenic interference with the climate system. Such a level should be achieved within a time-frame sufficient to allow eco-systems to adapt naturally to climate change."

At the international level scientists agree that in such circumstances average global warming of around 0.1% per decade can be viewed as just about tolerable. This is only a minimum demand. That figure is merely based on the capacity for adaptation of most but by no means all eco-systems. Establishing that criterion entails acceptance of the extinction of further species.

To be able to limit global warming, humanity must restrict the concentration of greenhouse gases in the atmosphere. Since most of these gases remain active in the atmosphere for many decades, stabilization can only be attained by drastic reduction of emissions. The German Federal Parliament's "Protection of the Earth's Atmosphere" commission of inquiry thus recognized that emissions of carbon dioxide would have to be reduced globally by between 50 and 60% by the year 2050.[6]

If the second aspect involved in the concept of environmental space, the principle of international justice, is to be observed, considerably greater reductions must be demanded of the industrial nations. With today's world population (5.8 billion) and levels of emission (around 29 billion tonnes of CO_2 annually[7]), "equal rights of emission" would signify 5 tonnes per head. A reduction of 50–60% by 2050 would entail – for today's world population – reduction to 2.3 tonnes. However, in today's Germany the per capita figure is around 12 tonnes. Meeting the target would thus involve cutting CO_2 emissions by 80% up to the year 2050. For Canada and the USA with averages of 15 and 20 tonnes of CO_2 per head annually, there would have to be reductions of between 85 and 88%. If the current forecast of a world population of around 10 billion by 2050 is added, then adherence to the principle of equal utilization rights would mean a reduction of 90% for Germany. As a medium-term objective, a reduction of 35% by the year 2010 is thought appropriate (figure 3.1).

That demand's relative independence of the assumptions made here can be demonstrated as follows. Suppose that we did not seek the same

Figure 3.1 Previous and sustainable development of German CO_2 emissions
Developments in recent decades must be reversed in order to make an effective contribution to protection of the climate. For the period up to 1950 the greatly oversimplified assumption was made that German emissions increased at the same rate as global emissions. (*Sources*: Keeling, 1994; Marland et al., 1994; Umweltbundesamt)

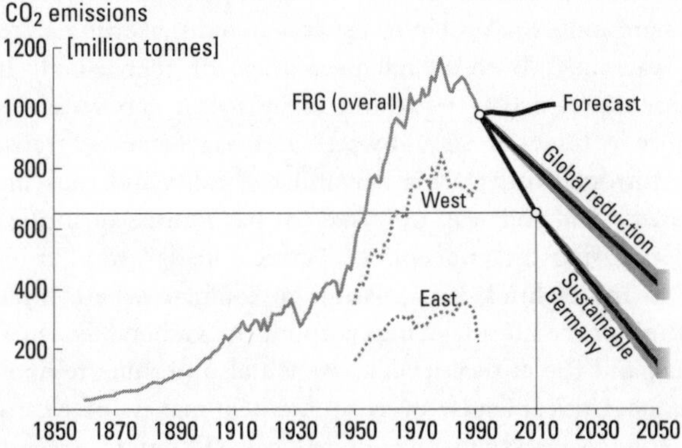

emission rights for everyone alive today and in the future, but instead advocated that:

1. the billions of people in the North, who have long existed with high levels of CO_2, could lay claim to twice as many emissions per capita as people in the South, and that
2. increases in population, probably mainly in the South, should be left out of account when calculating necessary reduction rates.

Even in that case – with the minimal ecological demand still for a 50% global reduction of CO_2 emissions by 2050, but without any provision made for particularly vulnerable eco-systems – Germany would have to make cuts of around 65%.

Acidification and nutrient deposition from the atmosphere

When forests suffered great damage in the seventies and eighties, research was intensified. The main problem is now thought to be prolonged exposure to airborne pollutants such as sulphur dioxide (SO_2), nitrogen oxide (NO_x), and ammonia (NH_3). Apart from directly damaging parts of plants above ground and leaching nutrients, the outcome includes enrichment of nutrients (eutrophication) and acidification of soils. Eutrophication shifts competitive relationships prevalent between species, leading to ousting or death for plants adapted to habitats poor in nutrients. Nitrogen-saturated forest soils discharge excesses into the ground as nitrate and into the atmosphere as nitrogenous gases. Acidification leads to a variety of consequences. Among these are leaching, with a consequent lack of basic nutrients and the release of pollutants such as toxic heavy metals including cadmium and zinc. The combination of excessive nitrogen deposits and acidification results in much greater – and at present considerably underestimated – amounts of N_2O in forest eco-systems, exerting a great impact on global warming.[8] Both a high percentage of increasingly intensively worked agricultural eco-systems and many forest eco-systems have lost their function as filters of air and water, and now serve as "transformers", converting nitrogen into forms harmful to health and the climate.

Eco-systems and soils can only keep at bay limited quantities of acids and nitrogen. Using the concepts of "critical loads" and "critical levels" developed in the eighties, it is possible to estimate where the ecological limits lie. Both procedures take into account the vulnerabilities of different eco-systems, and the critical level approach also permits temporal graduation of limits. Critical loads/levels should help makers of clean-air policy determine how far emissions must be reduced. Within a foreseeable period emissions of pollutants should be cut back to such an extent that ecological limits are no longer exceeded throughout this sphere.

Mounting soil acidification has been demonstrated almost everywhere in Europe. Critical levels are exceeded in over 85% of German forests, and the state of forest soils is similarly serious in Poland, the Czech Republic, and Slovakia.

Determining critical loads with regard to nitrogen is more difficult since airborne deposition results in several complex processes (development of biomass, fixing in humus, denitrification, and leaching). At present such deposition from the atmosphere totals between 20 and 80 (in extreme cases 200) kg of nitrogen per hectare annually (kg N/ha*a). However, natural eco-systems can on average only deal with around 20 kg N/ha*a.[9] Nitrogen deposits far exceed eco-systems' capacity for absorption – by factors of 10 to 15, and more in some cases. In many forest eco-systems a nitrate content of between 60 to 80 milligrams per litre, much above EU limits for drinking water, has been measured in water seeping through the ground.

Unlike the global problem involved in the greenhouse effect, in the case of acidification and eutrophication caused by airborne pollutants cause and effect are restricted to a limited area – such as the continent of Europe.[10] Targets for reduction and an equitable distribution of burdens – the two components of the concept of environmental space – can thus be determined within the continent. In 1979 the Geneva Clean Air Treaty was concluded as the outcome of European negotiations. Agreements on reductions were then laid down in various protocols.[11] One outcome was

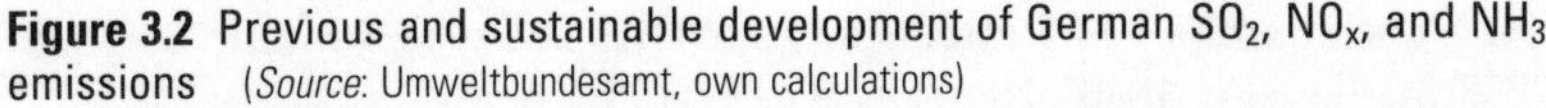
Figure 3.2 Previous and sustainable development of German SO_2, NO_x, and NH_3 emissions (*Source*: Umweltbundesamt, own calculations)

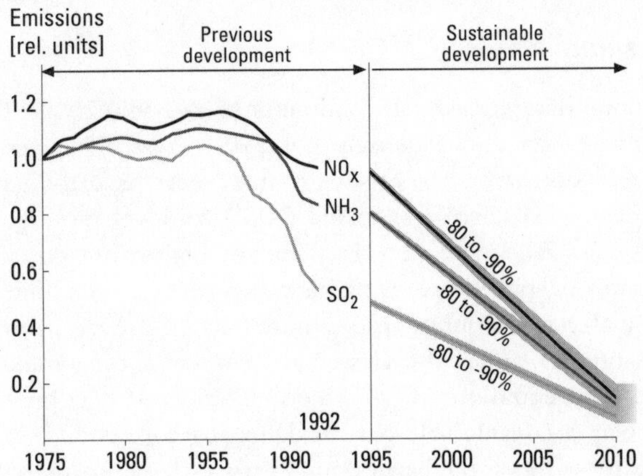

that SO_2 emissions in the continent sank by around 30% between 1980 and 1993. Revision of the sulphur protocol in spring 1994 provides for a further reduction of emissions so that the figure for the year 2000 is 60% less than discharges in 1980. Reunification once again made the German Federal Republic the chief source of SO_2 emissions in Europe, but this country has contracted to reduce such emissions by 83% (down to 1.3 million tonnes) by 2000 and by 87% (0.9 million tonnes) by 2005.

Even if those targets are achieved, around 7% of Europe's eco-systems are still excessively subject to SO_2. In some countries, including Germany, up to 20% of land-areas may be affected.[12] By now NO_x and NH_3 are responsible for most acidification. The relevant protocol laid down that 25 European countries should reduce NO_x emissions to the 1987 level by 1994. Eleven countries, including Germany, have now agreed to further reduce such emissions, cutting 30% of the 1988 totals by 1998.[13] However, NO_x agreements to date are far from fulfilling ecological requirements. For NH_3 no agreements exist.

Recommendations by the "Protection of the Earth's Atmosphere" commission of inquiry say that current emissions of NO_x (from transportation) must be reduced by 60% in the next 10 to 20 years, of NH_3 (from agriculture) by 55%, and of SO_2 by 25%. Over the longer term this means that SO_2 emissions must be cut by half and nitrogen emissions by 80% during the next 20 to 40 years.[14] Current increments sometimes exceed the critical loads by factors of 10 to 15, so far-reaching protection of eco-systems can only be guaranteed if sulphur dioxide and above all nitrogenous emissions are reduced more quickly, which means by 80 to 90% in the next 10 to 20 years (figure 3.2).

Summer smog

On very sunny days considerable amounts of ozone (O_3) are formed in the atmosphere just above densely populated areas. That results from mounting emissions of such precursor substances as carbon monoxide (CO), methane (CH_4), nitrogen oxide (NO_x), and volatile organic compounds (VOC).[15] The increasing frequency of high ozone concentrations in the lowest troposphere directly harms plants, animals, and human beings. This mainly affects the lungs among humans because of ozone's highly oxidative nature. Ozone is also viewed as a source of cancer and allergies.

Increased concentrations of ozones do not only endanger human health. They also play a considerable part in damaging forests and are thought responsible for 90% of the harm done to plants by airborne pollutants.[16] Several days of strong sunshine may sometimes be necessary for development of high concentrations of ozone, but then it takes several days for this ozone to disperse. Precautionary measures for reducing precursor substances must therefore be taken. Once the currently valid limits are reached, it is too late. Experts believe that emissions of NO_x and VOCs must be reduced by between 70 and 80% for low-level ozone impact to be kept at an acceptable level.[17] Along with the German Council of Experts on Environmental Issues we think it necessary to reduce the 1987 figures for NO_x and VOC emissions by 80% up to 2005 (figure 3.3).[18]

Figure 3.3 Previous and sustainable development of German VOC emissions
(*Source*: Umweltbundesamt, own calculations)

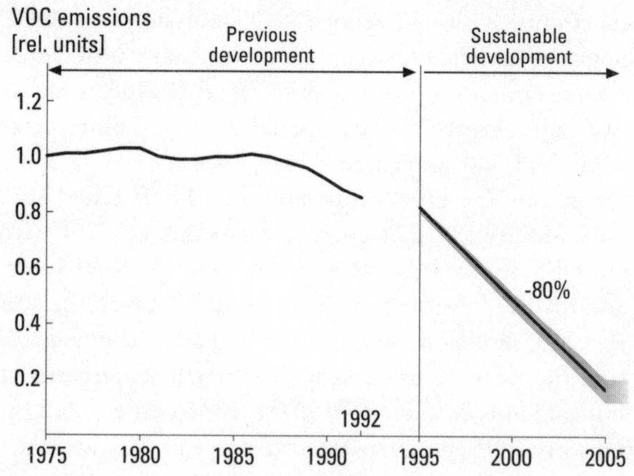

Water pollution through agriculture

In recent years greater purification of effluents and replacement of washing powder phosphates have resulted in a considerable reduction of the ammonia and phosphate content of running water in Germany. However, pollution of large areas of water by fertilizers, biocides, and eroded nutrient-rich agricultural soils continues unabated – even though the amount of fertilizers used per hectare has diminished since the end of the eighties. The nitrate content of ground-water continues to rise, and EU limits of 50 milligrams of nitrate per litre are exceeded in more and more areas. In 1995 over 270,000 tonnes of nitrogen from fields and meadows were washed away – only 17% less than in 1985.[19]

An average of 200 kg of nitrogen in the form of mineral and organic fertilizers is still used annually on every hectare of agricultural land. Added to that is airborne nitrogen and what is absorbed in the ground through microbes. If what harvests take from the soil is subtracted, there remain annual surpluses of between 88 and 167 kg N/ha.[20] These surpluses frequently exceed the amount of non-organic fertilizers used. This means that natural production of nitrogen through soil micro-organisms or the cultivation of pulses,[21] combined with airborne deposits and the use of organic fertilizers, could on average supply land with sufficient nitrogen. The precondition is establishment of largely closed cycles on farms where nitrogen mainly takes the form of home-grown forage returned to the land as organic fertilizers. By correlating the number of animals and size of farms, and thus assuring relatively equal distribution of animals instead

Figure 3.4 Previous and sustainable development of use of nitrogen fertilizers and biocides in German agriculture (*Source*: Bundesministerium für Ernährung, Landwirtschaft und Forsten, own calculations)

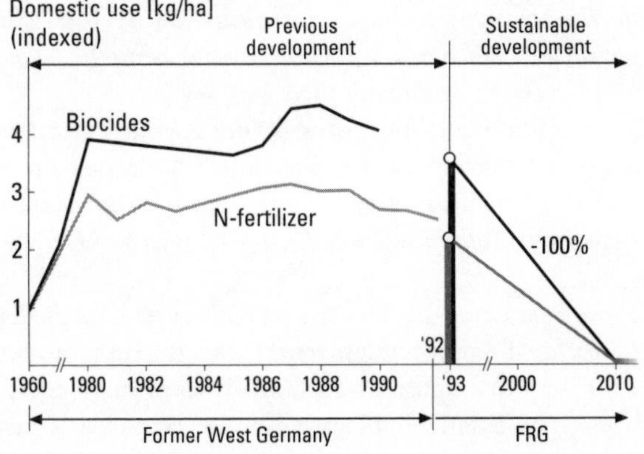

of the present concentration, it could and should be possible to renounce use of non-organic nitrogen fertilizers completely, thereby avoiding polluting surpluses after a transition period of 10 to 15 years.

Apart from drastic cuts in nitrogen surpluses, the use of pesticides must also be reduced if the pollution caused by agricultural residues is to be dealt with. Large amounts (little reduced in recent years) of herbicides, fungicides, and insecticides destroy biological diversity on neighbouring areas whether farmed or not, leading to contamination of ground-water by these poisonous substances.

The precautionary principle thus demands complete renunciation of the use of biocides in agriculture after an appropriate transitional period of 10 to 15 years (figure 3.4).

3.2 Targets for Risk Prevention: Reducing Extraction

In section 2.2 we showed in detail that a precautionary strategy for sustainability cannot be limited to control of pollutants with reductions of emissions harming health and the environment. The extraction of resources, the source and driving-force behind present and future environmental problems, should be reduced to a viable level in order to preempt the emergence of new problems. A distinction will be made here between energy, materials, water, and land.

Energy

Some 90% of Germany's energy supplies are still based on fossil fuels (see section on "Energy Consumption" in chapter 4) whose conversion leads to discharges of CO_2 and other pollutants. Development of practical and economically viable preventive technology is not to be expected in the foreseeable future, so the necessary objective of reduction of CO_2 emissions initially involves continuing exploitation of fossil fuels. However, in a sustainable Germany their use should be reduced by between 80 and 90% by the middle of the next century.

The objective of minimization of risk, put forward in the concept of environmental space, gives rise to demands for immediate withdrawal from employment of nuclear energy. We therefore assume that from 2010 nuclear energy will no longer make any contribution to Germany's energy supplies.

What are the main non-nuclear possibilities for a sustainable energy system? Expansion of energy from renewable sources – at present only contributing the very low figure of around 2% to primary energy supplies (see figure 3.5) – is an essential objective on the way towards sustainability.

Figure 3.5 Previous and sustainable development of German energy supplies
(*Source*: Bundesministerium für Wirtschaft, own calculations)

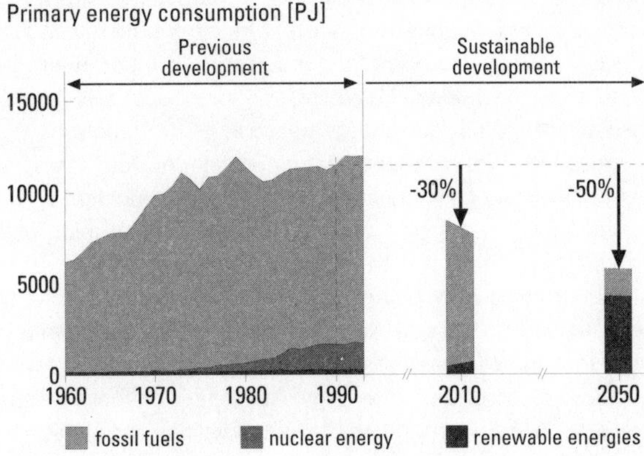

In order to maintain the current level of primary energy utilization – with use of fossil fuels reduced by 80 to 90% and renunciation of nuclear energy by the year 2050 – renewable supplies would have to be increased by a factor of over 40. That does not seem desirable for two reasons.

First, there is an ecological price to pay for utilization of renewable sources of energy. Expansion of solar energy infrastructure is dependent on non-renewable resources (such as materials for photovoltaic modules), utilizes land, and causes emissions elsewhere (during the construction and maintenance of infrastructure, or in the provision and conversion of fuels – in the case of energy-plants by way of erosion, use of fertilizers and biocides, and emission of carbohydrates). So alternatives should not be developed on a large scale without prior evaluation of the overall ecological consequences.

Second, relatively "cleanly" produced renewable energy will not automatically be used cleanly. A solar-powered car, for instance, will for the most part be constructed from non-renewable resources and use roads that seal off the soil and cut up the landscape. It is also unlikely that the fact electricity is "solar-generated" will stop people from using it for new and questionable purposes. Quite the contrary in fact. Depiction of renewable energies as an "environmentally neutral horn of plenty" would involve a danger of sparking off new services and thus calling in question the ecologically positive impact of transition to solar energy.

In view of the fact that neither the production nor the consumption of energy can be structured in a way that is environmentally neutral, we conclude that overall use (as an indicator of a society's level of physical

Why Germany Should Renounce Use of Nuclear Energy

In Germany social and political disagreement about the future role of nuclear energy persists, despite the fact that its contribution to world energy supplies – even when assessed by supporters – will not even reach 10% over the next few decades.[22] However, various people time and again call for intensified use of nuclear energy because of the problems involved in greenhouse gases. It is true that when individual nuclear reactors replace fossil-fuel power stations, they contribute towards reduction of CO_2 emissions, but continuing – as part of a strategy for minimization of risk – to employ a technology linked with high and partly incalculable risks is problematic. The reactors now being developed may promise greater safety, but cannot exclude catastrophic releases of radioactive fissile material. Apart from that the question of decommissioning is still unresolved after three decades of use of atomic energy. At present neither in Germany nor anywhere else in the world do there exist facilities for highly radioactive waste which could guarantee sufficiently safe storage of fissile products for thousands of years. The risk is also increased by the transportation procedures involved. In addition the utilization of nuclear energy is always linked with dangers of proliferation. So if the criterion of minimizing risk is taken seriously, nuclear energy must be abandoned as quickly as possible.

Those doubts about safety and risks are intensified by a number of arguments concerning industrial investment and research policy. System-analyses show that the necessary research and investment in innovative low-risk future technology (efficiency techniques, solar energy, co-generation) are obstructed by the constraints resulting from the existence of a high-tech system of nuclear power stations and associated facilities. In addition empirical testimony (from Denmark, Switzerland, Sweden, Austria, Italy, Canada, California) shows that renunciation of nuclear energy (or a moratorium on building additional nuclear power stations) is closely associated with innovative initiatives in energy policy and dealings with the climate. Many aspects of such theoretical and empirical considerations speak in favour of abandonment of nuclear energy because of – rather than despite – the need to protect our climate.

activity) should be stabilized at a sustainable but compared with today clearly lower level. For that, existing possibilities of savings must be exhausted and the development of energy-conserving technologies intensified. Halving primary energy consumption by the year 2050[23] would be a desirable goal within such a development. In conjunction with the targets for reducing the use of fossil and nuclear fuels that leads to the objective of considerable expansion of energy production from renewable sources with an annual growth rate of around 5% up to the year 2050.

Materials

In section 2.3 the "material input" indicator was defined as the totality of resources withdrawn from the environment during a specific period. To what extent should this withdrawal be reduced so as to meet the criteria of sustainable development?

A comparison between natural and humanly caused flows of materials provides the basis for setting a target. In many cases humanly caused flows of materials have today become as great as natural flows.[24] We have shown that in the geo-chemically highly important carbon, sulphur, and nitrogen cycles such massive interventions in formerly pristine processes affect basic functions within eco-systems and must thus be corrected. As previously mentioned, release of such pollutants is directly linked with resource extraction.[25]

For that reason (and following on from the global target for reduction of CO_2 emissions) the target would be to reduce global extraction of materials from the environment by 50% up to the middle of the next century.[26] Reduction of use of fossil fuels has already been called for so as to protect the climate (see above) and utilization of renewable raw materials is thought particularly important (see below), so we relate this target to use of abiotic (non-renewable) primary raw materials excluding sources of energy. Proceeding from the approximate assessment that "the rich fifth of the world's population in the North consumes around four-fifths of the world's resources", the criterion of equal utilization rights for all produces the requirement that Germany must cut its share by between 80 and 90%, amounting to reduction by a factor of 5 to 10 (figure 3.6).

Figure 3.6 **Previous and sustainable development of German consumption of abiotic (non-renewable) raw materials** Relating only to the former Federal Republic because of lack of more comprehensive data. (*Source*: Own calculations)

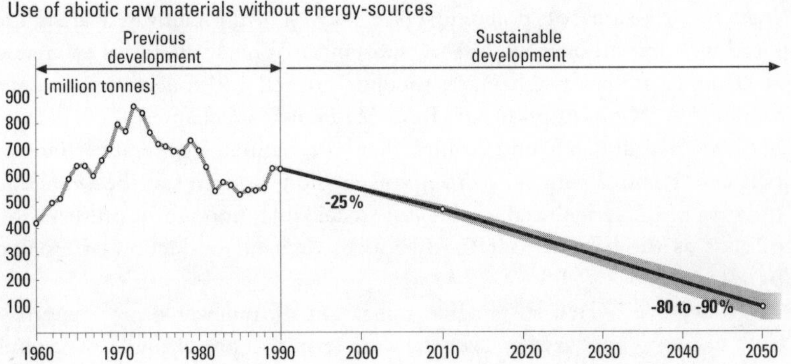

Other authors come to similar conclusions about sustainable utilization of non-renewable resources – but most of them argue that resources are finite and will become increasingly scarce.[27] Weterings and Opschoor take as their criterion availability of non-renewable resources for at least a further 50 years, thereby demanding that use of copper should be reduced by 80% by 2040.[28] The target in "Sustainable Netherlands" is only indirectly based on withdrawal of resources. The authors want at least 95% of non-renewable resources to be used in recycled form by 2010, deducing that the use of aluminium in the Netherlands must be cut by 80% up till then. Mounting scientific consensus about the magnitude of necessary changes is exemplified by establishment of the "Factor 10 Club", grouping 16 internationally recognized scientists who jointly call for reduction by a factor of 10 of raw materials and energy throughput in the industrial countries.[29]

Priorities will have to be established when drawing up targets for withdrawal of individual raw materials. Important criteria include the human and toxicological consequences of extraction alongside purely economic aspects – such as how long will known reserves last, and what could be used as a substitute? Extraction of rapidly dwindling materials (copper for instance) and toxic substances (or components in toxic products) should thus be reduced more quickly and comprehensively, especially when alternatives are already available.

Renewable raw materials

Targets are considerably more difficult to formulate for sustainable use of renewable raw materials.

The indispensable basis for lasting utilization of renewable materials requires preservation of the ecological functions of the soils in which they grow. That applies equally to forest soils (used for wood production) and agricultural land which to date has been almost exclusively used for food production. In Germany forests and their soils are mainly threatened by emissions of pollutants (see above), while cultivated areas are faced with the problem of loss of substance. Annual soil loss is estimated at 10 to 12 tonnes per hectare, totalling around 130 million tonnes (see section on "Consumption of Raw Materials" in chapter 4), which is between five and ten times more than the natural regeneration rate of between 1 and 2 tonnes.[30] From soil erosion alone it can be seen that today's use of agricultural land is not sustainable. Long-term preservation of soils as the basis of our food supplies demands reduction of erosion by 80 to 90%.[31]

To achieve overall sustainable utilization of renewable raw materials, both ensuring big harvests over the long term and preserving eco-systems and biological diversity, these targets for reducing use of non-organic fertilizers and soil-loss are necessary but not yet sufficient peripheral conditions. The way towards sustainable agriculture and forestry demands a series of measures and steps that will be described in detail elsewhere.

Water

If national consumption is taken as a reference-point when attempting to determine a sustainable level of water extraction, the following picture emerges for Germany. About a third of new water resources, added annually by rainfall and influxes from other countries, are used.[32] Taking "less utilization than replenishment" as the criterion, Germans should be allowed to use considerably more water than they in fact do. The water-use index would permit a 100% increase. On the other hand, in individual areas – such as the Berlin region or parts of South Hesse – water supplies are already much over-used. Acceptable use-rates can thus only be set for individual catchment areas and not nationally.

In establishing such use-rates the fact that the "water problem" involves a qualitative as well as a quantitative dimension must also be taken into account. Pollution with chemicals from agriculture, industry, and domestic use has led to high-quality "natural water" becoming scarce in Germany despite the relative abundance of water.

Expanding on the general guidelines for resource utilization (section 2.2), the following rules can be put forward for sustainable utilization of water:[33]

1. Annual extraction should not exceed annual replenishment within a water catchment area.
2. The impact of organic and inorganic substances should not exceed water's capacity for self-cleansing.
3. Account must be taken of seasonal differences between supply and utilization.
4. It then follows that balancing out between areas differing in size and potential for water utilization is only acceptable to the extent that these regulations have been adhered to in the catchment areas involved.[34]

Land use

Unlike flows of energy and materials where withdrawal from the environment must be greatly reduced, the amount of "land" remains unchanging and the need is for stabilization of utilization at a generally sustainable level. Even conservationists no longer view human interventions in nature as being intrinsically negative in ecological terms, so imposition of an absolute limit to ongoing growth in the most intensive form of land utilization – sealing off the soil through housing or transportation infrastructure – seems necessary.

This can be justified by the fact that this form of land-utilization virtually excludes others (agriculture and forestry, nature conservation, leisure activities). Building on land entails renunciation of utilization for other purposes. These areas are urgently needed for environmentally acceptable sources of food supplies, production of wood as a renewable raw material, and maintenance of biological diversity. In addition new settlement is accompanied by new transportation infrastructure, which entails loss of more land and additional traffic with accompanying noise and other emissions. The converse holds true too. A transportation system dominated by the motor car promotes development of settlement structures requiring large expanses of land. It favours scattered housing and separation of functions (accommodation, work, leisure), allowing firms greater freedom in choice of location. Feedback is thus intensified with an upwards spiral linking increased traffic and spreading areas of settlement.

The necessity of limits is confronted by forecasts of unrestrained growth: additional demand for accommodation, mounting needs for building land, establishment of new commercial zones, extension of transportation infrastructure as part of the European Union's expansion eastwards. All these trends indicate continuation of a great increase in built-over land.

On the other hand, alternatives are available: land-saving, high-density building, construction of multi-storey houses (shared by several families) instead of "energy- and land-consuming" detached homes, better utilization of office space, more emphasis on land-saving local transport systems than expansion of the road network, and, above all, re-utilization ("recycling") of redundant areas rather than fresh development.

Our quantitative target for land employed for settlement and transportation thus involves gradual reduction until no new land is used for that purpose from the year 2010 (figure 3.7).

Agriculture and forestry do not usually entail any loss of land. If managed in an environmentally sound way, they are compatible with many other soil functions or even further them. Land utilization during previous centuries thus positively shaped today's image of a cultivated landscape with its diversity of plant and animal species – at least up to the 1950s.

In recent decades that positive trend has been reversed. More intensive use of chemicals and machinery in some branches of agricultural production, reallocation of land use, more frequent cultivation of crops that

Figure 3.7 Previous and sustainable development of land used for settlement and transportation Referring only to the former Federal Republic for lack of relevant data. (*Source*: Statistisches Bundesamt, own calculations)

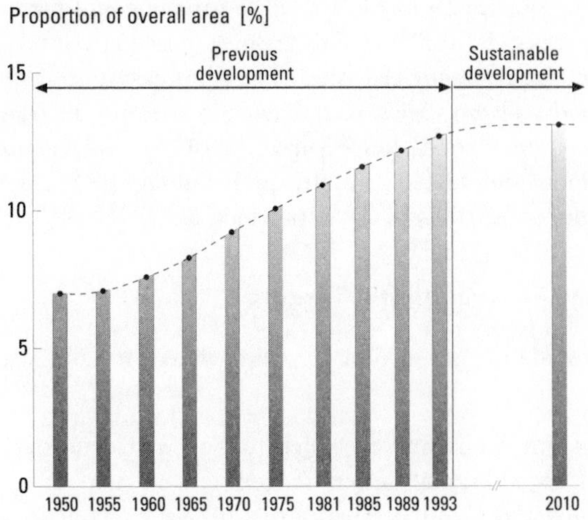

cause erosion, and large-scale monocultures in reafforestation have led to considerable damage to eco-systems and a decline in biodiversity. The leaving fallow of large areas, promoted by the 1992 European Community agricultural reforms, threatens to make the situation worse. Taking such areas out of use does not help protection of nature and the environment so long as most land is still intensively used. Conservationists thus increasingly recognize that the objective of environmentally acceptable structuring of agriculture and forestry (80% of the total area) is strategically more important than optimization of protection of nature in a low percentage of the landscape. A mere change in proportions (10% for conservation and 70% for agriculture and forestry) would not solve the problem. In fact it is to be feared that this would lead to strengthening the trend towards a "reservation agriculture", leading to the loss of historical landscape. Such a decline in farming would endanger the existence of many semi-natural eco-systems such as heaths, common land, and copses, which were not deliberately created but are dependent on human attention. What is therefore needed is large-scale extensive farming and protection (or restoration) of vulnerable, natural, or semi-natural eco-systems.

Organic farming has demonstrated for decades that economically viable and environmentally acceptable agriculture is possible, and that conservation and diversity of species can also be expanded again. Extensive and environmentally acceptable land utilization serves conservation far better than the present system of protected zones. Sustainable land use thus demands large-scale conversion of agriculture and forestry to organic methods.

Ecological agriculture and forestry in Germany could meet the needs of a population of 80 million. The greatest possible regionalization of raw material cycles is ecologically desirable. Unnecessary transportation is thereby avoided and emissions resulting from over-production of nutrients would be diminished. Regionalization of use of agricultural and forestry products should thus be striven for alongside a changeover to environmentally acceptable ways of production.

3.3 A Set of Environmental Targets

The findings made in this section are summarized in table 3.1. We again stress that:

- This set of environmental objectives is only a selection and must be augmented by additional targets (covering such matters as emissions of toxic substances and regional levels of water extraction);
- New findings within environmental research may demand a change of objectives;
- These observations and calculations refer to Germany but are methodologically applicable to other countries: magnitudes of necessary changes in dealings with natural resources are comparable for most countries in the North;
- The formulation of objectives is founded on scientific knowledge, but nevertheless also calls for value judgements (previously referred to) intended to promote public discussion of environmental targets.

This overview of environmental objectives demonstrates that the current level of German resource use and pollutant emissions is not sustainable. Such utilization far exceeds German environmental space and has long left behind the natural frame of reference which must be respected in long-term social and economic development. Maintenance of the natural foundations of existence, combined with an internationally equitable distribution of life-opportunities, demands changes in dealings with natural resources by a factor between 5 and 10.

If that objective is compared with the outcome of 20 years of environmental politics, the methods employed to date are shown to be insufficient, despite individual successes. This can be seen from patterns of resource consumption and emissions during this period. What has been achieved can in many cases be termed merely stagnation at a high level (energy, raw materials, additional use of land, and emissions of CO_2,

Table 3.1 Environmental objectives for a sustainable Germany

Environmental indicator	**Environmental target**	
	short-term (2010)	long-term (2050)
RESOURCE WITHDRAWAL		
Energy		
Primary energy consumption	at least –30%	at least –50%
Fossil fuels	–25%	–80 to 90%
Nuclear power	–100%	
Renewables	+3 to 5% per year	
Energy productivity [1]	+3 to 5% per year*	
Materials		
Non-renewable raw materials	–25%	-80 to 90%
Material productivity [2]	+4 to 6% per year*	
Land use		
settlements and transportation	• absolute stabilization • annual additional use: –100%	
Agriculture	• extensive conversion to organic farming methods • Regionalization of nutrient cycles	
Forestry	• extensive conversion to ecologically adapted silviculture • increased use of domestic timber	
SUBSTANCE RELEASE/EMISSIONS		
Carbon dioxide (CO_2)	–35%	–80 to 90%
Sulphur dioxide (SO_2)	–80 to 90%	
Nitrogen oxides (NO_x)	–80% by 2005	
Ammonia (NH_3)	–80 to 90%	
Volatile organic compounds (VOC)	–80% to 2005	
Synthetic nitrogen fertilizers	–100%	
Agricultural biocides	–100%	
Soil erosion	–80 to 90%	

1 Primary energy consumption per unit value added (GDP).
2 Consumption of non-renewable primary materials per unit value added.
* Assuming annual growth rates 2.5% in gross domestic product. It must, however, be stressed that continuing economic growth makes it impossible to achieve the long-term environmental targets.

NO_x, NH_3, and VOCs), while ecological necessity very clearly demands absolute reductions. It is thus more than doubtful whether the new magic concept of "decoupling" can deliver what is promised: increases in efficiency and innovation allowing continuing economic growth, accompanied by reductions in the destruction of nature and consumption of raw materials and energy. There are many signs that a revolution in efficiency – urgently needed though it may be – is not enough.

Strategies for sustainable German development must therefore call in question the ecological viability of constantly mounting production of goods and services. Such strategies must take into account the social and economic aspects of sustainability alongside the physical and technological dimensions. Success will depend on the degree to which ecological necessities can be made plausible and attractive in terms of social, cultural, and economic perspectives.

Notes

1. World Resources Institute, 1994.
2. Own calculations without CFCs, 1990; Intergovernmental Panel on Climate Change, 1994, p. 11.
3. ppmV = parts per million volume.
4. Intergovernmental Panel on Climate Change, 1994.
5. Intergovernmental Panel on Climate Change, 1996.
6. Article 2 of the climate convention also calls on signatories "to ensure that food production is not threatened, and to enable economic development to proceed in a sustainable manner". These two sub-conditions have not as yet been taken into account in the formulation of targets for reduction or stabilization and may thus make necessary further intensification of protection of the climate.
7. World Resources Institute, 1994.
8. Cautious estimates indicate that N_2O formation in forest eco-systems alone may already be more than 20,000 t N_2O/year, and thus amount to 10% of total national N_2O emissions. (Enquete-Kommission "Schutz der Erdatmosphäre", 1994a).
9. An initial survey indicates that the critical rates for nitrogen are between 5 and 35 kg N/ha annually, quoted in: Sachverständigenrat für Umweltfragen, 1994, p. 118.
10. Unlike the low-reaction and thus long-lived greenhouse gases, the reactive compounds – SO_2, NO_x, and NH_3 – are within just a few days deposited again relatively close to their place of emission.
11. 1985 protocol on sulphur compounds; 1988 nitrogen oxide protocol; 1991 VOC protocol.
12. Friends of the Earth et al., 1993, in: Enquete-Kommission "Schutz der Erdatmosphäre", 1994a, p. 586.
13. NO_x is also one of the most important precursors of ozone (see below).
14. Ulrich, 1991, in: Enquete-Kommission "Schutz der Erdatmosphäre", 1994a, p. 476 – relating to the anticipated 1995 level of emissions.
15. In Germany over the past 25 years ozone concentration in the troposphere

has increased by around 2% annually (Enquete-Kommission "Schutz der Erdatmosphäre", 1994a, p. 23).

16. Adams et al., 1986. In the USA annual ozone-engendered losses in harvests of cultivated crops are estimated at two billion US dollars (Stüben, 1992).

17. Ozone Symposium, 1991, in: Enquete-Kommission "Schutz der Erdatmosphäre", 1994a.

18. Sachverständigenrat für Umweltfragen, 1994, p. 274.

19. Ibid.

20. Haas and Köpke, 1994.

21. Certain micro-organisms exist symbiotically in the roots of pulses, forming airborne nitrogen which they supply to plants.

22. World Energy Council: Energy for Tomorrow's World, draft summary global report, London 1992; Grübler, 1993.

23. "Sustainable Europe" puts forward the same target at the European level: Friends of the Earth Europe, 1995, p. 20.

24. Schlesinger, 1991.

25. E.g. heavy metal emissions during mining, SO_2 emissions from slag-heaps.

26. Schmidt-Bleek, 1994a.

27. Ekins, 1992; Meadows and Meadows, 1992; and national environmental plans in the Netherlands (see: Ministerium für Wohnungswesen, Raumordnung und Umwelt der Niederlande, 1994) and Austria (see: Österreichische Bundesregierung, 1995).

28. Weterings and Opschoor, 1992.

29. Schmidt-Bleek, 1994b.

30. Fleischhauer, in: Burdick, 1994, p. 75.

31. Weterings and Opschoor, 1992, call for a reduction of 85% in the Netherlands.

32. See Kluge et al., 1995.

33. Hüttler and Payer, 1994.

34. This rule imposes tight limits on long-distance conveyance of water from conservation areas to densely populated urban centres.

4 Stock-Taking

4.1 Structures of Environmental Consumption

Drawing up national environmental accounts presents a difficult methodological hurdle. Today virtually all states are engaged in an ever more complicated network of reciprocal trade relations, and the ecological impact of running a nation's economy and ways of life extends from the local to the global. That raises the fundamental question of whether, and how, the outcome of importing and exporting goods can be attributed to a specific "environmental account". Such a concretization of the principle that the polluter should pay is difficult at the level of international trade since responsibility for the environmental problems linked with a product or a service can be assigned to both the consumer and the producer. Apart from that methodological difficulty there is also the question of availability of data. The forms of consumption and the emissions resulting from individual imports and exports are inadequately known.

As a pragmatic solution to this problem some authors recommend completely ignoring foreign trade when drawing up national environmental balances, merely taking domestic production into account.[1] An example of such territorial stock-taking is provided by the methods for ascertaining national carbon dioxide emissions used in the UN Convention on Climate. However, this means that no account is taken of pollution caused by trading relations whose impact occurs abroad. Worse still, transferring environmentally intensive spheres of production to other countries is even viewed as a success within these stock-takings. Such trends are of decisive significance in evaluating North–South trading relations. The environmental pollution caused by the extraction and processing of raw materials (iron, wood, agricultural products, etc.) later

Figure 4.1 Structure of environmental consumption Overall indicators of impact are assigned to different sectors of supply and demand.

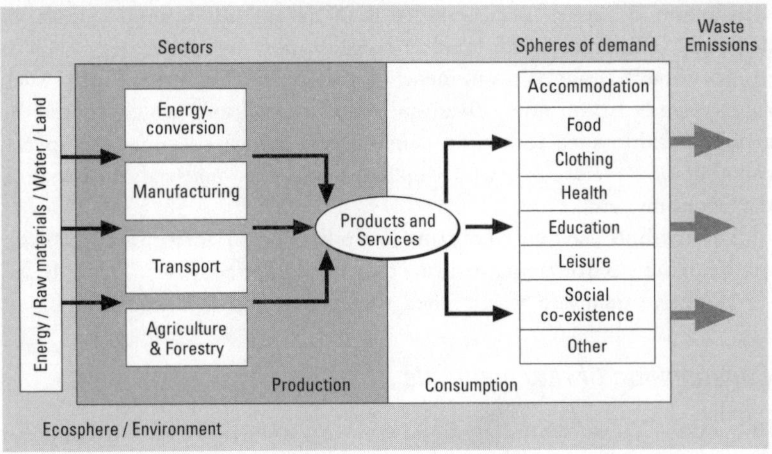

exported by the countries of the South is thus completely attributed to those states. On the other hand, shared responsibility for the consequences of German exports (vehicles and machines alongside pesticides and toxic waste) is insufficiently taken into account.

The structural causes of environmental stress will be examined here so as to offer an empirical basis for a change of direction. This will cover different sectors of the economy and private consumption. The relative impact of various aspects of demand will serve to provide adequately documented indicators of environmental impact. This dual approach reflects recognition that production and consumption should be viewed as reciprocal determinants in that sphere (figure 4.1).

The a priori non-material sectors of health, education, leisure, social life, etc., are considered alongside the material spheres of food, clothing, and housing. The degree to which a sphere of demand, such as energy consumption, contributes to a specific impact on the environment depends on the nature and quantity of goods bought to meet this demand.

Two steps are essentially necessary:

1. Calculation of cumulative environmental impact (by way of totalling the individual processes involved) in producing "end-use goods".
2. Establishment of a classificatory structure answering the question: "What demand is served by purchases of goods by the private economy or the state?"

The most important methodological decision in this context is that mobility should be comprehended as a secondary category, comprising satisfaction of other needs, rather than as an autonomous sphere of demand. Other decisions involve consumption by the state, which is proportionally assigned (in monetary terms) to private utilization of such categories as health and education. State expenditure which cannot be grouped within such realms of demand is summarized under the special category of "social life", which includes public administration, boosting the economy, etc.

The method used here constitutes a new kind of instrument for summarizing the environmental relevance of consumer activities. This is based on extensive data and was applied to Germany in this study.

Consumption of raw materials

In section 2.3 we defined withdrawal of resources as the criterion for potential impact on the environment, following the precautionary principle. We distinguish between resources subject to further processing (raw materials) and those merely displaced to make access to raw materials possible and then returned to nature ("ecological rucksacks") in order to indicate that utilization may often involve only part of what is extracted. We concretize the indicator of material extraction at the national level by taking into account both domestic withdrawals of resources and imports from other countries. The total figure for an economy thus entails domestic withdrawal plus imports and minus exports. This magnitude is termed a country's "global material consumption".

Development and present situation

In the period between 1960 and 1990 the former Federal Republic of Germany experienced its highest ever rates of increase in domestic withdrawals of raw materials during the sixties and early seventies (figure 4.2, top). By 1972 the annually withdrawn total had risen by around 60%. This fell by the end of the eighties to the sixties level and then rose again. However, since the ecological rucksack element of domestic withdrawals continued to increase during that period, the total figure (raw materials + additional impact) rose constantly rather than stagnating.

Imports and exports of raw materials and manufactured products increased sharply during the entire period, indicating ever greater integration of the German economy in the world market (figure 4.2, middle). Imports' share in the domestic total (withdrawals + imports) rose from 15% in 1960 to 38% in 1990. During the overall period the level of imports clearly exceeded that of exports (on the average by between 70

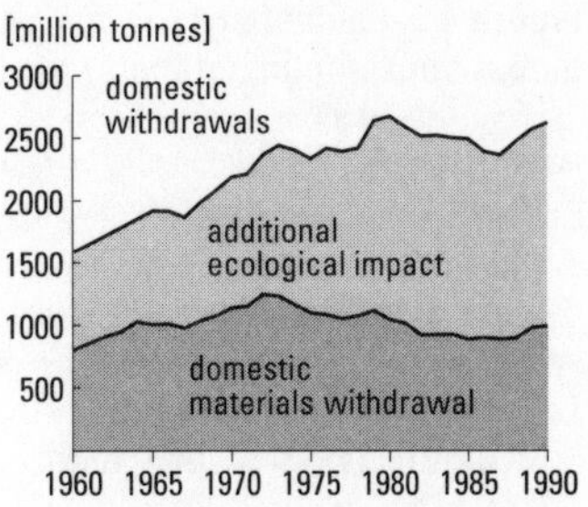

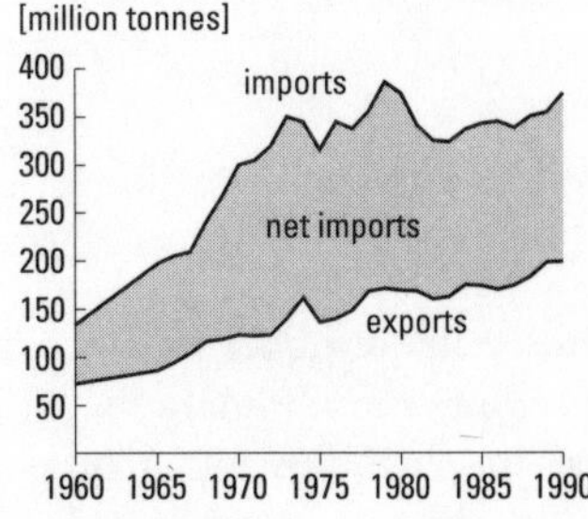

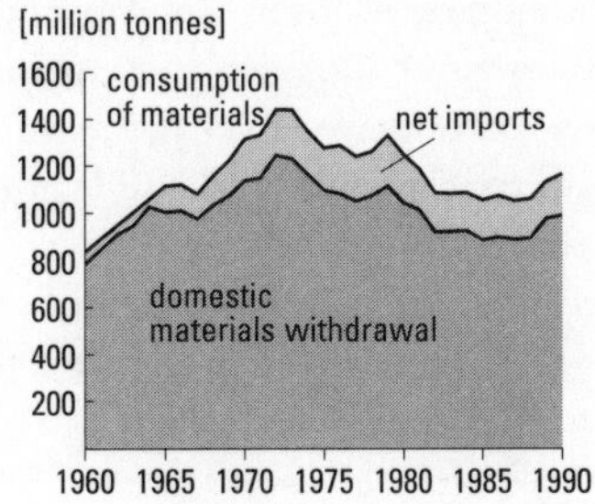

Figure 4.2 Development of domestic withdrawal of materials (inclusive of ecological rucksacks), imports, exports, and consumption of primary materials (without additional impact) in the former Federal Republic (*Source*: Own calculations)

and 100%), and visible consumption of materials accordingly exceeded domestic withdrawals by between 5 and 15% (figure 4.2, bottom, without taking into account ecological rucksacks whose contribution to this sphere is still unknown).

Foreign trade

In imports the "ecological rucksack" comprises all material flows "from the source to the frontier" which are not incorporated in the actual product. Such materials are usually returned, more or less unchanged, to the environment in the countries of origin – in the form of the waste accompanying extraction and emissions. The magnitudes presented here are estimates of the minimum amounts involved. The "ecological

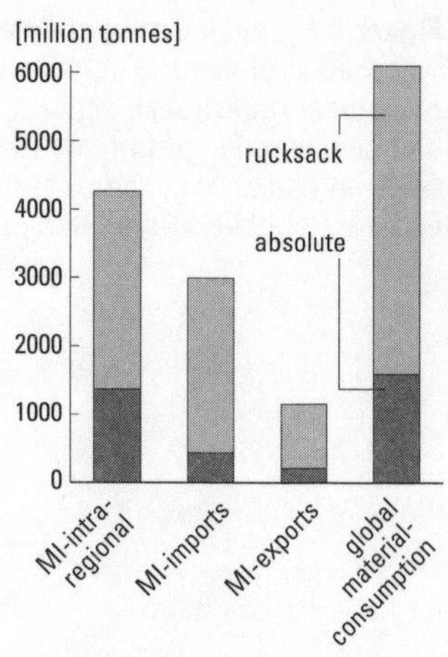

Figure 4.3 Estimate of Germany's global consumption of materials in 1991
This consists of the sum of withdrawals of materials at home and abroad (for exports to Germany) minus withdrawals for exports (MI = material input from the environment). The dark part of the bars represents exploited materials – i.e. absolute amounts of imports and exports. The light areas constitute their "ecological rucksacks". (*Source*: Bringezu and Schütz, 1995)

rucksack" resulting from Germany's imports is greater than the outcome of domestic withdrawals. This demonstrates a disproportionate impact on the environment in other countries.

If domestic withdrawals, imports, and exports (as in figure 4.2) are summarized (now incorporating ecological rucksacks), the upshot is Germany's global use of materials (figure 4.3). As long as more accurate data are unavailable, the assumption is that the "ecological rucksack" of goods exported and used at home is in general the same. In 1991 the Federal German economy's global consumption of materials was 6.1 billion tonnes (excluding water and air). That amounts to annual per capita use of 76 tonnes, which is taken from the natural environment and returned sooner or later.

Balance by sectors

This analysis of use of materials by various production sectors is based on official economic statistics relating to the former Federal Republic in 1990. The 58 production sectors distinguished are here summarized as 23 sectors so as to increase comprehensibility. This analysis considers material input in production spheres that supply "final use" (consumption by the private sector or state, investment in plant, changes in stocks, exports).

Figure 4.4 provides an indication of where great potential exists for reducing the quantity of materials used in manufacturing. Provisional findings show particularly great potential in building, finished metal products, and transportation by road, water, and air. In those spheres assessment of increasing functionality for the purchaser should be the priority rather than the highest possible turnover of material goods. ("Orientation toward Service", see sections 5.3 and 5.4.)

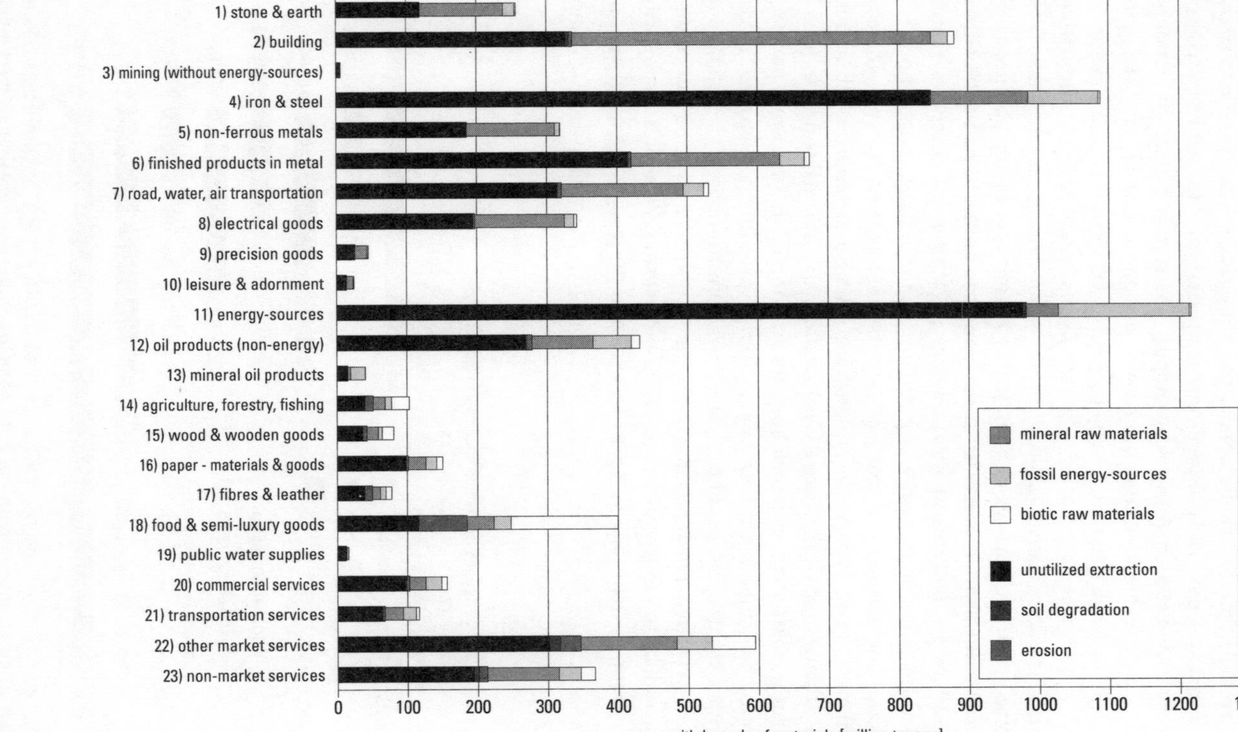

Figure 4.4 Material input in Federal German production sectors supplying final use (Former Federal Länder in 1990)

The overall material input was iteratively attributed to different branches of the economy on the basis of their share in supplies to other spheres, excluding water and air

Figure 4.5 Withdrawals of materials according to categories of demand, based on provisional data (*Source*: Behrensmeier and Bringezu, 1995b)

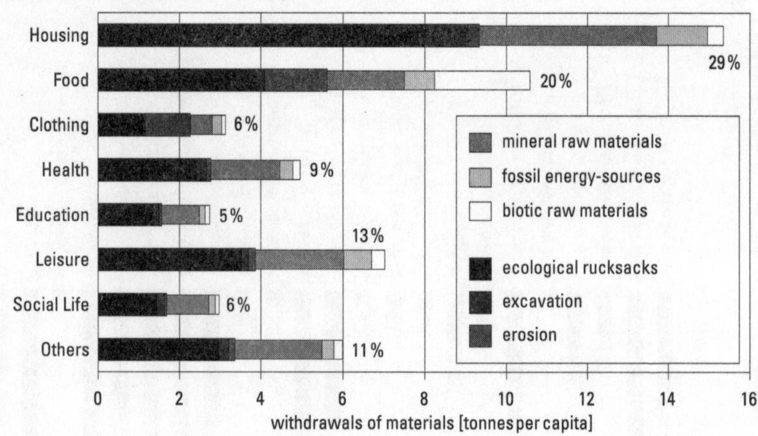

Balance by categories of demand

By far the highest level of withdrawals (29% of the total) is linked with demands for housing. This takes account of the annual use of materials for the construction of new houses, the extension and maintenance of existing buildings, and upkeep (heating etc.). Use of mineral raw materials and the ecological rucksack impact is clearly greater than in the other categories of demand – resulting from both the building materials themselves (stone and earth) and material-intensive preliminary work (steel etc.). Energy consumption (heating, electricity) beyond the associated flows in material (energy-sources, ecological rucksacks) also exerts a considerable impact.

Food is directly or indirectly involved in a fifth of material flows. Just under a quarter of that total derives from private use of energy for preparation of foodstuffs and shopping trips, and more than three-quarters is accounted for by processing and trading (a quarter by transportation, packaging, and infrastructure; and a half by production and processing in agriculture and the food industry).

Meat and meat products (with 17 kilos of materials per kilo of product) have the largest additional ecological impact because of the great amounts of animal feed used – followed by such basics as sugar, glucose, cocoa, and plant oils and fats. Fish and fish products, and vegetables and fruit, come off best. Overall the production and processing of meat and meat products amount to around 16% , and of milk and milk products to around 20%, of consumption of materials in the food category. These figures make clear that changes in eating habits most certainly could contribute towards a reduction in environmental impact. However, far-ranging relief can only occur if all levels of the product-chain – production, processing, packaging, transportation, and preparation of meals – are included.

In third place here (with 13%) is the demand category of "leisure". This reflects the long-observed trend towards material satisfaction of non-material needs. "Free" time is increasingly structured with material- and energy-intensive products and activities such as (long-distance) travel, hi-fi and video equipment, sports apparatus, and suchlike. Transition to the leisure society – with current trends continuing – thus by no means leads to resource-saving, sustainable consumption (see also section 5.4).

Consumption of materials in other industrial countries

Extensive calculations of use of materials (as above for Germany inclusive of additional ecological impact) are not yet available for all industrial countries. The usual stock-takings of environmental consumption do not take into account either the fact that damage is done during the stage of resource withdrawals in other nations, or that some use is exported and should be assigned to the final consumer.

Nevertheless, existing statistics about consumption of selected metals do permit a number of clear-cut conclusions. By far the greatest part of global consumption is attributable to a small group of countries – mostly industrial nations. For many metals 10 countries are responsible for between two-thirds and four-fifths of world consumption. Only some newly industrializing states, such as China or Mexico, are to be found in the top 10.

The overview also shows that shortages are to be expected within the foreseeable future for a number of materials (copper, zinc) on the basis of today's known reserves and extraction technologies – especially if the high levels of consumption in existing industrial states are increasingly followed in countries pursuing industrialization.

Energy consumption

Development and the present situation

In the former Federal Republic primary energy consumption increased by 85% between 1960 and 1980. During the eighties it stagnated at a high level, and then rose again slightly at the start of the nineties (see figure 4.6). Despite growing utilization of nuclear energy, even today Germany is still almost completely dependent (90%) on fossil fuels. Nuclear energy's low-level (10%) contribution to primary supplies demonstrates what an enormous increase in the number of reactors would be

Figure 4.6 Primary energy consumption in Germany (1993) and the contribution made by renewable energies (1994)
(*Sources*: Bundesministerium für Wirtschaft; Nitsch, 1995; own calculations)

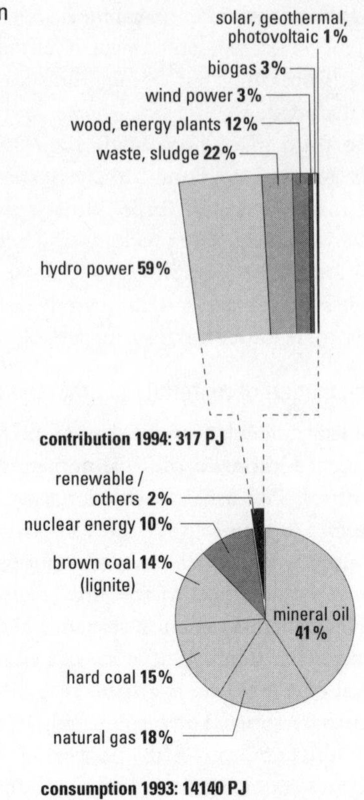

necessary to replace an appreciable percentage of fossil fuels (see section 3.2). Viewed in absolute terms, utilization of renewable energies increased by about a half during the past 30 years. However, their proportional share (in 1994 still around 2% – figure 4.6) declined because of the great increase in overall consumption of primary energy. As already shown with the indicator for withdrawals of materials, a rapid and evident rise in use of renewable resources only seems possible if at the same time the level of overall utilization is reduced through making the most of existing potential for savings (see section 3.2).

The minor contribution made by renewable energies largely derives (95%) from the "classic" forms of water power, wood-burning, and waste-incineration (wrongly termed renewable). Despite great increases, new technologies such as wind and solar power today merely meet a thousandth part of German requirements for primary energy (figure 4.6).

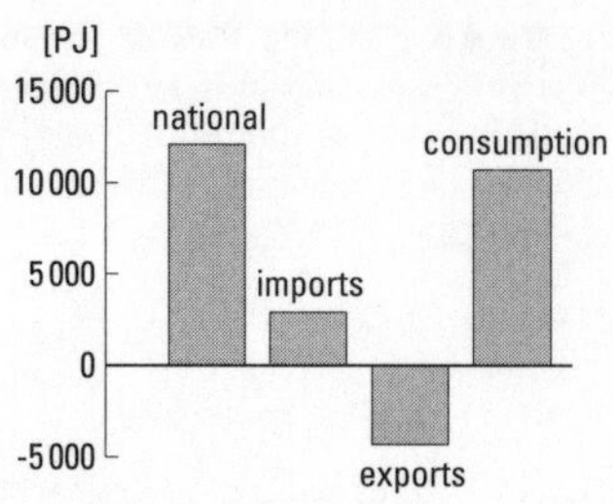

Figure 4.7 Estimate of primary energy use in domestic production, imports and exports, and domestic demand (= consumption) for the former Federal Republic in 1988 (utilizing an input–output audit) (*Source*: Weber and Fahl, 1993)

Foreign trade

National energy statistics have to date been based on energy-sources, and do not take into account what is known as "grey" energy, hidden in products imported and exported. Even though such an expanded balance cannot be completely implemented for the foreseeable future because of insufficient data, at least an estimate of the export/import balance is possible (figure 4.7).

This shows that the energy expended on production of exports in 1988 amounted to around 35% of the figure for domestic production. Outside Germany energy was also used in the preparation of goods for the German market, amounting to around 24% of the domestic figure (all figures relating to the former Federal Republic). This high exchange-quota is a consequence of the German economy being embedded in the world market. In 1988 the energy trade balance (exports minus imports) was positive with the energy-content of goods exported exceeding that of imports. More recent surveys indicate that the situation is changing during the nineties because of an increase in imports of energy-intensive products.[2] Deployment of energy usually involves local environmental impact (including use of water and toxic emissions), so this trend is an indication of increasing displacement of environmental burdens onto other countries.

Balance by sectors

Despite ongoing technical improvements even today around 30% of primary energy in the conversion sector (in generation of electricity and district heating, in refineries, and in delivery of natural gas) is "lost" – almost exclusively in the form of unused waste heat (figure 4.8). The profitability of utilization of waste heat depends on the distance from potential place of utilization, so the causes of this state of affairs are to be sought in centralized electricity generation in big power stations.

End-use energy consumption[3] is today roughly equally split between industry, households, and transportation with low-level consumers (including agriculture) accounting for the rest. End-use consumption by

Figure 4.8 Primary energy consumption by sector, former Federal Republic
(*Source*: Bundesministerium für Wirtschaft)

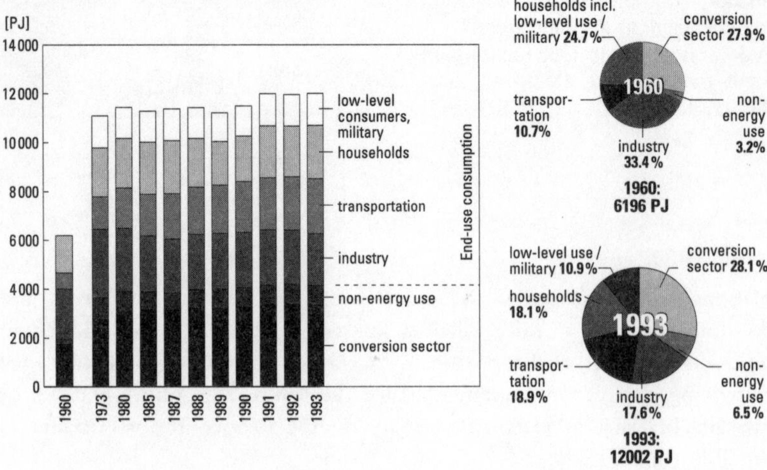

private households and low-level users has been stagnant over the past two decades, sinking by around a third in industry, but increasing by over a half in transportation. The large growth-rates in transportation mainly result from the increase in road traffic where end-use consumption in the former Federal Republic has risen by around 700% since the start of the sixties, and today comprises two thirds of the total usage in that sector.

Balance by categories of demand

Almost a third of total consumption of primary energy is accounted for by housing, far outstripping other categories (figure 4.9). Almost 70% is attributable to direct use of energy sources in households (mainly heating, and to a much lesser degree electrical appliances and lighting – table 4.1). Just under 20% is still accounted for by the erection and maintenance of buildings.

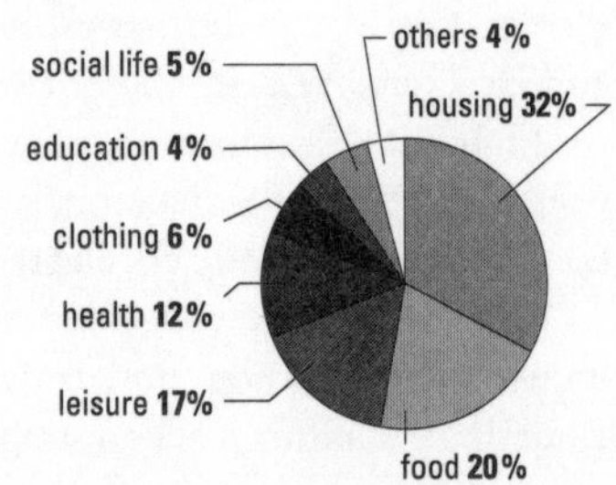

Figure 4.9 Primary energy consumption according to demand categories in the former Federal Republic, 1988
(*Source*: Weber and Fahl, 1993)

Table 4.1 End-use energy-consumption[4] in private households, listed in accordance with service and category of demand, former Federal Republic, 1987 (*Source*: Bach, 1993; ordering in demand categories after Weber and Fahl, 1993)

Energy service	**Demand category**	**Sum (PJ)**	**Share (%)**
Space heating	Housing	1760.7	80.7
Hot water	Health, food	192.6	8.8
Cooling/freezing	Food	65.7	3.0
Warm meals	Food	48.1	2.2
Lighting	Housing	27.4	1.3
Laundry	Clothing	23.6	1.1
Television	Leisure	19.0	0.9
Washing up	Food	12.0	0.6
Drying laundry	Clothing	8.6	0.4
Appliances	Leisure/housing/food	20.9	1.0
Total		**2178.5**	**100.0**

The food category accounts for a fifth of primary energy consumption. However, around four-fifths involves cumulative energy use in the production of foodstuffs, and only one-fifth preparing meals.

In third place is "leisure" (17%) where over 50% of energy consumption derives from transportation. The rest is divided between a large number of very diverse groups of goods and activities in accordance with a wide range of leisure pursuits.

These three categories of demand – housing, food, and leisure – account for just under 70% of total primary energy consumption – as with the indicator for "material input". The other categories will not be examined more closely here.

Energy consumption in other industrial states

Dependence on fossil fuels is a global phenomenon. In 1993 90% of global consumption of primary energy was covered by such sources.

Figure 4.10 Development of water extraction in the former Federal Republic
(*Source*: Statistiches Bundesamt)

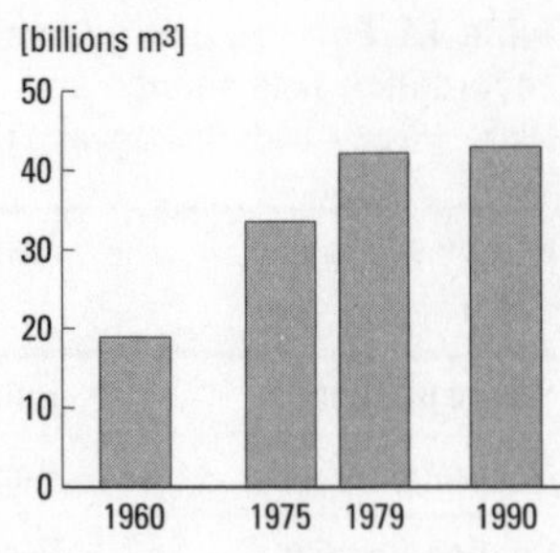

Water use

Water is a renewable resource. After human beings have made use of water, it is returned (varying in quality) to nature's water cycle. The relevant magnitude for the amount of water used is the annual extraction from rivers, lakes, and ground-water reserves.

Increased water extraction in the former Federal Republic is shown in figure 4.10. After a doubling between 1960 and 1980 there followed high-level stagnation.

By far the greatest consumer of water is the electricity industry, whose need for coolants (almost all running water) accounts for 60% of water use. The second largest group of users (around a quarter) is formed by mines and associated enterprises. Consumption by the chemical industry alone (around four billion cubic metres annually) is as high as use in private households – each less than 10% of total extraction.

Even though ground-water only accounts for a small percentage of the total, consumption is of particular significance since renewal takes a long time. Today less than a third of the water used for supplying the population is taken from rivers and lakes since they are much polluted by many substances discharged by industry and private households or airborne – despite all the successes achieved by precautionary treatment of effluents. Seventy per cent of Germany's drinking water is pumped from wells. Supplies are thus moving away from the surface towards groundwater, and public consumption has continued to increase in recent years, albeit somewhat more slowly, exerting fluctuating pressure on reserves. One of the causes of that ongoing increase is the fact that the same high quality water, fit for human consumption, is used for a diversity of purposes (flushing toilets, washing cars, cooking), and waterworks are thus forced to extract large amounts.

Water utilization in other countries

Over-utilization of precious water supplies in many parts of the world as an outcome of increased irrigation (following population growth) and industrial and private use has become a serious ecological problem. National statistics often conceal the incidence of regional or local shortages. The South-West of the USA – in general a land rich in water – is afflicted by chronic shortages. In California annual over-utilization of ground-water amounts to 1.6 billion cubic metres, which is 15% of total utilization. Two-thirds of that over-utilization occurs in the Central Valley, the region's "vegetable basket", which depends on intensive irrigation. The result is sinking land-levels (up to 8 metres in the south of the Central Valley) and the slow drying up of entire eco-systems (e.g. Lake Mono).

Land utilization

Settlement and transportation

Compared with the areas used for agriculture and forestry, taking up over 80% of Germany, the proportion of land devoted to settlement and transportation (13%) initially seems of lesser significance (figure 4.11). However, as has been shown in section 2.3, this form of land use by human beings is of particular ecological relevance, involving, among other things, paving over land surfaces, fragmentation, and noise pollution and toxic discharges along transport links.

The amount of land used for settlement and transportation in the former Federal Republic almost doubled between 1950 and 1993. During that period an average of around 100 hectares of land (130 football pitches) was newly built-up daily. By 1993 the total area amounted to 11.3% of the Federal Republic, i.e. bigger than North Rhine-Westphalia and about twice as large as Rhineland-Palatinate.

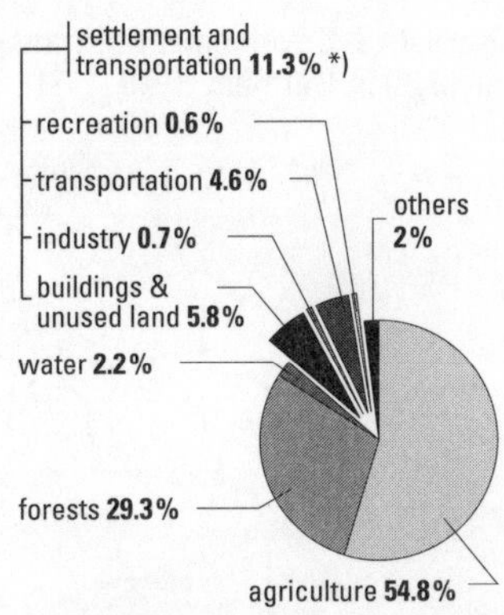

Figure 4.11 Use of land in Germany in 1993 (*Source*: Statistiches Bundesamt)

Figure 4.12 Development of living-space per person in the former Federal Republic (*Source*: Statistisches Bundesamt)

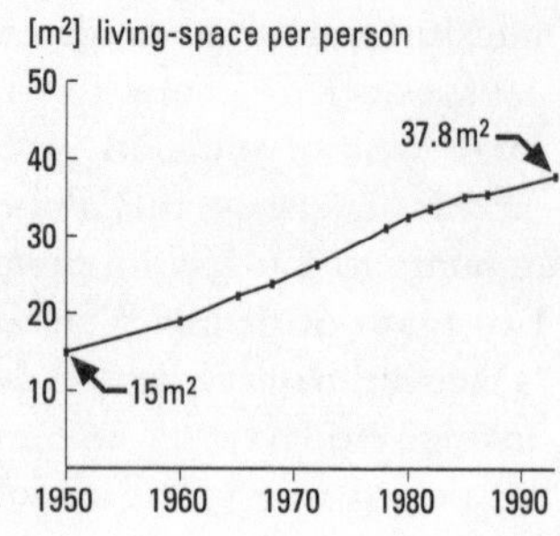

One of the driving-forces behind constant expansion of settlement is unrestricted growth in demands for living-space and size of building plots. The average living area per person in 1950 was still only 15 square metres, while the figure today for the former Federal Republic is over 37 square metres (figure 4.12). In new settlements detached one-family homes predominate with around 200 square metres of net residential building land per inhabitant – roughly three times as much as would be required for land-saving, high-density construction.[5]

This trend towards greater living-space and detached houses helps account for the fact that energy consumption in private households has not gone down during the past 20 years despite better heating and insulation technology (see figure 4.8).

Figure 4.13 Development of transportation infrastructure (main roads and railways) in Germany 1948–1991 (*Source*: Bundesministerium für Verkehr)

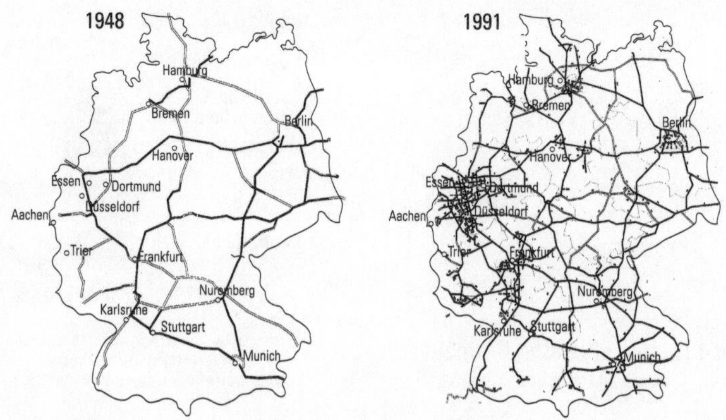

The transportation system, which now covers around 5% of the total area, was at least equally important in determining land use for settlement and traffic. Rapid growth since the fifties has largely been the result of giving preferential treatment to the automobile, which takes up an exceptional amount of land, rather than to any overall increase in transportation efficiency.

Purely quantitative growth in areas of settlement and transportation was paralleled by large-scale expansion of infrastructure, accompanied by increasing fragmentation of related areas (figure 4.13).

The number of non-fragmented, low-traffic areas of over 100 square km in the former Federal Republic declined by 15% (to 296) just in the period between 1977 and 1987. In the former Länder in 1987 there were only just under 300 areas where one could walk in the same direction for two hours without having to cross a relatively busy road. These low-traffic areas then constituted less than a fifth of the total area.

Agricultural utilization

In recent decades employment of fertilizers and biocides has increased alongside greater consumption of energy, raw materials, and water (figure 4.14). Utilization rose sharply between 1960 and 1980, and was followed by high-level stagnation or a slight decline. The application of nitrogen fertilizers and pesticides thus roughly tripled between 1960 and 1980, and then remained constant during the eighties. The high degree of correlation between those trends is striking. Only since the end of the eighties has use of such substances fallen.

The third indicator under consideration here is soil erosion – the amount of top-soil carried away annually by water and wind. Soil-renewal is a very slow process – formation of a layer 2 or 3 cm deep takes several hundred years – so erosion means an irreversible long-term reduction of soil fertility and an endangering of food supplies for future generations. The main causes of soil erosion are enlargement of fields, accompanied by elimination of natural barriers to erosion (such as hedges and trees), "re-allocation of land use", the conversion of nature into arable land, intensified cultivation of erosion-promoting crops such as maize and sugar-beet, and loss of humus through a decline in use of animal dung and in more intensive husbandry. Average soil losses today are between 10 and 12 tonnes per hectare annually, which amounts to a total of around 120 million tonnes a year. That scarcely conceivable amount is roughly equivalent to the total biomass (around 190 million tonnes) produced by German agriculture annually.[6] This comparison makes clear what a burden today's agricultural methods are heaping onto the shoulders of future generations.

Figure 4.14 **Development of national use of nitrogen and phosphate fertilizers and pesticides on agricultural land in the former Federal Republic** (*Source*: Bundesministerium für Ernährung, Landwirtschaft und Forsten)

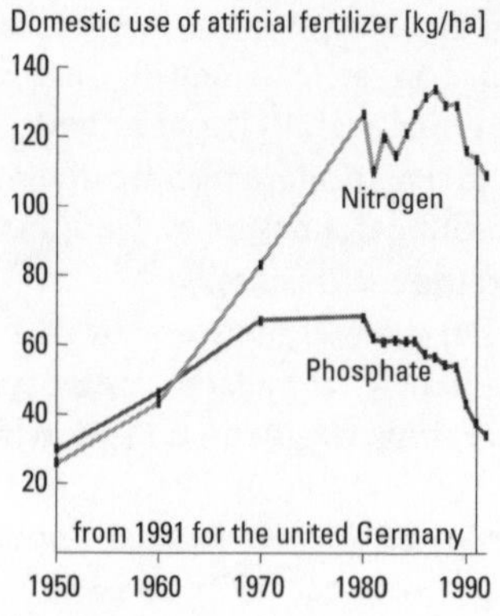

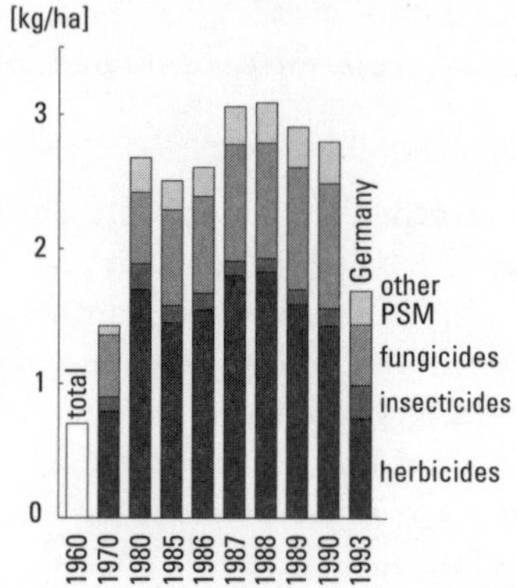

Foreign trade

Use of land for agriculture in the former Federal Republic declined by around 15% between 1970 and 1990 – for the most part in favour of expansion of areas of settlement and transportation (see above). Imports and exports of agricultural products rose greatly – exports by 50% and imports by 30% – as a consequence of increasing integration of German agriculture in the European and global markets. Despite higher rates of increase for exports, in 1990 the land devoted in other countries to production of German imports was still more extensive than the German land used for cultivation of produce for exporting. This means that German consumption of agricultural products is based on a net claim to farming areas in other countries. In 1991 that German claim (inclusive of the former GDR) amounted to around 30% of agricultural land at home.

In 1991 Germans used 0.26 hectares of arable land per head for consumption of agricultural products – a little less than the global aver-

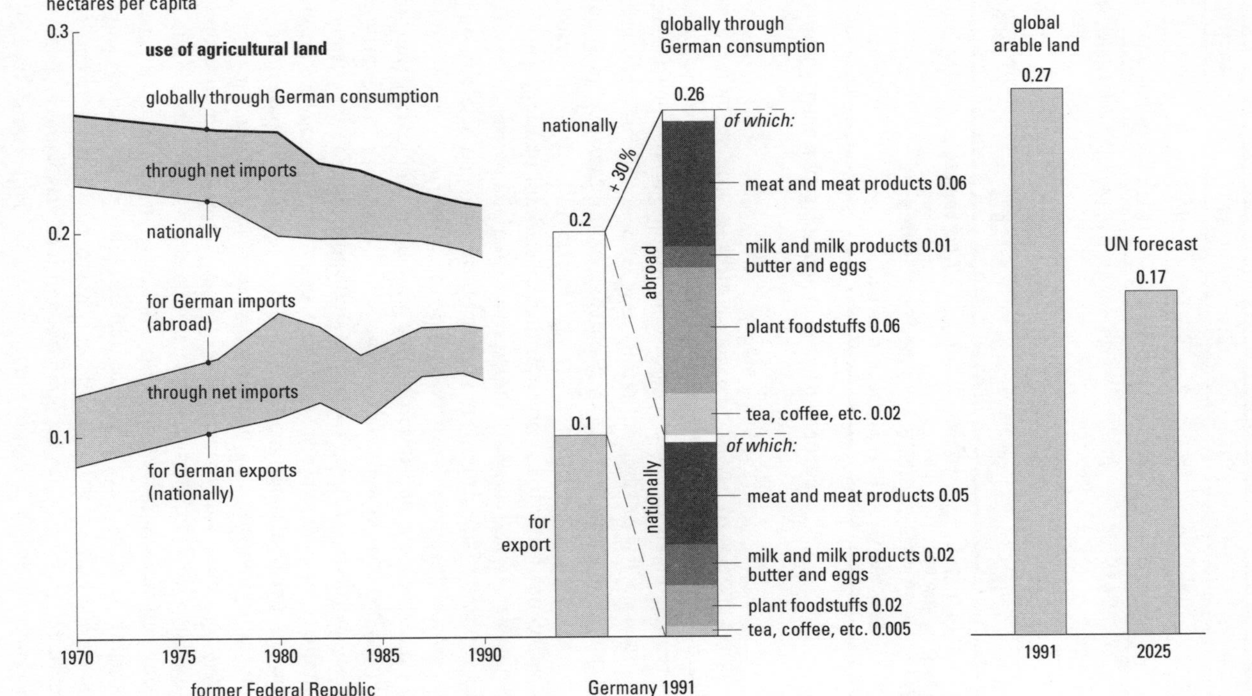

Figure 4.15 Development of land use in agriculture in the former Federal Republic between 1970 and 1990, based on extensive analysis of agricultural, production, and foreign trade statistics Plant and animal products consumed in this country were followed back to their country of origin. The amount of arable land needed for supplying all biotic products was calculated on the basis of statistics for harvests and animal foodstuffs. (*Source*: Own calculations)

age of 0.27 hectares. However, the latter magnitude will be much reduced during the decades ahead as world population increases – with the United Nations forecasting around 0.17 hectares per capita in the year 2025. That does not even take into account irreversible losses of arable land, particularly in the countries of the South.[7] In view of that development, which constitutes a threat to future global food supplies, today's overall level of land use in Germany does not seem sustainable and should therefore be reduced through changes in structures of consumption. A reduction in meat-eating, which in 1991 accounted for about 40% of the land used outside Germany, would make an important contribution.

Increased integration of German agriculture in international markets in recent decades has resulted in almost half the land used for farming serving cultivation for export, while only just over a third of the agricultural produce consumed in Germany originates in this country. Bearing in mind that around 170 million tonnes of agricultural produce originate in Germany annually, the enormous expenditure on transportation becomes apparent. The raw materials and products that are transported could for the most part be produced and consumed within a regional cycle. The land devoted to such German imports as tropical fruits, coffee, tea, and cocoa – which cannot be grown in Germany for climatic reasons – is less than a fifth of the total, and very little compared with the land used for animal products (see figure 4.15). Trade in agricultural products makes clear how contradictory and ecologically counterproductive increasing integration of international markets is. The slogan here should be: as much regional market as possible, as little world market as necessary (see section 5.1).

Table 4.2 Continental distribution of soil degradation

		Share of degraded land for various uses			
	Land area (million km²)	**Degraded (%)**	**Arable land (%)**	**Unspoilt nature (%)**	**Woods & savannahs (%)**
Africa	29.66	17	65	31	19
Asia	42.56	18	38	20	27
Central & South America	21.91	14	51	14	14
North America	18.85	5	26	11	1
Europe	9.5	23	25	35	26
Oceania	8.82	12	16	19	8
World	**130.13**	**15**	**38**	**21**	**18**

Figure 4.16 Available arable land per capita (hectares)

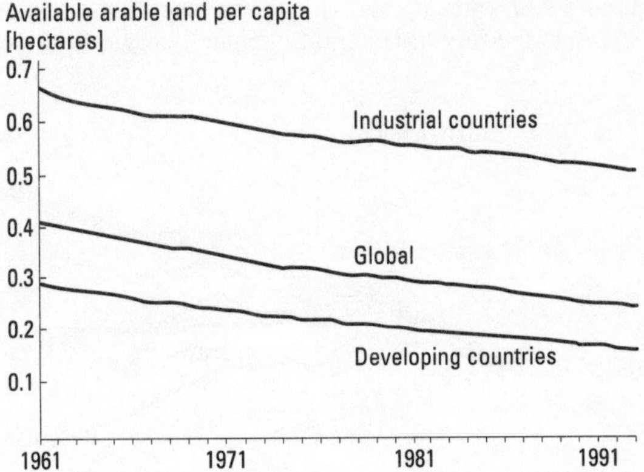

Worldwide land utilization – future shortages of fertile soils

The German trend in land utilization is paralleled across the world. Expansion of areas of settlement and transportation infrastructure plus over-use of agricultural areas are to be observed in both industrial and developing countries, albeit to widely differing degrees. The nature and extent of soil degradation vary widely from place to place. The share of degraded arable land thus extends from a quarter in Europe (or 16% in Oceania) to three-quarters in Central America; of unused green areas from 11% in North America to 31% in Africa; of woods and savannahs from 1% in North America to 38% in Central America (Table 4.2).

The loss of fertile arable land is particularly serious because safeguarding global food supplies is increasingly called in question as the world population continues to rise. One indication of that is the decline in arable land available per capita from 0.41 hectares in 1961 to 0.24 in 1993 (figure 4.16). Developing countries are particularly affected. For them the amount of agricultural land per head in 1993 was only 0.16 hectares – below the mean for meeting minimal human needs for plant-energy (0.17–0.3 hectares).

Selected emissions

The emissions selected in section 2.3 for inclusion in a system of environmental pollution indicators do not provide a complete picture, but they cover most of the physical causes of today's environmental problems.

Development and present situation

Over the past three decades highly disparate trends have become apparent with regard to emissions. In some cases considerable reductions have

Figure 4.17 Development of selected emissions and gross domestic product (GDP) in the former Federal Republic (*Source*: Statistisches Bundesamt, Umweltbundesamt)

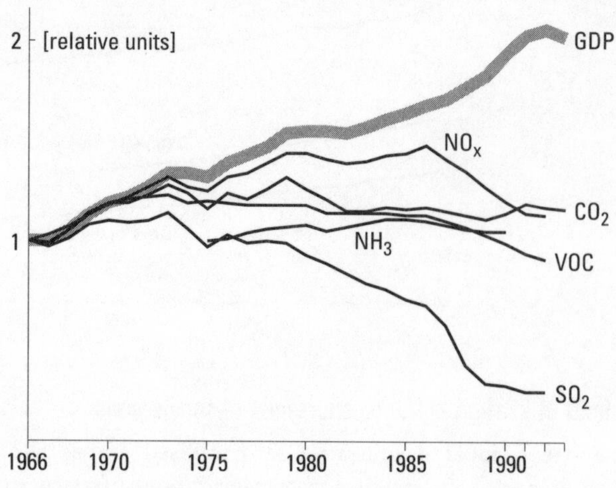

been achieved through application of environmental technology and replacement of pollutants by less toxic substances. For instance, SO_2 emissions in the former Federal Republic were reduced by over 80% between the sixties and the nineties through sulphur filtration and increased use of liquified and gaseous fuels. Comparable successes were also achieved through incorporation of dust-extraction systems (decline of 75% between 1960 and 1992) and better car engine technology, catalysers, and the changeover from coal to gas heating, leading to a 50% cut-back in carbon monoxide (CO) emissions between 1975 and 1992. An equally important success was achieved in 1994 when production of CFCs and halons was ended in accordance with the Montreal convention on protection of the ozone layer. However, this agreement permits utilization of old equipment as well as "essential uses" and trade in recycled substances, so a close watch must be kept on future developments.

Despite those important individual successes it is impossible to speak of a general improvement since emissions of many ecologically significant substances have only been reduced slightly or not at all (figure 4.17). Discharges of carbon dioxide (CO_2), the main cause of global warming, thus declined by a fifth during the eighties, but have been rising again since then and approaching the high level of the seventies. Ammonia emissions, which contribute towards ongoing degradation of forests, have changed little since the mid-seventies. Discharges of nitrogen oxides and

Figure 4.18 Estimate of the CO_2 balance in foreign trade (indirect emissions from imports minus exports) for the former Federal Republic (*Source*: UPI, 1994)

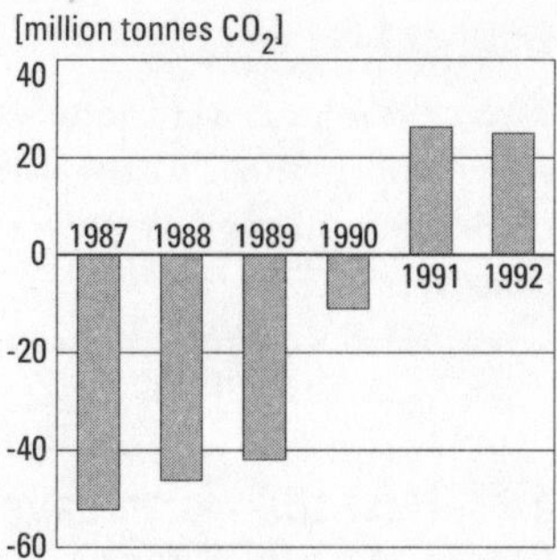

volatile organic compounds (VOCs) declined from the mid-seventies but recent summers have shown that these reductions are not sufficient for dealing with seasonal smog.

The findings in section 3.1 allow the overall situation to be summarized as: reduction in individual instances while the general problem remains. The decoupling from economic growth achieved for some emissions is not sufficient in most cases. Emissions stagnating at a high level signify ongoing discharges into eco-systems incapable of coping.

Foreign trade

The relation between imports and exports of CO_2-intensive products was reversed in the former Federal Republic between 1987 and 1992. In the latter year Germany imported considerably more CO_2-intensive products than it exported (figure 4.18). Domestic production also increased during the same period so it is inaccurate to speak of a displacement of production. Nevertheless, mounting German demand for energy- and CO_2-intensive products is increasingly met by way of imports. Local pollution (emissions of SO_2 and NO_x) linked with production thus takes place in other countries.

Balance by sectors

German emissions of carbon dioxide (CO_2), sulphur dioxide (SO_2), and nitrogen oxides (NO_x) are largely linked with utilization of fossil fuels. The amount of carbon dioxide and sulphur dioxide per converted energy-unit basically depends on the specific carbon or sulphur content of the energy-source. The amount of nitrogen oxide changes with combustion temperatures. Release of SO_2 and NO_x into the environment can be largely prevented by employing suitable filter technology, but financially viable means for dealing with slow-reaction CO_2 will not be available for the foreseeable future.

Emissions in other countries

Toxic emissions were reduced in most Western countries in the eighties – but not in all or to the same degree, depending on national legislation on desulphurization of power station emissions and introduction of vehicle catalysers. Reduction of CO_2 emissions constitutes a general problem since the necessary technology is not available.

4.2 How the North Lays Claim to the South's Environmental Space[9]

It is quite possible for a state to pursue ecologically sustainable development within its own borders, largely preserving its natural resources for present and future generations, while at the same time calling on resources from other countries to a degree that deprives them of the possibility of sustainable development and endangers the overall world situation.[10]

In an interdependent global economy, considerable effort is in fact required for recognition of connections between one's own actions and consequences elsewhere, particularly in the South. It may be obvious that shipping toxic waste from Germany to Africa is an ecological crime. However, the cutting down of Indonesian rainforests by Japanese timber companies is also a form of ecological exploitation, even though this example is already less clear-cut because felling takes place by mutual agreement. Things become more difficult in evaluating imports of raw materials from developing countries. Most of us do not usually know whether mining metals there destroys landscapes or not. With imports of flowers, animal feed, and citrus fruits, are the fertile soils used for cash crops being exhausted and poisoned by pesticides? Are they taken away from the poor who must then try to survive in areas of minimal productivity or jungles? We do not know for sure.

Climate change and destruction of the ozone layer

The man-made greenhouse effect is mainly caused by emissions of CO_2, chlorofluorocarbons, halons, methane, laughing gas, nitrogen oxides, and hydrocarbons, the substances that precede ozone at near-ground level. The major part of those emissions comes from the industrialized world. At present the G7 countries and the former Soviet Union are responsible for a good 55% of CO_2 emissions caused by energy production, even though only a sixth of the world population lives there. A citizen of the United States produces 25 times the annual per capita carbon dioxide emissions of someone living in India (tables 4.3 and 4.4).

Table 4.3 Absolute, per capita, and relative CO_2 emissions and percentage of world population in the G7 states and the former Soviet Union (*Source*: World Resources Institute, 1992 and 1994)

Country	CO_2 emissions (billion tonnes) 1991	Per capita (tonnes) 1991	% of global CO_2 emissions 1991	% of world population 1995
Japan	1.1	8.8	4.8	2.2
Canada	0.4	15.2	1.8	0.5
USA	4.9	19.5	21.6	4.6
France	0.4	6.6	1.7	1
Germany	1	12.1	4.3	1.4
Italy	0.4	7	1.8	1
Great Britain	0.6	10	2.6	1
ex-USSR	3.8	13.3	17*	5
Total	**12.6**	–	**55.6**	**16.7**

* Data for 1989

Table 4.4 Absolute, per capita, and relative CO_2 emissions and percentage of world population in selected developing countries (*Source*: World Resources Institute, 1992 and 1994)

Country	CO_2 emissions (billion tonnes) 1991	Per capita (tonnes) 1991	% of global CO_2 emissions 1991	% of world population 1995
Brazil	0.22	1.4	1	2.8
China	2.55	2.2	11.2	21.6
India	0.7	0.8	3.1	16.2
Egypt	0.08	1.5	0.4	1
Total	**3.55**	–	**15.7**	**41.6**

Figure 4.19 National/regional contributions to global increases of carbon dioxide in the atmosphere (1800–1988)

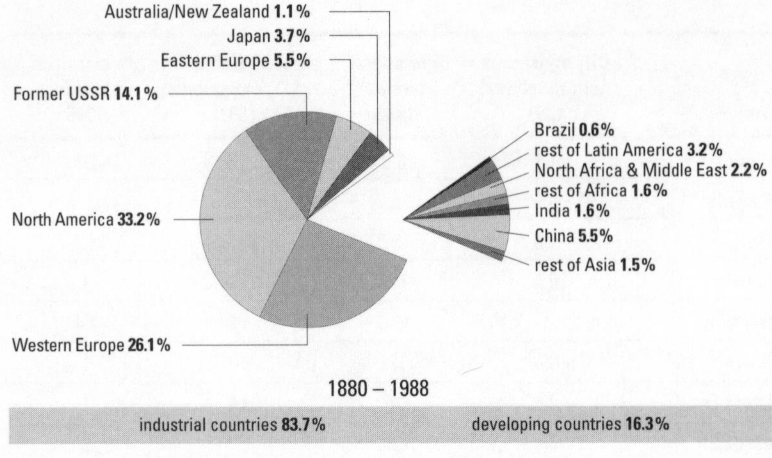

The disparity between industrial and developing countries becomes even greater if seen from a historical perspective. Lunde,[11] for example, estimates on the basis of available data and plausible assumptions that about 90% of the man-made greenhouse gas emissions in the past 150 years were produced by industrial states. The United Nations Environment Programme ascertained that over 80% of the global increase in carbon dioxide in the atmosphere between 1800 and 1988 was caused by those countries (figure 4.19).

Only in the case of methane emissions, mainly resulting from wetland rice paddies and cattle rearing,[12] are developing countries significantly involved, particularly India and China (each 15%). However, the methane emissions produced by an Indian subsistence farmer growing rice are not comparable with CO_2 discharges by the German owner of a big limousine. The former are "survival emissions", the latter "luxury emissions".[13]

Disparities are not limited to the greenhouse effect. The impact of global warming will most probably also be very unequally distributed. A wide range of research has shown that poorer countries will be particularly affected by droughts, a rise in sea-level, and more frequent storm-tides or hurricanes.[14] There are numerous reasons for this. Many developing countries are situated in parts of the world already subject to extreme climatic conditions (as in large parts of Africa) or liable to natural catastrophes (e.g. Bangladesh and the Philippines), so further global warming and a rise in sea-level will aggravate this situation.

The greenhouse effect also entails particularly negative consequences for agriculture and food supplies in the developing countries. The primary sector there often constitutes over 50% of the gross national product, and export revenue is largely dependent on agricultural produce. In industrial states agriculture, forestry, and fishing generally account for less than 5%. Global warming threatens the very existence of low-lying island-states like the Maldives or Barbados. If the sea-level rises by just one metre, large parts of such countries would vanish from the map. Nations such as Egypt, Bangladesh, and Senegal, whose most fertile regions are in river valleys and coastal deltas, are similarly endangered.

Opportunities for combating the consequences of global warming are also unequally distributed. If a wealthy country like the USA has poor harvests for climatic reasons, it can usually meet its needs on the world market. A poor country has very little chance of that. If a rich country like the Netherlands is threatened by a rising sea-level, it has technology and funds available to protect itself, for instance by strengthening dykes. A poor country is deprived of such possibilities. In short, those who have as yet contributed very little to the development of man-made global warming, but will probably be especially affected by it, lack the means to protect themselves.

Even more extreme is the discrepancy between those who cause depletion of the ozone layer in the stratosphere and those who suffer the consequences. This layer, surrounding the earth like a protective mantle and filtering ultra-violet radiation from the sun, is mainly attacked by chlorofluorocarbons (CFCs) and halons.[15] These substances, which have an extremely long life, were previously produced and used exclusively in industrial states. In 1991 only 12,000 tonnes of fully halogenated CFCs were used in the entire African continent, compared with 23,000 tonnes in Germany, 64,000 tonnes in Japan, and 90,000 tonnes in the USA.[16]

The consequences of ozone depletion in the stratosphere are again mainly to be felt in the Southern hemisphere. The possible impact of increasingly intense ultra-violet radiation – skin complaints, eye diseases, reduced photosynthesis in plants, and decline of marine plankton – will in all probability be greatest close to the Poles: in Chile, Argentina, Southern Africa, and South Australia. The general link remains constant: the consequences of what is produced in the North are mainly borne in the South, which has no effective means for countering them.

Exploitation and pollution of the oceans

The world's seas also belong to the global commons, which can in principle be used by everyone – within certain limits and economic/

technical possibilities. Defined property rights only exist with regard to coastal waters, which according to international law (see below) are assigned to the adjacent state.

Today the ocean, which has always seemed infinite, covering almost three-quarters of the earth's surface with its diverse eco-systems, containing 97% of the world's water and deeper in some places than Mount Everest is high, is in extreme danger: because of the input of pollutants, nutrients, sediments, oil, and waste; because of over-fishing and the extraction of raw materials; because of construction of dykes and the reclaiming of coastal wetlands for building purposes; and because of ozone-depletion in the stratosphere and the man-made greenhouse effect.

The countries of the South are singularly dependent on fishing for protein supplies. At the turn of the century around 5 million tonnes of fish were caught across the world annually; today the figure is around 84 million tonnes – an increase of nearly 1600%. However, the annual growth rates have been falling for years now. Between 1950 and 1970 the increase was still 6% annually, but between 1970 and 1990 it fell to 2.3%. In recent years the annual catch has even declined in absolute terms.

Obviously exploitation of fish-stocks has reached a limit. That is also confirmed by the FAO, whose assumption is that sustainable exploitation of sea fish would amount to around 100 million tonnes annually. However, that estimate must be viewed as being over-optimistic since the same organization believes that even today all 17 of the world's main fishing-grounds are close to, or have already exceeded, the limits of exploitation. High-tech fishing and the sheer number of boats are mainly responsible. The United Nations estimates that the fishing-power of the existing fleet is twice what is required for sustainability. The people who suffer most from this industrialization are traditional fishermen and small and medium-size businesses – especially in developing countries.[17]

The coming into force of the International Convention on the Law of the Sea[18] in November 1994 could make possible better management and protection of fish-stocks. Among other things this convention provides for extension of territorial waters from 12 to 200 miles. Coastal waters, wetlands, and deltas are of particular importance for oceans' biological productivity. About 90% of the fish caught come from the third of the ocean near land. In principle, creation of the 200 mile zone creates a possibility of utilizing fish-stocks in such a way as to maintain a dynamic balance. This hope may prove to be a false one since nearly all fishing nations systematically built up their fleets in recent years by way of subsidies and tax advantages. This expanded capacity wants to be used to the full, despite the obvious fact that over-fishing will in the long run deprive fishermen of the basis for their existence.

Industrial and developing countries are equally responsible for protecting the ocean and its ecological functions. Over-fishing is by no means a "privilege" of the industrial states, but because of their technological power they clearly make disproportionate use of the "fruits of the sea". Japan, the USA, and Europe (including Russia) thus account for over 40% of the catch – for somewhat over a fifth of the world's population.

At the same time these countries are largely responsible for doing ecological harm to the world's seas. A study by the University of California comes to the conclusion that more intense ultra-violet radiation has reduced the ocean's biological productivity (the production of phytoplankton) by between 6 and 12% in the area beneath the Antarctic ozone hole.[19] That hole is caused almost entirely by industrial activities. Discharges of refuse and toxic substances into the sea – by way of coastal industries, rivers, or the air – also derive to a very high degree from industrial states. Such pollution includes nitrogen from road traffic – and 80% of the world's automobiles are to be found in Europe (excluding Russia), Japan, and the USA. Chemical fertilizers play a large part in eutrophication of the ocean. The amount used per hectare of arable land in Germany is 25 times as much as the African average, five times as much as Pakistan, and more than twice as much as China.

Industrial nations are using considerably more than their share of the world's seas and contributing disproportionately to their pollution. Those states must therefore reduce discharges of refuse and toxic substances into oceans and cut back on consumption of fish-stocks to a sustainable level. For fishing fleets that primarily entails "technical disarmament" so that they will not be able to pursue fish to the remotest corners of the world's seas.

Ecological rucksacks in German raw material imports

The countries of the South are not only put at a disadvantage by industrial states' over-utilization of such shared assets as the atmosphere and the oceans. Less obvious, but no less significant, is unequal distribution of the pollution resulting from extraction of raw materials. The countries of the South bear the brunt of the ecological consequences since they are mainly suppliers of raw materials in world trade.

Unprocessed agricultural products

In 1991 about 30% of Germany's imports of unprocessed agricultural products came from the countries of the South. However, this percentage involved around two-thirds of the "ecological rucksack", depicted here in simplified fashion as erosion of the land used[20] (figure 4.20).

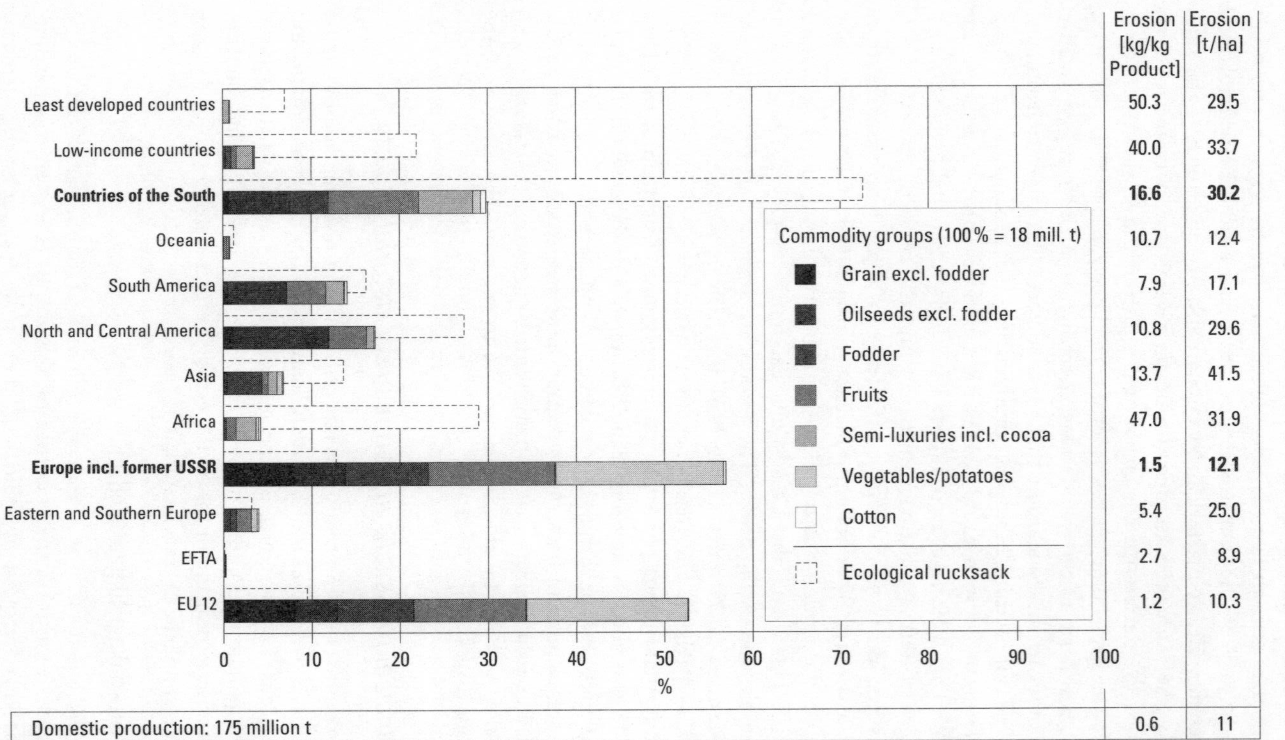

Figure 4.20 German imports of agricultural commodities Classified according to country and categories, showing the associated soil loss in producer states; the erosion figures are projections. (*Sources:* Foreign trade statistics, own calculations)

The reason for this is that imports from the South are handicapped by above-average erosion rates. In Germany the ratio of land erosion to harvest is on the average around 0.6 to 1. The equivalent magnitude in the case of German imports is about 10 times greater, and for countries in the South 25 times greater.

Tropical timber

Trade in forestry products provides another example of asymmetry in economic relations between North and South. In 1991 34% of Germany's imports of unprocessed forestry products (primarily natural rubber and tropical timber) came from countries of the South, while only about 1% of processed goods came from there. The bulk of Germany's imports of tropical timber originate in Africa where the wood is harvested in forests rather than plantations, thereby devastating large and richly diverse areas.

Abiotic raw materials

The unused by-products of raw materials extraction (including overburden and soil excavation) can serve as a measure of the additional ecological impact entailed in imports of abiotic raw materials (minerals, ores, sources of energy). This yields a qualitatively similar but not quite so stark a picture as in the case of unprocessed agricultural products. In 1991 a quarter of Germany's imports came from the countries of the South, but the ecological rucksack due to these imports was again higher, amounting to 43% of the total.

The ratio between additional ecological impact and the raw materials actually used is on the average twice as high in imports of abiotic imports (three times as high for imports from the South) compared with national raw materials. The figures for imports from other European countries are more favourable. This is not due to old, environmentally destructive technologies being used to extract raw materials in the countries of the South. The decisive factor is that the minerals whose extraction causes exceptional environmental damage are mainly mined in the South and then exported to countries whose viable resources have already been exploited.

Unlike agricultural products, which can be grown again and again on the same piece of land by using sustainable methods, deposits of ores, minerals, and fossil fuels can only be mined once. The ecological follow-up costs, left out of account at that time, may be enormous. Natural habitats may be lost for ever and important eco-systems polluted for a long time. Sooner or later there will have to be compensation for this ongoing exploitation (even in the post-colonial era) to the advantage of the industrial countries and to the detriment of local eco-systems and the people dependent on them.

Commercial exploitation of biodiversity in the South

The countries of the South are home to a large percentage of biological diversity.[21] Tropical forests[22] in particular offer natural habitats for over 70% of all known species.[23] The "Wawilow Centres", areas with an exceptionally great variety of economically useful plants (agrobiodiversity), are mainly to be found in the countries of the South. Depending on the perspective, biodiversity is of value per se as precondition for the stability of eco-systems, or as an almost inexhaustible supply of useful raw materials. However, our knowledge about this is very limited. Of the hundreds of thousands of plant species, humanity has made use of just a few thousand, cultivated a few hundred, and feeds a population of five billion plus their working animals with barely a dozen.

This makes clear that preserving biodiversity involves more than conservation of nature. For many societies ongoing utilization of biodiversity constitutes an indispensable aspect of social and economic development. For the rural poor in the South biological resources – as food and medicine, source of income, and an aspect of cultural integrity – are often the only or the most important means of survival. Societies in industrial countries are also highly dependent on biodiversity – in combating cancer and AIDS, or in producing healthy foodstuffs.

Biological and genetic resources are of mounting economic importance, especially for the pharmaceutical, agrobusiness, and cosmetic industries. In the USA the active ingredients in 25% of all prescription drugs derive from higher plants. Their total value was estimated at 15.5 billion US dollars for 1991.[24] The worldwide annual turnover of medicaments originating in the tropics is estimated at up to 30 billion DM. In the realm of agrobusiness genetic material from the Third World by now accounts for more than two billion US dollars annually in the earnings of American wheat, rice, and maize producers.

The "Green Revolution" led to modernization of agriculture in the South, following the Western model so as to ensure food supplies for the mounting population. That also marked the beginning of gene erosion in the countries of the South, the centres of genetic diversity. Large-scale introduction of new varieties,[25] producing large yields in favourable conditions, led to vast destruction of locally adapted methods of cultivation and ousting of traditional varieties of plants.

For centuries biological and genetic resources were discovered and collected all over the world without thought of any compensation for the country of origin or the people living there. Declared to be common goods, even today plants are often still collected for research or economic utilization, animals trapped, and traditional knowledge exploited without scientists or professional collectors having to seek permission, let alone pay compensation.[26]

The Convention on Biological Diversity signed at Rio de Janeiro in 1992, which came into force in December the following year, is the most comprehensive attempt so far to subject the protection and ongoing utilization of overall biological diversity to international regulation. One of the convention's objectives is equitable distribution of the economic benefits derived from biological resources. Issues within technology transfer and the related question of patents and (intellectual) property rights play an important part here.

The political controversy over biological diversity mainly involves three forms of knowledge which, if taken into account, go beyond the limits of classic agreements on protection of nature: (a) the well-guarded powers of control among representatives of the new biotechnological industry (intellectual property rights); (b) traditional knowledge of breeding and healing among indigenous peoples and farmers in genetically rich countries ("Farmers' Rights"[27]); and (c) the descriptive and evaluative information stored in global gene banks.[28]

The impact of the Green Revolution on genetic diversity and growing awareness of the importance of genetic resources for breeding purposes triggered off a global rescue operation. The assumption was that genetic diversity would not survive out in the fields, so "experts" decided that this should be stored in what seemed to be the safety of gene banks away from its natural habitat (*ex situ*). At present 53% of stocks are in gene banks in the North and 12% are stored at the 18 agricultural research centres co-ordinated by the Consultative Group on International Agricultural Research (CGIAR), the Western-dominated instigator of the Green Revolution.[29]

At a time of advances in biotechnology and gene technology biological diversity in the countries of the South is under increasing pressure. Annual increases of up to 25% in turnover are anticipated for these technologies. By now over 200 companies have bought and secured utilization rights through what are known as "prospecting contracts" with Third World countries.[30]

A fundamental problem is at stake. Even though the knowledge and skills of indigenous farmers and fishermen in Africa, Asia, and Latin America play a considerable part in the development of new agricultural and medical products, there is no sign of any general trend towards extension of protection of intellectual rights, treating local populations more justly. Even if the convention recognizes the traditional biological and breeding skills of indigenous peoples and local communities for the first time, and also assigns them a central role in sustaining ecological productivity, it is apparent that state and/or inter-state organizations will largely be in control, and profits derived from utilization of biological diversity will be divided between national elites and private companies.

Protection for industrial patents motivates scientists and big companies to pursue innovation. The local population, however, may supply its knowledge free of charge and almost always receives nothing in return. While the biotechnology industry prospers, patent rights on living organisms were not expanded until the 1993 GATT negotiations. What began at the start of the century with patenting of decorative plants today comprises patent applications for entire crops (as in the case of genetically engineered cotton) and even human cell groups.[31] This has provoked discussion of whether worldwide patenting of living organisms should be permitted at all since many cultures find such actions completely incomprehensible.[32]

When the convention came into effect in December 1993, this issue became even more politically controversial. Will the countries of Africa, Asia, and Latin America – as administrators of by far the greatest share of the world's biological diversity – devote the profits from marketing their genetic resources to boosting economic development while simultaneously protecting nature? Or will nature, and with it indigenous peoples and other local communities, once again lose out?

Notes

1. Opschoor and Costanza, 1995.
2. Teufel et al., 1994 (based on selected energy-intensive products).
3. End-use energy consumption = primary energy consumption minus use/distribution losses in the conversion sector plus/minus statistical differences.
4. If energy use is related to primary energy, the share of electricity-backed services increases.
5. Apel et al., 1995, p. 36.
6. Bringezu and Schütz, 1995. See figure 3.3.
7. See Wissenschaftlicher Beirat für Globale Umweltveränderungen, 1993.
8. Another problem results from increased production of HCFCs as a substitute for CFCs. These may cause considerably less harm to the ozone layer but they exert as great an impact as CFCs in terms of global warming.
9. The term "South" is used here for the totality of developing countries in awareness of its great inadequacy at a time when those states are becoming increasingly different. Actual examples will therefore be used wherever possible in what follows (see also section 5.8).
10. Covered in greater detail in Pearce and Warford, 1993, pp. 281ff.
11. Lunde, 1991. pp. 199–210.

12. Alongside wetland rice paddies and cattle rearing, gas from mines, landfills, and losses during extraction and transportation of natural gas are mainly responsible for increased concentrations of methane in the atmosphere.

13. Covered in greater detail in Agarwal and Narain, 1991.

14. Niang-Diop, 1994.

15. In addition CFCs and halons at present contribute around 20% of the greenhouse effect.

16. Figures from World Resources Institute, 1994.

17. *Newsweek*, 27.4.1994, Special Report: "Fished Out", pp. 30–3.

18. The International Convention on the Law of the Sea was passed as long ago as 1982, but 12 years went by before it came into force. With the Climate Convention that period was less than two years (June 1992–March 1994).

19. Smith et al., 1992, quoted in World Resources Institute, 1992.

20. Specific forms of pollution, such as fertilizers in ground-water or the consequences following use of pesticides, are not taken into account. However, the overall picture does not change essentially if, for instance, the use of mineral fertilizers is also quantified. Erosion as a governing factor within agricultural ecological rucksacks constitutes a minimal estimate of its potential impact on the environment.

21. The concept biological diversity comprises diversity of species, genetic diversity, and diversity of eco-system (living-space). Biodiversity usually has to be viewed in terms of different hierarchical levels, but any overall evaluation requires consideration of interactions between those levels.

22. As in Columbia, Ecuador, Peru, Brazil, Zaïre, Madagascar, China, India, Malaysia, Indonesia, Australia, and Mexico.

23. McNeely, 1990.

24. Reid et al., 1993, p. 7.

25. For instance a single high-performance variety of "Green Revolution" rice (IR 36) is cultivated across the world (under different names) on almost 11 million hectares of reallocated land (*Frankfurter Allgemeine Zeitung*, 9.11.1994). It is estimated that there are (or used to be) around 100,000 local varieties of rice.

26. Cf. Heins, 1993.

27. "Farmers' Rights" entail on the one hand an intellectual property right for groups and individuals as a counterweight to industrial countries' patent rights and resource protection, and, on the other, farming communities' right to have a say in agricultural development.

28. Heins, 1993.

29. Flitner, 1993; Kumar, 1993.

30. The discovery and collection of biological material for industrial uses – primarily pharmaceuticals, agriculture, and cosmetics. Gettkant, 1995, p. 116.

31. Crucible Group, 1994.

32. Shiva, 1993.

5 Paradigms

What might a sustainable country be like? The answer that it would involve a "reduction of resource use" provides a framework for action. But what would such restructuring actually mean? Who should make a start? And why should people want to? Up to now these questions have not been addressed. In answering them, a merely quantitative approach remains remarkably powerless. Fyodor Dostoevsky skewered that weakness: "What kind of pleasure should people derive from acting in accordance with statistics?"

It is both the strength and the weakness of quantitative presentations that they are highly abstract. Such depictions ignore the great diversity of natural processes. Instead they put the emphasis on shared and measurable sub-strata: energy, materials, land. Nevertheless, the strength of these representations of the environmental crisis is founded on that very conceptual simplification. It orders a complex world in terms of data about specific states and sequences; it promises objective statements; and it is capable of laying down clear-cut, quantitatively controllable objectives. That creates a stock of knowledge whose data cannot be ignored. Every strategy and every good intention has to be measured against those criteria.

However, this abstraction also gives rise to the weakness of representations. People are rarely moved by this approach. Remarkable and surprising aspects of nature, its sounds, colours, and structures, are left out of discussion of levels of consumption; people's organizations, interests, and wishes are lost to view. At most they are stumbled upon during the follow-up process when implementation and acceptance of scientific conclusions become a gaping problem. Only when the environmental crisis is understood as a historical process will insights about why and how society became ensnared in high levels of material consumption become accessible. Only then will it be possible for quantitative reduction to become part of the world people live in. What social innovations, intellectual projects, models of behaviour, and institutional restructuring can give expression to the search for moderation in using nature? What kind of society should arise in tandem with reduction of consumption? Such questions demand an answer if the social imagination necessary for change is to flourish. By themselves targets for cutting consumption at best serve as a source of information but do not arouse anyone's enthusiasm. Curiosity, delight in experimentation, and commitment only come into play when people's sense of possibility is intensified and when images of change gain ground in many spheres of life. That is why targets must be converted into qualitative objectives, or else this study will remain bogged down in ascertaining limits without involving ordinary people. People do not only want to be forced to act; they also want to exercise their free will.

In the following section we attempt to illustrate the desired transformation to a sustainable society, utilizing a number of qualitative and historical scenarios. Eight paradigms, relating to different areas of social renewal, will be presented. Even though the different guidelines are clearly related, they do not together comprise an all-embracing utopia. The change sought is presented as a polyphonic process serving a shared objective over the course of time. In a multi-structured, complex society there does not exist any single observation-point from where society can be seen as a whole, nor is there any single control centre from which society-wide changes can be programmed and implemented. It would thus not be appropriate to conceive of change as the outcome of a comprehensive and rationally executed strategy, even though such an approach must play a part. Transformation comes about when a large number of people set up different priorities in the large and small arenas of society, establishing new routines and structures despite conflicts and set-backs.

It would be particularly wrong to envisage change as being predominantly motivated by the state. For a start, the state consists of very diverse protagonists (from the village mayor to the European Commissioner), and citizens will be equally involved in ecological transformation – as professionals and participants in the market, as private people and social activists. Anyone who places too much dependence on state regulations makes citizens into mere recipients of incentives, thereby easily underestimating the crucial resource within transformation: human interest and pride in acting as the times demand. The following paradigms are thus conceived as creative possibilities for people active in different social spheres – businesspeople, consumers, public utility staff, legislators, city-dwellers, the rural population, and development policy activists. They are founded on ideas and initiatives which ecologically aware people in these areas have put forward, developed, and tried out over the years.

These directions also contain a number of scenarios, presenting specific projects in greater detail. These scenarios add concrete objectives to the more programmatic guidelines. Qualitative and quantitative arguments are brought closer together since the changeovers provide direct recognition of the character, and sometimes the magnitudes, of reductions in consumption of energy, raw materials, and land.

Despite all the different aspects involved, an underlying theme is constantly apparent in these directions and scenarios – a dramatic motif permeating the search for a sustainable civilization. What is at issue is to change limits into opportunities. On the one hand all the guidelines derive from recent decades' epoch-making insight that nature and global justice impose limits on conventional forms of progress, and those have to be accepted by any form of sustainable development. On the other hand, all the guidelines discover the creative power unleashed by limits. Restricting one dimension creates the basis for developing others. Taking leave of former patterns of development opens up new spheres of possibility, inviting previously uncalled-for technical and social inventiveness. At any rate limits constitute opportunities. Everywhere – in art and architecture, in psychological development and in biological evolution – examples of limits constituting the condition for qualitative leaps are to be encountered. Why – asks Paul Hawken[1] – should the bio-physical limits to which progress is subject be any more constraining than, say, the confines of a canvas for Cézanne or the number of holes in a flute for Jean-Pierre Rampal?

5.1 Moderation in Time and Space

"Faster", "Further", and "More" could be seen as the main leitmotifs in the progress driven by fossil fuels. Trains, limousines, and jets promised high speed; and railway lines, motorways, and air-routes easy passage. The greatest possible movement in the shortest possible time – that is the utopia which moves people in the age of transportation. Across decades, unnoticeably and yet programmatically, the restless society was created – with rare agreement between popular demands, economic interests, and political planning. As if self-evidently, a huge number of individual decisions implemented a form of progress whose basic assumptions ran: Come what may, it is better to increase speeds and to augment the permeability of space. From the motor vehicle by way of aeroplanes to the Transrapid express and supersonic flight, engineers everywhere have been driven onwards by the demand for mastery of time and space.

However, even utopias grow old – and the utopia of acceleration and interconnection is particularly unlikely to be spared that fate. Against the background of a slow and sedentary society that had to seem like some brave new world, but viewed in the light of a restless high-speed society it at best offers repetition of what is always the same while wishes for change latch onto new images.

Slower speeds and shorter distances

Success turned out to be the greatest set-back for the utopia of all-embracing mobility. So long as only a few people owned cars, the individual motorist was highly satisfied, but since most people have now become motorized the advantages of being quicker and able to travel further than everyone else have shrunk. As soon as speed is a general expectation, gaining time is frequently no longer a pleasure because it becomes an obligation. The power over space and time made possible by mass mobilization is in process of becoming a duty rather than a privilege, so the fascination of utopia vanishes with its triumph.[2] More of the same also offers little hope. It is true that higher speed leads to saving time, but a look at the history of transportation shows that such gains are quickly converted into longer distances and/or an increase in what has to be done. And then greater distances and more tasks in turn demand greater speeds which allow further increases in distance and work-load. Out of the logic of acceleration there thus develops for many people a feeling of futility: every expansion increases effort but seems to achieve less and less.

None of the usual "more of the same" prescriptions help against systemic over-development. It is intelligent self-regulation that seems most likely to bring relief. Contemplating limits to further growth is a rational strategy in such circumstances since restraint makes possible a slowing down of rampant growth, avoids additional burdens, and allows discovery of new possibilities for shaping the situation. Renunciation of further acceleration and interconnection will open up opportunities for creating a socially appropriate transportation system for the twenty-first century.

The general increase in speed also has consequences on the level of personal experience. Consistently pursued acceleration has a regrettable tendency to cancel itself out. People arrive ever more quickly at places where ever less time is spent. The attention devoted to arrival and departure takes over from the actual visit. Acceleration thus fails to fulfil its purpose. A life constantly on the move is similarly afflicted. When everyone is busy travelling, people increasingly move around to see others who are met less and less frequently. The ability to be in many places quickly is rapidly succeeded by difficulties in co-ordinating meetings. The more people circulate, the more complicated synchronization of meetings becomes. In a mobile society special efforts are required in order not to derail the whole purpose of the enterprise: coming together. With this general foreshortening of space and time, particularly among more mobile social groups, it becomes apparent that beyond a certain threshold acceleration and interconnection are counter-productive.

Beneath the official compulsions of acceleration a cautious interest in greater slowness is beginning to stir. Not as a programme, not as a strategy, but rather as a subversive demand viewing all the glorification of speed as old-fashioned and out of touch with the times. If such experiences accumulate, then the familiar trend might conceivably be reversed and affluence become associated with deceleration.

All kinds of rapid transportation accelerate part of society while the rest becomes relatively slower. That is even true of the most widespread source of speed, the automobile. By no means all people are motorized. Contrary to appearances over a third of the population do not have a car at their disposal for everyday activities. Children, the young, and the old predominate, but some people cannot afford or do not want a car, and there are housewives whose husbands require the family car for going to work. With motorization all such people must accept drastic restrictions on their mobility. They are endangered and displaced, and also have to put up with longer and more inconvenient journeys because of the precedence accorded the car. The price of mobility for some is increased immobility for others. Men with jobs and (increasingly) women with sufficient income are speeded up, while children, young people, housewives, and often old people are slowed down.

Policies aiming at limiting the contracting of space and time will therefore restrain the privileged world of work in favour of everyday living. The infrastructures of rapid covering of distances were established to meet the demands of the business economy whereas the needs of the everyday world and its maintenance are primarily supplied by way of local structures. Short distances and slow speeds generally characterize the procuring of household supplies, the life of children, the neighbourhood, and the local environment. The expansion of infrastructures planned by men has thinned out the local aspect of providing for needs. Ring-roads separate urban districts, noise makes parks and gardens unbearable, shopping centres are built close to towns, and everywhere danger threatens. Policies that wish to establish a new weighting in the relationship between the two aspects of economic life, employment and the household, will therefore plan for local, low-speed, and low-powered mobility.

Systemic over-development, creeping counter-productivity, and inbuilt inequality have already undermined the fascination exerted by the utopia of ever-increasing speed, which has become an obstacle in the way of developing an appropriate transportation system for today. Transport experts have realized for years that the politics of opening up bottlenecks and expansion of supply – as has predominated since the sixties and seventies, and is still practiced today – basically only creates new flows of traffic. However, volumes of traffic constitute the decisive variable in consumption of nature, so strategies merely involving optimal distribution and rational administration do not meet the demands of sustainability. Computer-backed direction of traffic flows, planning systems for efficient selection of means of transportation, or other plans for traffic management do not strive for anything except optimization of the unsustainable. Genuinely ecological transport policies primarily seek to influence the underlying conditions so as to attain step-by-step reductions of traffic volumes to an acceptable level. Avoidance of transportation is at the heart of ecological transition. The more accessible higher speeds are and the more distant destinations, the greater is the demand for transportation. Deceleration and disconnection are thus the corner-stones of planning seeking to avoid superfluous and enforced traffic.

That could also lead to development of a social aesthetic where a relaxed attitude to time and shorter distances is thought a particular achievement, slowly influencing what progress means for our age. After a long period when it was thought unquestionable that improvement meant reducing the obstacles associated with time and distance, now the view is gaining ground that progress can also involve leaving such obstacles as they are or even deliberately increasing them. Such a transformation would demonstrate that our society has moved beyond compulsively dragging nineteenth-century desires into the twenty-first century.

Designing for moderate speeds

Technical development of vehicles can follow different priorities. Engineers can design them to be comfortable and spacious, economical and inexpensive, or robust and durable. During the predominance of utopian acceleration, engineers' skills were primarily focused on constructing comfortable means of transport with high top speeds.[3] That was particularly the case with the automobile. Between 1960 and 1993 the average power of engines in German vehicles shot up from 34 to 85 h.p. The situation is similar with German Railways (Bundesbahn). For 15 or so years now innovative efforts have concentrated on Intercity routes with the development of ever more high-speed trains. The planners follow European visions of speed. The intention is that by the year 2015 there should be a 30,000 km high-speed network in Europe – with 19,000 km for speeds of between 250 and 300 km.p.h. and 11,000 km for speeds of between 160 and 250 km.p.h.[4] It is obvious – even without the planned 500 km.p.h. Transrapid – that mercurial speed remains the guideline for transport engineering.[5]

With a finite earth such a guideline is nothing but rapacious mortgaging of the future. Of course all transportation entails gigantic consumption of nature, but top speeds demand extensive energy, raw materials, and land. The increase in a vehicle's energy throughput (inclusive of emissions) is not simply linear; it rises disproportionately because of resistance and friction. A car that uses 5 litres of fuel at 80 km.p.h. needs not 10 but 20 litres at 160 km.p.h. Even when a vehicle is equipped for higher speeds (using comparatively less fuel than other vehicles), in normal usage it will consume more fuel than a less powerful car. The weight of a vehicle also significantly influences fuel consumption. More powerful car motors lead (for safety reasons) to demands for greater sturdiness, in turn entailing greater weight. Similar laws apply to railways. Energy consumption is almost doubled for ICE (and TGV) trains when speeds are increased from 160 to 250 km.p.h., and again from 200 to 300 km.p.h.[6] So anyone who is concerned about long-term reduction of energy turnover by a factor of 10 will contemplate restriction and reduction of technically possible speeds before striving for more efficient motors, new materials, or a rational choice of means of transportation.

For a society seeking sustainability, the power of equipment and technologies will be a major political issue. If "moderation" is not publicly debated, leading to general agreement, this society is unlikely to succeed in living within its considerable means. As the age of fossil fuels comes to an end, the great historic challenge facing politicians is to achieve political consensus on once again controlling the unrestrained dynamism unleashed when the limits set by nature were exceeded. Setting upper speed limits as design-criteria for cars and railways opens up enormous potential for reducing energy consumption and use of materials in transportation since comfort and safety would then no longer require excessive technical facilities. The construction of roads and railway lines will also require fewer materials and less land since new straight stretc.hes, large-radius curves, a multitude of tunnels and bridges, etc., are often the outcome of demands for high speeds. Designing moderately powered vehicles and engines will give technical expression to the twenty-first-century utopia of living elegantly within limits.

Scenario 1: A Moderately Powered Automobile Fleet

The technology and design of the new generation of automobiles will reflect the aspirations of a society striving to link moderation, intelligence, and aesthetics. This will involve the following technical concepts.

Speed: Moderately powered motors will put an end to the culture of high speeds and competitive behaviour on the road. Technology will be oriented towards speed limits: on motorways of 100 km.p.h., on secondary roads 80, and in built-up areas 30. Acceleration will be limited to 1 to 1.5 m/s^2, and the highest possible speed will be technically restricted to 120 km.p.h. Vehicle construction and motor performance will be optimized accordingly.

Consumption: Assessment of energy consumption will be based on primary energy-use. The provisional upper limit to consumption should be set at 2.5 litres per 100 km for a car with four passengers and luggage. Weight will be reduced by replacing non-load-bearing steel parts in the chassis with aluminium and/or glassfibre-strengthened synthetics and a smaller motor.

Engines: Petrol, diesel, electro, and hybrid-powered vehicles will be manufactured, meeting the regulations on consumption and emissions. An output of 15 to 20 kw will be sufficient. Reduced demands for performance and speed will establish more favourable possibilities for using alternative sources of power.

Transportation of goods: Use of vehicles as a general means of transportation must not be restricted. The greatest possible flexibility of interior space – for passengers or goods – is important. Additional means of expansion (such as alternatives to roof-racks) are also envisaged.

All demands apply to every size of vehicle from small car by way of family saloon and minivan to transporter and minibus.

Emphasizing regional scale

Easily attainable speeds exerted a paradoxical impact on the history of transportation. The time saved was usually not devoted to other purposes but rather taken up with more travelling. Anyone who can gain time at high speeds travels longer distances.[7] People now travel right into the city centre to go to a pub, commute between 50 and 100 km to study, fly right across Germany for a conference lasting just a few hours, and supply German milk products to markets on the European periphery. Innumerable minor and major choices of location then adapt to easily manageable distances. Moving out into the country, the spatial concentration of administration and retail trade, and dispersal of centres of production for a single item over one or even several continents all exemplify long-distance structures of settlement and manufacture. It is not surprising that over the past 30 to 40 years the average length of journeys has increased from about 2 km to between 10 and 15 km.

Scenario 2: Disincentives for Transportation of Goods by Road

The costs resulting from road transportation of goods are in no way covered by vehicle and petrol taxes. Such transportation thus receives a concealed subsidy since the prices demanded do not reveal the "true" costs of carrying goods.[8] To rectify this, heavy goods vehicles with a total weight of over 12 tonnes should pay a graduated charge per kilometre on all roads. For a 40 tonne lorry a progressive increase over the next 10 years up to at least 1 DM per kilometre would be appropriate.[9] That reduces the profitability of transportation but increases overall economic efficiency. Reduced speeds, smaller vehicles, and a long-term reduction in road capacity will also cut back expenditure on transportation.

That would provide an important stimulus towards expansion of transport-saving economic structures, mainly based on regional circulation. Everyday foodstuffs would then come from the locality to the shop around the corner rather than, as today, from an average distance of 278 km. Door panels may then once again be made in Lower Saxony and not in Portugal. Higher transport costs at least invite "regional sourcing", a development that will be supported by labelling local products.

In addition transportation of goods will be shifted from road to rail. If rail facilities are sufficiently prepared, by the year 2010 reduction of road transportation by around 40% and up to a threefold increase in rail traffic would be conceivable.[10]

A policy of regionalization has two objectives: de-emphasizing long-distance links and intensifying short-distance connections. At the end of our century it is sufficiently clear that further opening up of distant destinations is ecologically (and possibly also socially) unacceptable. Plans for land use, settlement, and transportation will therefore seek to increase disincentives for long-distance forms of transportation. The frequently neglected planning variant of the zero option is often to be recommended. Tunnelling, road-straightening, and extensions, justified in terms of saving hours and minutes over long stretc.hes (regardless of the other costs involved), do not make a country like Germany any more sustainable by generating traffic. Planners' concentration on long-distance road and rail transportation, or on domestic flights within Germany, has thus become inappropriate.

A traffic-saving city structure is another objective within a politics of transport avoidance. Surveys of different kinds of settlements have shown that medium-sized communities, districts on the edge of inner cities, and areas with local diversity and many retail outlets generate what in relative terms is the lowest amount of traffic.[11] Such a close-knit mixture of functions within a limited area, opening up the locality as was long characteristic of the European city, today also invites establishment of "the city of short distances". Mixed-use and decentralized concentration are thus important principles for traffic-reducing urban structuring, taking seriously a citizen's right to be able to lead a pleasant existence without a car. Assessment of the impact of traffic on new settlements could operate in this spirit to ensure that shopping and leisure centres reachable only by car belong to the past.

Scenario 3: Local Railway Networks[12]

Over the past 40 years German Railways has lost 30% of the network – as has happened in many other countries. A total of 4,500 stations and halts and 4,000 freight depots have vanished during a period when road transportation of both people and goods has increased dramatically. A sustainable society cannot afford any further loss of rail connections. Quite the contrary. Development of a technologically innovative and logically optimized regional rail network – if need be at the expense of long-distance facilities – is the primary infrastructural necessity within a sustainable transport system.

A decentralized rail service is characterized by a dense network with stations, halts, and freight transfer facilities where they are needed. All the important areas of settlement and employment, inclusive of shopping and leisure centres, would be linked up with this network. The objective will be to develop connections, sometimes using former roads, to create a high-density system so that between 80 and 90% of the population are within easy reach of this (within a 6 km cycle ride in the country and a 3 km walk in towns). This system will be hierarchically structured on three levels. For local traffic within a radius of 30 to 50 km regional railways will be developed in highly populated areas and the surrounding countryside. On the second level an inter-regional railway will link small towns and medium-sized centres with bigger connurbations, covering distances of 50 to 300 km. On the third level rapid long-distance trains will connect big cities and regional centres, like the present Intercity network. As far as time is concerned, the decisive factor will be the total time taken from door to door rather than a train's top speed. Journeys include the time taken going to and from stations as well as the time taken up by changing trains and waiting, so the objective will be greater overall speeds for journeys with reduced maximum speeds (not exceeding 200 km.p.h.). The provision of stopping-points and making changing trains easier by way of an integrated timetable is decisive. Rolling stock will be renewed too. A railcar system, pendolino technology, lightweight construction, modular components, double-decking, and low-slung carriages can combine flexibility, economical use of materials, and comfort for passengers. A railcard will be developed at the same time, offering discounts for local and long-distance services plus payment without cash, so that one day the number of card-holders will considerably exceed the total of car-drivers.

This "Concept for a New Railway" anticipates a switch in transportation to rail in conjunction with a decline in road traffic. Roughly calculated, by the year 2010 individual car use could have declined by half while rail use will have quadrupled.

Electronics instead of traffic?

Do new and future generations of electronic means of communication possess a potential for replacing actual transportation? Today that question can only be affirmatively answered in a few narrowly circumscribed cases – such as an international organization's conference system. Scepticism is appropriate in the largest spheres of utilization – teleworking, long-distance access to data, and the Internet – and ambiguous outcomes can be anticipated. The history of the telephone shows that long-distance communications replace actual travel but then create additional face-to-face meetings because this dense new network extends so far. Both developments – reduction in travel and growth – are also to be expected from telematic infrastructure.

What kind of outcome predominates largely depends on how the transportation system is structured. The ecological opportunity offered by information systems' reduction of the need for travel can only bear fruit if the new physical links accompanying expansion of electronic networking are restrained as much as possible. Perhaps, however, the information revolution is opening up a new area of freedom, bringing about slower speeds and shorter distances for the transportation of people and goods. If spatial deterrents blocking communication vanish, then it should be easier to make deliberate use of such obstacles, even cultivate them, in pursuit of transportation policy.

5.2 A Green Market Agenda

How must the economic system in Germany be organized to satisfy ecological and social demands over the long term? And what structure of economic incentives would be appropriate?

A greening of the market economy must comprise two dimensions: domestication of market mechanisms, on the one hand, and their ecologically acceptable promotion, on the other. Euphoric advocates of the market, who reduce the ecological issue to a struggle for future markets and technologies, easily forget the simple fact that economic expansionism and the demolition of social and cultural barriers through division of labour on a global scale are exceptionally destructive. Market sceptics, on the other hand, only see the latter and do not recognize what creative potential may lie in the environmentally acceptable unfolding of market forces. The objective must be a market economy that is (once again) embedded in a greater whole we call society rather than a market society where the rules of supply and demand determine all of human existence.

No reason for market euphoria

In most industrial societies competitive ability and local improvements enjoy the highest priority in the political process. There may be much talk of global responsibility at international conferences on the environment, but national politics remain crudely oriented towards growth. The debate about Germany's competitiveness provides an illuminating example. Development of building land, road construction, and establishment of industries and centres for gene technology are assisted by laws speeding up this process. The Transrapid railway is likely to be built, an attempt at rehabilitating and revitalizing nuclear energy may be forced through, and nature conservation could be reduced as an obstacle to investment.

Much of the environmental movement is opposed to that view of economic growth, maintaining that future competitiveness will no longer be determined by the motorway network or sheer output of goods but rather by capacity to use energy and raw materials economically, to manufacture eco-efficient installations, machinery, equipment, and vehicles, and to offer environmental services. Alternative thinking thus lays claim to a more modern understanding of competitiveness and criticizes the lack of foresight in traditional politics. Journalist Franz Alt has probably expressed this approach most succinctly:

> Those industrial nations which take the lead in comprehending that deriving energy from the sun, wind, water, and biomass will be at least as economically important in the 21st century as automobile production in the 20th, will do

> business with the entire world, have no worries about jobs, assure national well-being, and help nature. Which will take the lead?[13]

Such arguments are very influential in the current discussion of strategies for energy and environmental policy. Ecological thinking has at long last gone onto the offensive. More important still, it is finding allies in what are known as the winner industries which will profit from following ecologically oriented objectives. Nevertheless the ecology movement should not forget the reasons why it was established. It is in favour of solar electricity because that is more environmentally acceptable than current from fossil fuels or nuclear power, not because world markets can be conquered with photovoltaic technology. It is in favour of rational use of energy because it avoids emissions and protects people, forests, and climate, not because it strengthens Germany's competitive position. It is in favour of preservation of man-made landscapes because of their beauty and the fact that they provide homes for many kinds of animals and plants, not because executives' liking for attractive countryside has become a factor in deciding on industrial locations.

When specific market interests concur with ecological demands, that is a stroke of good fortune which can be put to use in the current dispute with apologists of the status quo. However, this does not mean that what is good for the market (even the world market) is also good for ecology. The expansive thrust of today's business is no more reconcilable with the principle of natural cycles, where unlimited growth is an alien concept, than economic globalism is compatible with cultural and ecological diversity. This insight is by no means new and was already to be found in classic economists.

As early as 1857 John Stuart Mill, one of the originators of liberal economics, wrote on the necessity of limiting growth:

> A state of constant capital (meaning an economy without growth) ... is not equivalent to a stoppage in human inventiveness. There would be great latitude for all kinds of intellectual culture, for moral and social progress, and just as many possibilities of improving the conduct of life; and it is more probable that this would also occur.[14]

Demarcating the market

Anyone who wants to define the areas where the dynamics of market forces should operate is well advised to first demarcate them negatively. Where should laws other than those of supply and demand, cost and utility, hold good? There are plenty of examples in the human sphere, far from ecology. Lovers do not usually conduct a cost–utility analysis before falling for one another. Parental support does not involve first asking how much of their "investment" will later be paid back by the children. Being good neighbours is not based on only giving what has previously been received or will certainly be returned.

A society where everything is calculated in financial terms seems a horrific vision to most contemporaries. Nevertheless increasingly many areas of human co-existence are being drawn into the economic sphere: care of the old and domestic work, looking after children and the organization of celebrations, keeping healthy, use of free time, exploring spirituality (through self-discovery courses and drum holidays) and one's own body (mountain-biking with the appropriate gear). Our society will have to decide what mixture of individual freedoms and communal obligations, of self-organized and commercialized social relations, is good for it. If that discussion does not take place, economic rules will ultimately determine the organization of community life.

It is also frequently argued that protection of the natural foundations of life can only be assured by way of the price-mechanism. If the external costs of our economic activities are ascertained and included in prices, protection of the environment will become financially viable and thus be implemented. Much of that argument is correct, and in this study considerable emphasis will be put on tax reform favouring ecology. But can and should a price really be put on everything, measured by the same yardstick? The utility involved in draining a wetland area or constructing a motorway cannot be offset against the value of the life thus dispersed.

Priorities among value judgements can be contemplated from various vantage-points but these remain value judgements. Why the Münsterland landscape with its hedges, slopes, and high meadows should not be transformed into large areas devoted solely to maize, why the fruit orchards in the Schwäbisch Alb should not be broken up by more roads and industrial development, why Mecklenburg's lakes should not be sacrificed to mass tourism, why there should be no oil drilling in mud-flats, and why farming should be preserved in the Alps are all questions where answers cannot be based on cost–benefit analyses. These are questions of value, social issues, political problems, which require personal, social, and political responses and decisions.

Anyone who does not want poisons in mothers' milk must ban production of toxics; if the preservation of a specific landscape is desired, the preconditions must be established. That starts with a value judgement. Only then can it be asked how an objective viewed as being right can best be achieved. And only after that will it also be relevant to determine what contribution the possibilities open to a market economy can make towards attaining what seems an ecologically meaningful objective.

Market and sustainability

Can the market mechanism be used for implementation of ecological objectives? That must be split into two sub-questions. First, where today is an environmentally acceptable development of market economy principles obstructed by state intervention or monopolistic structures? Second, what political framework could be established to redirect market dynamism towards ecological objectives?

Visible and concealed subsidies

A strategy of sustainability, aiming at reducing consumption of energy, raw materials, and land, must review all subsidies. It then becomes apparent that all subsidies assisting measures and technologies which do not satisfy the criterion of ecological sustainability must simply be gradually eliminated. One example would be the ecologically questionable subsidies for maintenance of a mine that causes enormous environmental damage, is not competitive, and calls on state funds which could be deployed much more effectively elsewhere. If some of the subsidies for coal and nuclear energy flowed into assistance for rational use of energy and renewable energies, the impact on the environment, employment, and the budget would be positive.[15]

The case of photovoltaic electricity is enlightening. Without massive subsidies for the foreseeable future this will not achieve a breakthrough. In order to be able to attain mass production of solar cells, and thus achieve clear-cut reductions in specific costs, increased demand must be created by way of subsidies, but these must not be perpetuated over the long term by the state – i.e. ultimately the tax-payer. It is conceivable that public electricity companies might be ready to devote some of their surpluses to assisting photovoltaic programmes. The state can also independently ensure that individual production of still very expensive solar electricity will be stimulated by other subsidies.

Subsidies that are thought indispensable – as in housing and regional economic assistance – would be increasingly linked with ecological objectives. For instance, land- and energy-saving construction must become a criterion for housing; local integration and energy- and raw material-saving production methods for regional economies.

An ecologically oriented subsidies policy would thus involve three elements:

- elimination of subsidies harmful to the environment;
- ecological restructuring of justified subsidies;
- availability of new and degressive means of assistance for limited periods.

Such a systematic thinning-out of subsidies in terms of ecological criteria should lead overall to a clear-cut decline in volume and thus relieve national budgets. The reason is simple. In many respects ecological objectives call for the virtue of refraining from taking action. Abstinence as a key to sustainability is an argument that will often be put forward in this study.

However, official state subsidies are both quantitatively and qualitatively exceeded by what are known as shadow subsidies, meaning costs whose originators or beneficiaries are known but which are pushed onto the general public because the state does not want to directly burden those who profit from this situation. Such costs include the damage done to health, forests, buildings, and climate by vehicle emissions or the free (but certainly not cost-covering) provision of roads and car-parks. Estimates of the social costs of road traffic in the former Federal Republic range from 50 to 200 billion DM (exclusive of long-term damage such as changes to the climate).[16] Estimates of the total external costs involved in our way of running the economy fluctuate between 100 and 600 billion DM annually.[17] A degree of deviousness is at work when self-proclaimed supporters of the market economy talk about reduction of public subsidies but seldom mention the considerably more lavish shadow subsidies. Anyone who is serious about true costs and clarity cannot talk about the one and pass over the other in silence.

The market economy offers efficient and often well-tried means of reducing shadow subsidies. In the case of clearly identifiable problems, such as over-utilization of our streets and inner cities by cars, very specific market measures are available: charges for utilization of roads or parking fees. With general problems such as the use of fossil fuels or discharges of carbon dioxide, there are such broad possibilities as taxes on energy/ CO_2 and tradable permits.

Scenario 4: Reduction of Ecologically Damaging Subsidies and Tax Provisions

In a recent comprehensive study by the European Commission, tax provisions with a potential impact on the environment in all 15 EU member states were investigated by tax consultants. This provides in-depth analysis of the environmental and budgetary impacts of each of the tax provisions examined. It reveals many environmentally counter-productive provisions within other taxes, often not intended to have an impact on the environment – alongside the known environmental taxes. Often VAT rates are reduced for the use of water, energy, pesticides, fertilizers, and other damaging products. Exemption of aviation fuel from taxation exerts a highly negative impact on the environment.[18]

The Ecological Tax Reform Association (ETRA) has proposed that ecologically counter-productive elements in the tax system should be eliminated. The most important suggestions include:

- a graduated tax deduction for journeys to work, dependent on distance rather than type of transportation (as in the present system);
- annulment of exemptions from sales taxes and mineral oil taxes for commercial air traffic, inland shipping, and agriculture;
- ecological restructuring of motor vehicle tax.

The IFO institute estimates that in 1993 alone the cost of quantifiable counter-productive regulations was around 65 billion DM. Over 95% derives from subsidies within the law on taxing mineral oil.

Liability for large-scale risks

Civilization is a risky business, which is why most people have got used to voluntarily insuring themselves against adversity – against fire and theft, invalidity and death, carelessness at home and in public, and much besides. That is a truly market-oriented approach. No-one is forced to insure themselves against such risks, but everyone has the possibility of doing so. The situation is different on the road. The state obliges car-drivers to take out limited-liability insurance. In view of the fact that in Germany alone more than half a million people have been killed in car accidents since the war, and millions more have suffered physical and psychological injury, hardly anyone would think of calling compulsory insurance into question.

What is demanded of individual citizens by no means generally applies in the business world. For instance, such provisions are systematically excluded in the operations of nuclear power stations. Those who run such plants do not have to meet the real costs of insuring on the free market against the risks of nuclear accidents let alone catastrophes. Indeed, that would hardly be possible. The costs of an extensive nuclear accident in the Rhine–Main area, greater Hamburg, or the Neckar region would be very high, so there is almost no free market insurance company ready to cover such a risk. If premiums were set realistically and included in cost calculations, nuclear energy would be unaffordable.

However, in the case of nuclear energy state policy views possible risks as less important than industrial development, so for 30 years now all German governments have implicitly accepted liability, thereby shifting the risks involved in nuclear energy onto society and future generations.

No-one who believes that this form of energy is basically acceptable will be able to maintain over the longer term that a technology uninsurable on the real market (because of the risks entailed) is sustainable.

There are plans for extension of exclusion of market mechanisms to other spheres of risk, to the Transrapid, to gene technology and biotechnology. Even though complete absence of risk is unattainable, there remains a crucial difference between whether technological breakdown causes losses amounting to huge sums and innumerable ruins, or whether it even causes disaster and death for thousands of people and irreversible ecological damage. The question of the degree of risk a society is ready to take on consciously is a political issue, not a matter of economic calculation. If, however, one accepts the primacy of economics as in our society at present, then the least that can be expected – from the perspective of warding off dangers – is realistic calculation of insurance premiums for risky activities, in other words consistent adherence to the principle of "the polluter pays" rather than "paying the polluter".

Moreover, the insurance business is increasingly supporting ecological demands – just because of its sober evaluation of risks. That becomes particularly clear in discussions about the consequences of man-made global warming.[19] An important role is played here by the reinsurance companies which ultimately have to cover the costs of increasing incidence of hurricanes, storm-tides, and extremes of weather. Because the prices of fossil fuels are kept artificially low – with no surcharge for climatic risks – there is little incentive to save energy and avoid greenhouse gas discharges. The outcome is changes in climate and the consequent damage, for which insurance companies are expected to pay. These cover themselves with reinsurers who have no possibility of buck-passing.

It is evident that the interests of different branches of industry clash. Energy-intensive companies' interest in energy prices being kept at the lowest possible level, and the insurance business's wish to keep payments for damage and catastrophe within controllable limits, are not reconcilable. A realistic risk surcharge must therefore be paid by the various sources of energy. As long as nuclear energy is still used contrary to the population's wishes, that will entail sufficiently high premiums for liability. Taxes on the use of energy and on greenhouse gas emissions are the appropriate form for internalizing the risk-costs involved in fossil fuels.

Competition to protect the climate: the energy sector

In Germany today the generation, transportation, and distribution of electricity as a cable-based source of energy is organized in a way that is irreconcilable with the principles underlying a market economy. The state grants the supply companies protected areas where only they have the right to offer electricity. In return these companies guarantee supplies at all times. State supervision of charges, half-heartedly implemented by the Länder, accords approval to prices for the general public. Suppliers' charges to big customers are largely unregulated.

Decentralized and locally based generation of electricity and heating is systematically obstructed by such a monopolistic structure. In the past energy-suppliers' monopoly of generation may have been weakened by minor modifications – such as the law obliging acceptance of and appropriate payment for electricity from renewable sources of energy – but the basic pattern of favouring sources of supply against demand, and centralized against decentralized structures, continues to apply.

A policy of ecologically oriented competition in the electricity sector would change that situation. The state must establish new regulations so that companies' objective is not to achieve the greatest possible turnover of electricity but rather to meet the services demanded (for room lighting, refrigerated foodstuffs, and operational appliances and machinery) with the least possible expenditure of energy. Such a change could be brought about through ending the existing monopoly and systematically favouring ecologically sustainable forms of energy generation – through state supervision of prices and investment, realistic conditions regarding feeding in electricity from renewable sources and co-generation, and changes in the law on taxes and charges, and so on. Energy supply companies should be transformed into energy services companies (see section 5.5).

Scenario 5: Cost-Covering Prices for Electricity from Independent Producers

The main obstacle to massive introduction of photovoltaic units is high production costs, expressed in prices of 1.60 to 2.20 DM per kW of solar electricity. According to studies made by the German Parliamentary Commission of Enquiry on the Earth's Atmosphere, the crucial breakthrough for solar electricity "essentially depends on transition to mass construction of units".[20] Electricity costs could then fall to between 0.23 and 0.30 DM per kW by the year 2005 – not under the Californian sun but in German climatic conditions.

Nevertheless mass production of solar cells and implementation of the solar age will remain unattainable without large-scale financial assistance. The "Aachen Model" increasingly seems a more viable form of financing than direct subsidies for solar energy.[21] Here payment for both solar electricity and current from other renewable sources covers the costs involved.

At present the city electricity works pays suppliers 2 DM per kW for solar electricity and 24 pfennigs per kW of wind power. Inexpensive and well-maintained sources of power can thus be operated viably. Payment is regularly adjusted in accordance with the cost of producing power so as to allow for new equipment which will reduce prices. The city electricity works can spread these additional expenses among all customers – both private and industrial – but price increases are not allowed to exceed 1%.

Cost-covering prices are to be seen as a complement to ecological tax reform. While tax reform makes fossil fuels more expensive, prices for solar equipment, and thus for solar electricity, will fall as an outcome of cost-covering reimbursement and mass production. The price-difference between "conventional" and solar electricity will become less, leading to market-competitiveness for the latter.[22]

Steering with taxes

Ecological tax reform offers one of the best examples of diversion of market dynamism to environmental objectives. This is a key element in transition to a sustainable economy. That possibility has been discussed for almost a decade and has now reached a phase of great political relevance.[23] Here too the energy sector is crucial.

Such tax reform is both ecologically and economically desirable,[24] and fulfils the precautionary principle. Environmental policy over the past 25 years has focused on elimination of toxic substances already in existence. Bureaucratic efforts have been directed towards implementing this very expensive way of protecting the environment after the damage has been done. Firms have had to instal expensive filters and purification systems, involving costs without any direct impact on profitability. That was not always the best strategy for the environment either since total elimination of toxic substances is usually not possible and entails very high costs. Wanting to transfer such a prohibitively expensive system to the developing countries would mean renouncing environmental objectives. This system cannot be harmoniously implemented internationally.

Environmental scientists urge the necessity of cutting emissions of greenhouse gases and consumption of nature across the world by at least half before the middle of the next century. At the same time the developing countries are striving for a clear-cut improvement in their material affluence. That dilemma might be alleviated through a considerable increase in resource-productivity. Such a revolution in efficiency cannot, however, be achieved through setting targets and imposing bans. Instead such market incentives as ecological tax reform must be deployed because price is the most effective means of steering the market economy.

Wrong signals have been given in the tax system to date. State budgets (inclusive of social insurance) were increasingly financed by levies on labour as a factor in production. That unavoidably led to today's high level of subsidiary wage costs, which must be seen as one of several causes of high unemployment. In comparison the much lower levies on use of nature (such as taxes on mineral oil) have even declined in relative terms.[25]

The Washington-based World Resources Institute estimates that the economy becomes half a dollar richer for every dollar of fiscal relief for "good things" and every dollar of fiscal burden for "bad things". If it is justified to view work as a "good thing" and consumption of nature as a "bad thing", then cleverly structured ecological tax reform offers an opportunity for becoming economically (i.e. monetarily) richer rather than poorer. That opinion is supported by the previously cited study by the European Environment Agency (see note 24).

Ecological tax reform can deliver advantages in five key areas of public policy:

- the environment;
- employment;
- reinforcement of regulations;
- innovation and competitiveness;
- the tax system.

However, ecological tax reform must fulfil two conditions:

1. It must be introduced in small steps which are socially and economically tolerable. This must be founded on an all-party social consensus, laid down for at least 20 years. A reasonable starting-point would involve introduction of a general energy tax and its incremental rise by 5% annually in real terms. At a later point similar taxes on primary raw materials and use of land could be introduced. Such taxes should be based (for administrative reasons) on quantity rather than value with various starting-points:
   - energy use in energy-intensive industries;
   - energy use in the rest of industry and in commerce, households, and minor uses;
   - fuels in transportation.

   However, a distinction should also be made between energy use for processes and for space heating since the latter often offers great potential for savings.

2. Ecological tax reform should not result in any overall increase in the amount of money flowing to the Ministry of Finance. In fact other

levies must be reduced so as not to add to the already high burden facing tax-payers. In particular, levies imposed on the labour factor should be decreased[26] – with social insurance as the obvious possibility.

European and international harmonization should be striven for and is desirable for ecological reasons. The assertion that competition will be distorted if one country acts alone cannot be upheld, provided that the total tax yield is not increased and slow implementation assures economic viability.

Other elements in a strategy to overcome perceived barriers to implementation due to potential negative impact on competitiveness are (see note 23):

- exemptions for energy-intensive processes;
- border tax adjustments through the application of a non-discriminatory tax on imports produced energy-intensively abroad;
- tax-free thresholds for initial consumption;
- recycling revenues, e.g. by reducing other taxes;
- international harmonization;
- reforming energy-cost provisions in business taxation as an incentive for reducing energy consumption.

The model of ecological tax reform put forward here is also acceptable socially and economically because it promises technical and social progress where the productivity of energy (and of resources in general) will increase each year (varying from sector to sector) as soon as the necessary investment has been made and bears fruit. In transportation in particular an increase in fuel efficiency of around 5% annually can be maintained for at least 20 years. During this period the necessary long-term switch of budget funds to local networks and long-distance rail traffic can be made.

It is essential that this tax reform does not compel anyone to throw away existing goods since that would be wasteful. Consumers – knowing that energy and resource prices will long continue to rise – will then always procure what is ecologically most efficient when making new investments or purchases. The main impact will be on new investment rather than existing capital stock. Long-term predictability will very quickly change the nature of goods demanded and supplied. Firms' research and development sections will thus receive a general indication of the direction their endeavours should take. The number of innovative products developed will play an increasingly important part in national and international trade.

Scenario 6: Ecological Tax Reform

In 1992 the European Commission (EC) advocated introduction of a tax on CO_2 and energy, and an amended proposal was put forward in 1995. However, this had not been approved by all member states by the end of the following year. The EC commissioned several studies on the consequences of such a tax, showing that the overall impact on the environment, economy, and employment would be positive.

According to a 1994 study, increased employment of around 12% in lower income groups would result from reduction of employers' social security contributions.[27]

More and more countries have acted unilaterally in introducing a modified version of this tax because of the EU deadlock. A core of eight countries (Austria, Belgium, Denmark, Finland, Germany, Luxemburg, the Netherlands, Sweden) met at The Hague in January 1996 and made a fresh attempt at introducing the tax throughout the EU. At the beginning of 1997 the Commission came up with a third proposal so as to profit from the existing administrative tax system and the wish to harmonize indirect taxes. This involved a twofold approach to raising energy prices: (1) broadening of the tax base to include other fuels (coal, gas, electricity, and aviation fuel) will be used as a means of increasing prices; and (2) an increase in the minimum excise rates (every two years).

5.3 From Linear to Cyclical Production Processes

In years of disputes between protectors of the environment and representatives of the economy, normally only one question has been raised: How can we save the environment? Strange though this may sound, we must also ask: How can we save the economy?[28] The current way of managing the economy is the central problem. Economic institutions are the most powerful forces across the world, so the necessary changes can only be introduced with their support. They must play an active part in fundamental processes of transformation. For that a far-sighted and far-reaching conceptual framework is necessary where the most important concepts are dematerialization and industrial ecology.[29]

The main idea behind dematerialization is to reduce by a factor of 10[30] (see section 3.2) the material and energy flows humanity takes from nature over the next few decades. In other words, the material- and energy-intensities of all products and processes – from the cradle to the grave – must be massively reduced so as to keep "natural capital"[31] relatively intact, and also to assure good prospects for future generations.

The main concept within industrial ecology is that both the natural and the economic system can co-exist and develop without threatening the other's viability. Nature is the undisputed mistress of complex systems, almost completely powered by solar energy, where substances circulate and are converted at differing speeds. Within this natural cycle eco-systems constantly develop further. Over the long term great changes occur in the composition of these flows. Materials are extracted (deposits of mineral oil and coal), and further employed in other configurations (genes and proteins), while species die out and appear in new forms. Nature itself is anything but a closed system where substances are statically and regularly recycled. There are also great losses of energy, mass, and heat. These are minimized as far as possible by utilization of solar energy, or only tolerated to the extent that the eco-system's viability is not impaired.

Four characteristic principles apparent in nature indicate a possibility of restructuring the way we have managed our economy to date:

1. Nature does not produce any waste products in terms of something that cannot be constructively absorbed and utilized elsewhere now or in the future. In a sustainable economy very many waste products could provide valuable material for other production processes – just as in nature "waste products" are constantly transformed with a minimum of expenditure (through bacteria and fungi) into (re)usable nutrients for other forms of life.
2. A sustainable economy must gradually be founded on solar energy – just as all natural processes are driven by the sun's power, continually and productively converting raw materials.
3. Nature permits to every individual within a species a form of independent activity, but co-operatively links the activity patterns of all species. Co-operation and competition are interlinked and maintained in a dynamic balance.
4. Just as nature depends upon diversity for healthy functioning, and flourishes and blossoms through differences, so too must human ways of life and economic activities be similarly structured.

These and analagous principles make it possible to reduce material- and energy-intensities in processes of production and consumption, to complete material cycles, and to combine different qualities of energy. The emphasis is thus put on forms of technology that operate with, rather than against, natural systems.

Material cycles

A distinction must be made between two forms of cycle: cycles for valuable substances (recycling) and cycles for products (extending durability and utilization). Both have in common the objective of reducing

Scenario 7: Recycling (the Example of Steel)

Like other metals (such as aluminium or copper), steel calls on large amounts of resources during the process of primary extraction. However, metals have the advantage of being usable time and again through low-cost, intelligent recycling. A car body can be re-used if the product is designed for a long life-cycle. Use of recycled metals can often reduce consumption of materials by a factor of 100 or more. For this, individual resources must be regained in a pure form. It is also important that the quality of the material is not reduced during recycling. Products must thus be made in such a way that materials can easily be separated from one another.

This possibility is demonstrated in the case of masts for overhead cables (figure 5.1).[32] Both masts are produced and used at present, serving identical functions and producing the same output – but the pre-stressed concrete mast requires about three times as many primary raw materials as the steel girder mast. The composition of materials can vary in accordance with the output required and the site. The costs for both variants, inclusive of starting operations, are similar. The decision on which is bought thus usually depends on suppliers' company policy or even the purchaser of electricity. The calculations presented here can easily be applied to bridges or other high-rise buildings.

demand for raw materials on the input side and of cutting the volume of waste at the end of processes of production and consumption – but there are fundamental differences with regard to the consequences for sustainability, choice of technology, and profitability.

In current discussions of waste, the emphasis is clearly on sorting and utilization rather than avoidance. Avoidance would entail producing less and smaller turnovers. Consistent pursuit of avoidance can harm economic interests so the apparent solution of re-use is very convenient. The "German Dual System" supposedly provides an ingenious way out of the waste products emergency. It is maintained this would permit consumption to continue at present levels in a world free of waste. The motor of ever greater and ever faster production and consumption could then remain active.

A sustainable economy instead demands a clear-cut reduction and slowing-down in flows of materials and energy, or of turnovers in production and consumption.[33] That is why the distinction between the viability of recycling and re-use of products is crucial. If, for instance, at the end of its cycle of use a washing machine is not dumped or demolished but instead stripped down so that parts can be re-used, then this "waste" becomes a source of income rather than a cost-factor. In addi-

Figure 5.1 Materials used in production of masts for overhead cables

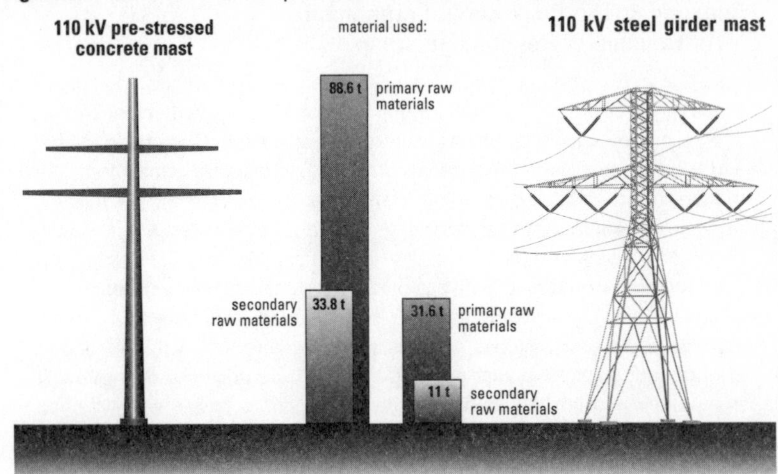

tion re-use of products is a substitute for expensive new goods whereas recycling frequently competes with cheaper raw materials. Firms that concentrate on maintaining products and extending their length of life quickly found out that they can make these products better than the original manufacturer because of their focus on utilization. Konica, for instance, has slowed down its product cycles since 1989. Now only three (instead of nine) new items of camera equipment are brought onto the market annually. That allows time for creativity and innovation, and also provides greater security for consumers and better training for service staff. Konica deliberately chose deceleration of its product-cycles as a management strategy for maintenance of market viability. However, most German enterprises still put the emphasis on acceleration and waste-management.

Firms which are active in recycling soon call for state subsidies. Companies that develop "end-of-pipe" technologies quickly seek legislation prescribing utilization (as with catalysers). State subsidies for recycling or state regulations in the realm of "end-of-pipe" technologies are modern forms of indulgences which prevent substances, goods, and materials being taken back by manufacturers and re-used. Even worse, they obstruct responsibility throughout the system – a principle constituting an essential aspect of sustainability.[34]

System-wide responsibility for products involves development of corresponding cycles of responsibility alongside the most intelligent circulation of products and materials possible, so that valuable materials

Scenario 8: The Rank Xerox Corporation – An Example of Re-manufacturing

Xerox does not sell photocopiers or talk about such products any longer. Xerox now calls itself a "document company" and markets customer satisfaction by way of a mixture of rentals and leasing. Ownership, costs, and the risks involved in maintenance and waste disposal remain with the manufacturer. This solution meets customers' needs; it offers flexibility in utilization, requires no investment, provides transparency of costs, demands no greater expenditure than alternative solutions (purchase), but guarantees economically and ecologically optimal durability through the refurbishing of old equipment. If a customer needs the capacity for making copies, Xerox concludes a "satisfaction agreement" with him or her, offering a three- to five-year guarantee and a fixed price per document. If the customer is not satisfied with the equipment, a phone call will bring a service engineer to put things right. The existing equipment will be repaired, upgraded, or in extreme cases exchanged. No matter what costs may be involved, the customer still pays the agreed amount for each copy.

In order to be able to sell this "trouble-free copying service" profitably, a company must re-organize its technical and commercial strategies. Xerox views continued existence of its equipment as the primary asset. Asset management (keeping these products on the market) is of central economic importance. If a customer does not want or need a machine any longer, then it is serviced by the salesperson, who has become a consultant, and leased to another customer as quickly as possible. The last thing that should happen is its return to the works. Only technically superseded or no longer reparable equipment returns to the factory for re-manufacturing. Such re-manufacturing units are regional – with Holland as the European centre. During this process a 1090 copier, by now about 10 years old, becomes the latest 5088 model, 80% of whose parts come from the earlier equipment.

That is possible thanks to standardization of components throughout the entire range, modular construction based on easy dismantling, long-term utilization of parts, and systems construction. If equipment can no longer be upgraded or re-manufactured, it is not recycled but rather "converted". Standardization of components makes it possible for fax equipment to be turned into a printer, or a photo-copier into a fax machine, since the paper-transport system is the same in all of them. Goods can be dismantled and components reassembled in a different way so as to become different equipment – just like Lego.

Even though less is produced, earnings are satisfactory because rentals are steady. Turnover is dependent on stability of income from leasing rather than production. Profits can mainly be increased through savings. Two factors are involved: reduction of purchases of raw materials and lower expenditure on waste disposal. If 80% of components in new machines can be re-used, then 80% fewer have to be purchased and at the same time there is 80% less waste. New parts are made out of recycled materials so that a target of nil waste is no longer an unattainable vision. Xerox estimates that savings of up to 800 million dollars annually will result from the company having learnt to utilize its products in a closed cycle.

and products are taken back at the end of their service-life by the retailers or manufacturers who initially benefited economically from putting them on the market. They or others will use these materials again. They will repair or improve used products, or make new ones out of old components. Re-use is exemplified by the multi-use bottle; repairs by replacing individual components in a modular office chair; and technological improvement of used products by integration of a new resource-saving cooling unit in an old refrigerator.

All this makes absolutely new demands of product-design. Products will be devised in terms of modular construction. Then ongoing improvements can be implemented relatively easily by exchanging components, and at the end of its life-cycle the product can easily be dismantled into its parts, which can then be re-used for new products or other purposes.

Of course even the longest-lived product at some stage reaches the end of its life and must be recycled. These two cycles of materials thus complement one another, but recycling is always secondary to extending products' durability and utility.

Environmental management and competition

An essential precondition for a firm's survival is attainment of competitive advantages. In order to achieve that either well-established products must be offered more cheaply or new products made available.[35] There thus exist two fundamentally different marketing alternatives: either offering a product or service at the lowest price or presenting something unique.

In the former case a successful firm must constantly maintain or increase its share of the market. This leads to accelerated product-cycles, especially when several companies are competing to achieve a lower price. Only one firm can offer the most favourable price in this sphere. If this strategy is consistently pursued, it leads to ever more products and constantly mounting production volumes because that is the only way of achieving the necessary cost reductions through economies of scale. This kind of growth-oriented business still predominates today.

Another not unproblematic way of running a business involves specialization. Even with only a small share of the market it is possible to make profits through specializing in specific services or unique products. Such an approach does not demand an increasing share of the market, and promotes creative products rather than emphasis on costs. It leads to previously homogeneous groups of products becoming increasingly individualized. The disadvantage is that the number of variants gets out of hand and products become incompatible. Customers thereby lose their overview of the market and may stop using completely functional products. It is obvious that this way of setting about things results in greater flows of material in production, ever-shorter cycles of product-life, and more waste.

So how can firms use competition to establish ecological, acceptable, and keenly priced products on the market, meeting real human needs?

Green companies

A small but growing number of "green companies" already accept that challenge and are taking on the role of ecology-oriented leadership. They respond proactively and strategically by restructuring products and processes, avoiding pollution and waste, and seeking co-operation and alliances with other organizations.[36] In other words, they plan over the long term and attempt to deal with the root-causes of ecological problems by assuming responsibility for products' entire life-cycle and in general advocating green approaches (for instance by supporting eco-taxes). They emphasize product quality and think in terms of function/services, responding to demand and context (e.g. short distances in transportation), and linking up with needs (such as mobility).

Active environmental management can be implemented by way of firms' ecological use of resources even when starting-points differ greatly. A number of these starting-points are shown in figure 5.2. Active environmental management involves both internally and externally directed strategies for implementation of a company's ecological policy.

Internally firms can make a difference during production, shaping their range of products, distribution, and works management. In concrete terms purchasing policy can be restructured on the basis of knowledge of specific ecological demands – with the flow of information from production, assembly, after-sales service, etc., used as the broadest possible basis for decision-making. The development department can design ecologically acceptable goods and services, and also establish production processes with less impact on the environment. That need not be more cost-intensive than previous planning and development procedures if ecological demands

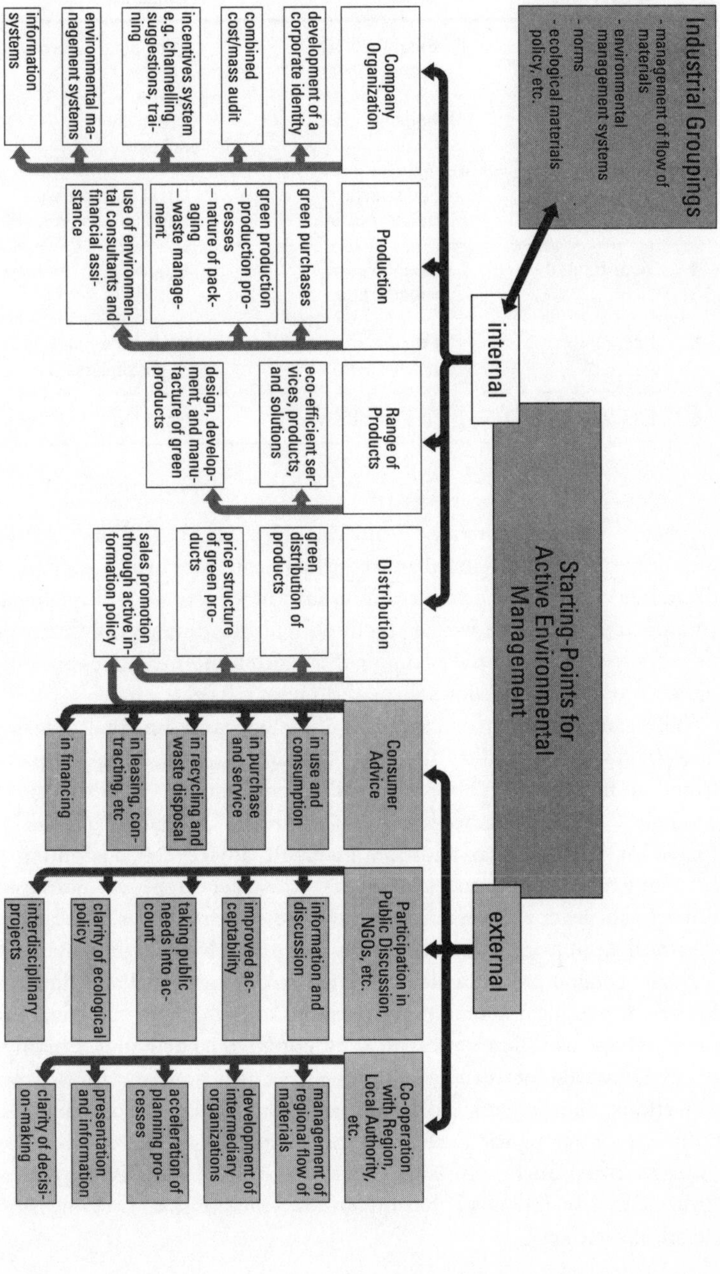

Industrial Groupings
- management of flow of materials
- environmental management systems
- norms
- ecological materials policy, etc.

Starting-Points for Active Environmental Management

internal

Company Organization
development of a corporate identity
combined cost/mass audit
incentives system e.g. channelling suggestions, training
environmental management systems
information systems

Production
green purchases
green production
– production processes
– nature of packaging
– waste management
use of environmental consultants and financial assistance

Range of Products
eco-efficient services, products, and solutions
design, development, and manufacture of green products

Distribution
green distribution of products
price structure of green products
sales promotion through active information policy

external

Consumer Advice
in use and consumption
in purchase and service
in recycling and waste disposal
in leasing, contracting, etc
in financing

Participation in Public Discussion, NGOs, etc.
information and discussion
improved acceptability
taking public needs into account
clarity of ecological policy
interdisciplinary projects

Co-operation with Region, Local Authority, etc.
management of regional flow of materials
development of intermediary organizations
acceleration of planning processes
presentation and information
clarity of decision-making

Figure 5.2 Starting-points for active environmental management

Table 5.1 Guidelines for firms (*Source*: Pfriem, 1995)

	Impact area	Criteria	Guideline
1	Ecological	Sustainability, reproductivity	Ecological diversity
2	Social	Equity, health	Creativity, solidarity
3	Space-related	Local links, decentralization	Local network with experienceable feedback
4	Time-related	Deceleration, regeneration	Openness to the future
5	Economic	Efficiency, productivity	Welfare, wealth of possibilities
6	Ethical	Responsibility	Good life

are taken into account right from the start. Local staff are usually very well informed about installations which can be further extended and diversified with appropriate communication structures and qualifications. In such a concept the management should in principle only manage and be responsible for central planning. Structures and incentives for everyday operations should be devised at the factory level.

The starting-point for externally directed environmental management is a firm's active policy towards consumers, presenting simple, well-founded information about goods' environmental viability and other ecological qualities as well as possibilities of recycling and acceptable forms of disposal. In addition in-depth advice for customers about financing complex services, such as construction of an energy-saving house, can reduce uncertainties about new technologies.

Another important external possibility involves a company's contact with the general public, which apart from customers includes direct neighbours, non-governmental organizations, and the regional and national press, which are often very critical of commercial activities. Finding ways of working together can sometimes save much time and money, prevent objections, and accelerate planning approval. Co-operation with the local authority or regionally based enterprises can also lead to further reductions in costs. Such companies have succeeded in jointly organizing the flow of raw materials so that quantities, emissions, and waste have been drastically reduced.

Creative enterprises' understanding that their activities also generate meaning or culture – with material production also entailing the creation of symbols – extends business rationality and opens up entirely new social and ecological aspects, guidelines, and possibilities of action in other spheres of impact (table 5.1).

Areas of ecological action and freedom of decision can only be utilized if suitable organizational structures and a generally creative environment come into being. Rigid hierarchies, long lines of communication, absence of exchanges of information, lack of co-operation, and individual striving for power stand in the way. Unrestricted areas of innovative thinking could instead come into existence at all levels of a firm as an indispensable precondition for realistic potential for change. This is far from being a single act or mere implementation, but rather an ongoing process which is seldom without conflicts and for that very reason demands time, composure, and prudence. This calls for such key qualifications as readiness to give and receive criticism, ability to communicate, understanding of and sensitivity to systemic environmental relations, creativity, readiness to learn, and orientation towards the future.

Ecological product policies

Durability and quality must be linked. Products made to be usable for a long time will only be profitable if this alternative is more interesting for customers than short-term use of throwaway goods. If the mounting costs of disposal make short-life products more expensive, the customer has to carry those costs – either directly when he or she wants to get rid of the old product, or indirectly when manufacturers attempt to pass on disposal costs in the sales price. The more expensive throwaway goods thus become, the more attractive long-life products are as an alternative. A large number of users would like to combine consumption and ecology, wanting enjoyment without remorse. Quality products are an achievement, not a renunciation. They last for a long time, give satisfaction, and are economically and ecologically successful. That is why the aesthetic quality of products is so important. People with a feeling for quality want to be surrounded by products with which they can live for a considerable time, goods that can tell a story. Even if one day an owner does decide to part with such a product, not infrequently he or she will find a taker at a flea market or similar set-up, attracted by the object's aura.

Against that background a durability strategy constitutes a new and fascinating task. Management, engineers, development teams, designers, marketing people, specialist workers, etc., devote knowledge and abilities to making products ecologically acceptable. Characteristics such as durability, modular construction, reparability, extendability, re-usability, and freedom from toxics are of central importance.

Durability encounters its limits when a genuine technological alternative emerges, fulfilling the same purpose better, more elegantly, more cheaply, or more environmentally acceptably so that it can replace the existing product. Extension of product-life would then be meaningless since the object of durability is the longest and most intensive utilization possible, not everlastingness.

Dematerialization, regional cycles, plural economy

Mounting costs of waste disposal, raw materials, and energy constantly push forward the process of dematerialization. Rising transport costs will also result in the shipping of all kinds of goods half-way round the world becoming increasingly unviable. The outcome is that more and more products, materials, and substances are circulated, processed, and re-used regionally.

Decentralized workshops are coming into existence instead of global robot factories, "mini-mills" instead of huge steelworks, and above all new decentralized markets for used goods, components, and valuable materials. Jobs may be lost in the sphere of centralized manufacture, but new and more demanding forms of employment are being established. Reconditioning and repairs take place close to customers. Qualified skilled workers are required. Small quantities of goods can be manufactured more quickly and flexibly by skilled workers than by fully automated assembly-lines – and usually more cheaply too. More and more people are sought for reconditioning and overhauling old products. This demands manual skills to a much higher degree than highly rationalized new production, so this has a positive impact on the labour market. It also serves ecological tax reform, making more expensive use of new raw materials and energy and reducing the labour element in the tax burden. Labour-intensive repairs and restoration become cheaper, and remain a local activity.

Scenario 9: Regional Management of Raw Materials Flow

Kalundborg in Denmark offers an example of regional management of raw materials flow.[37] Here some waste products become raw materials for other manufacturers in the region. Gypsum from the power station goes to a plaster-works, district heating to the local community, steam to a biotechnical factory whose yeast is in turn used for feeding pigs, etc. The investment necessary for linking individual production units was paid off in three to five years. Large amounts of primary resources have also been saved and emissions avoided. To make such a development possible economic and ecological indicators are needed for all aspects of the regional economy. Saving resources in one area should not lead to accumulation of special kinds of waste in others. Easily comprehended environmental reporting is accompanied by development of active marketing, demonstrating the reliability and innovative nature of the region. Qualitative environmental objectives are part of the developmental concept. This promotes the settlement of firms dedicated to increasing resource-productivity, boosting the region's image and improving competitive advantages. Such qualitative environmental objectives thus become an incentive, leading firms to set up in this area.

The transition to durable products and the changeover to selling utility rather than objects strengthens a trend towards jobs in services rather than production. If, for instance, a firm sells "individual transportation" rather than "cars", it is advantageous to have workshops and sales or rental offices in towns or larger villages. That opens up fresh possibilities for part-time work, and also opportunities for older workers and the handicapped. People who had previously been left behind can now be more easily integrated in gainful employment.

In addition work fulfilling personal interests is becoming increasingly important. Alongside part-time jobs and autonomous enterprises, many people take up farming or gardening where they use alternative technologies (such as water-recycling in fish-breeding) for producing food; become carpenters making furniture and other utilitarian objects of wood; or work in the realm of community welfare, training, and culture.

This gives rise to a plural economy which makes possible diverse forms of production and consumption, is ecologically acceptable over the long-term, and promotes and supports cultural autonomy and social coherence.

5.4 Well-Being instead of Well-Having

Ambiguous change of values

Ever since the seventies empirical social researchers – starting with Robald Inglehart – believed they had discovered a "silent revolution"[38] in values. In developed consumer societies well-educated younger people in particular seemed to incline increasingly towards post-material values. They strove for self-development, *joie de vivre*, and good societies and environments, rather than fulfilling responsibilities by way of work, possession through consumption, and economic security within society. Researchers presented two explanations for this displacement of needs. The socialization hypothesis suggests that people whose early years are spent amid poverty and deprivation develop greater material needs than those who lacked nothing when young. The shortages hypothesis takes as its starting-point that people who live amid material affluence experience non-material goods as being in short supply and accord them higher status. It can thus be concluded that if a consumer society prevails, former wishes fade and new ones arise. Against a background of shortages people yearn for goods, while at a time of affluence they seek self-realization.

In the meantime it has become obvious that the triumphal progress of the post-material citizen must have come to a stop somewhere. In its pure form such a character is only to be found here and there, and certainly not among the majority, even though all kinds of interminglings of individual aspects are to be encountered across society. Researchers into changes in values were both right and wrong. Post-material value orientations have in no way generally replaced material values, but they do influence life-styles and have contributed to pluralization of attitudes and milieus. Shopping addicts exist alongside the socially committed, careerists alongside dropouts, ordinary folk alongside the highly educated, and family people alongside yuppies. A collage-like co-existence of value structures has developed, sometimes superimposed and sometimes contradicting one another. If "post-material" is comprehended as meaning an attitude involving relatively few goods and putting compatibility with nature and society before further affluence, then it can be assumed that in Germany this group of persons amounts to somewhat less than 20% while the clearly pro-material group adds up to around 25%. "Partly-sensitized affluent citizens", valuing both goods and environmental and social compatibility, constitute somewhat over 30%, while the 25% labelled "apathetic" are neither fixated on goods nor interested in non-material demands.[39]

The idea that economic development might one day be succeeded by satiation, with people in a position to devote themselves to free and fulfilling activities, is a venerable hope, even the basis for struggle, with which both conservatives and socialists have for 200 years sought to counter the dynamism of blind accumulation. However, the principle of non-saturation constitutes the cornerstone of economic thought. Economics inherited from the Enlightenment the basic assumption that human needs are (firstly) infinite and (secondly) directed towards increased utility. That contrasts polemically with the classical view of humanity, concerned with embedding needs within a successful life, and with the classical concept of happiness founded on implementation of a non-material ideal.[40] Moderns see things differently. For them needs always precede the means for their satisfaction, so means must remain insufficient. All their passion is thus devoted to perfecting means. The assumption of shortage of means in the face of unlimited needs is the founding myth of economics. That is why all theoretical efforts are focused on efficient deployment of ever-better means (such as technology, capital, and labour) while thought about objectives is systematically excluded. Whenever during the past two centuries economics' mounting claims to power have been attacked – whether by conservatives or social revolutionaries – this way of looking at human beings and their needs has been called into question. The conviction that happiness does not involve a constant increase in needs, and that the means could therefore one day be sufficient, has long been a thorn in the flesh of the growth society. It makes itself felt again subterraneously in hopes of a transformation of values.

However, like so many previous revolutions the "silent revolution" remains ambivalent. On the one hand, the detached consumer has made his or her appearance, buying modestly and selectively, seeking quality rather than quantity, bearing in mind nature and community rather than merely his or her own benefit. On the other, there is the consumer addicted to new experiences who uses up goods and services in terms of their hedonistic and theatrical value. The ideal of self-realization, the dominant value within post-materialism, can be embodied in both figures. From home furnishings to culinary taste, from shoes to therapies, the possibilities of choice are highly subtly differentiated – a landscape of options inviting everyone to construct their own life-style: the doctor riding a Harley-Davidson, buying clothes at both boutiques and flea-markets, and IKEA in a Jugendstil villa. A transformation of values has certainly happened, but it is both post-materialistic and neo-materialistic. Scepticism about consumerism goes hand in hand with a new level of commercialization.

Whoever expects that one day the consumer society will after all reach a saturation-limit greatly underestimates the symbolic power of goods. In the "experience society" (G. Schultze) products are less than ever simply vehicles of instrumental utility. Instead they serve an expressive function. What counts is what goods say, not what they do. Ethnologists studying pre-modern societies have also always read material possessions as symbols of social allegiance and cultural meaning.[41] In modern societies the same principle applies. Goods are loaded with significance. They constitute a system of signs with which a purchaser makes statements about the self and friends. Until the sixties this system was largely hierarchically structured in its communication of status, but since then a horizontal and temporally differentiated system has been superimposed, signalizing life-

Scenario 10: Saving Electricity

Electricity is a particularly high-value form of energy. It has many applications but is extremely expensive. What happens before it reaches household outlets is crucial. Around two-thirds of the primary energy involved is lost during conversion of fuels such as coal or oil into electricity, or during overland transmission. Consumers who bear in mind both their purses and use of resources will treat domestic saving of electricity as a necessary routine. They will assess whether the technology employed serves the purpose desired; they will take care that electricity is efficiently applied; and they will only make considered use of it.

Using electricity for purposes where it is not absolutely necessary means squandering resources. Only lighting and electrical appliances specifically demand electricity. Other sources of energy, such as gas, district heating, and solar energy, can be employed for domestic heating, warm water, and cooking. It is thus worth bearing in mind the degree of efficiency of hot-water tanks, household appliances, and lighting when installing them. Gains in domestic efficiency through more intelligent technology amounted to between 30 and 40% during the past 15 years, and similar savings will be made up to the year 2010. That entails considerable potential even for someone who is not yet ready to contemplate changes in life-style. Nevertheless the prudent consumer is well advised to consider the utility-value of household appliances rather than simply energy consumption. Such equipment may save work but often surprisingly little time. Preparation of operations and clearing up afterwards often swallow the time saved.

The specific amount of electricity used is not the only magnitude determining consumption. The facilities involved and user habits can also result in increased energy-efficiency being cancelled out or not fully utilized. More dishwashers, dryers, microwave ovens, or innumerable smaller appliances can easily nullify savings. Nothing is as efficient as appliances which are not purchased. In addition people are inclined to use eco-efficient equipment more thoughtlessly. The link between more technology and increasing demands is notorious. With a vacuum cleaner, washing machine, etc., demands for cleanliness, hygiene, and freshness easily mount. For that reason it is not enough to establish potential for savings; implementing them also demands a modest life-style. Here too efficiency must be stabilized by sufficiency. Prudent behaviour opens up additional possibilities of saving. If the demand for washed clothes and warm showers were to decline by 20%, and if dishwashers were 90% full (instead of the current 70%), then – leaving aside all technological improvements – environmentally committed households could make additional electricity savings of between 10 and 20%.

milieu and up-to-dateness. In addition these signs and social differences are constantly in flux. Identities and their forms of expression are unstable and constantly have to be renegotiated. Against that background it becomes understandable that the consumer society is striving for anything but a point of satiation since the interplay between goods and imagination is a never-ending process.

Green consumers

And yet – or to be accurate, for that very reason – during the past decade and a half the demand for an end to the plundering of nature has become a market force. The times are past when the organic shop in the student quarter or the plant centre on the outskirts of town could only count on ecologically inclined buyers. Today even giant concerns have to take into account customers' environmental demands. Ecology has moved from a niche existence to an established factor on the market. The food business offers organic products, manufacturers of electrical goods provide energy-saving appliances, the holiday industry speaks of green tourism, car manufacturers resort to environmental arguments, department stores remove non-ecological washing powders and cleaning agents from their shelves, clothes shops present eco-collections, and new product-lines become available in paints and varnishes, cosmetics and body-care.

Ecological motives impel a variety of life-styles. They become effective because on all sides the aspirations of the new consumer go beyond increasing numbers of possessions. He or she wants to fulfil with goods and services what for the person concerned are important qualities. That is the gateway to ecological consuming. To exaggerate a little, buying is transformed from an act of consuming into an act of creative expression, and thus a means of moral and political manifestation. Today already 50% of consumers would like to have more information about companies' environmental commitment.[42] Only when the customer has the means – in the form of independent advice and environmental labelling – to make a really informed choice is the way open for transition from an economy of affluence to an economy of influence.

A surfeit of affluence

As early as 1930 one of the master thinkers in twentieth-century economic theory, John Maynard Keynes, wrote in his "Essays in Persuasion" that the crises of the future would involve the premisses underlying economics. In this view economics, based on optimizing scarce means in the struggle for survival, would over the long term lose significance because of its splendid successes. In a world of superfluity the imperative of production had to yield its predominance in social life. It could be said that Keynes' expectation accords with the scepticism found in healthy human understanding: Why all the stress? Some time affluence really must suffice!

For the moment the economy – despite all that master thinkers say – has averted the danger of loss of importance by unleashing the consumer society. Products no longer serve the struggle for survival; they serve a struggle for experience. Many products have now been perfected and cannot be developed any further, so they can only find new buyers if they promise additional symbolic uses. Cars that cannot become faster and more comfortable are styled to give technological pleasure. Watches which cannot show the time more accurately take on a sporting aspect with a built-in stop-watch. Television sets whose images cannot become clearer mediate a cinematic feeling with big screens. What counts in the "late consumer society"[43], where potential for improvement of goods is gradually becoming exhausted, is creating possibilities of new experiences and identities while goods' objective utility becomes a secondary matter taken for granted.

The consumer's relationship with the product is thus changed. It becomes volatile and unclear. Means are no longer in short supply and objectives clear as in more deprived times; instead possibilities are plentiful but objectives are unclear. A poor person does not have to worry about whether to take trumpet lessons or go kite-flying, while the rich person constantly has to question intentions and shape the self. Satisfaction depends on an act of self-reflection, on an inner compass, and not simply on outer equipment – a situation that easily leads from surfeit to superfluity. "What do I want?" and "Who would I like to be?" are questions that arise daily during decisions about what to buy, but the answers constantly remain uncertain and illusory. The suspicion that one has not chosen rightly, the fear of missing out, and the stale after-taste when the yearnings projected onto purchases meet reality – all that makes disappointment a twin-sister of pleasure in consumption. In fact studies show that anyone who is particularly oriented towards materialistic consumption is most likely to be disappointed.[44] The coupling of sales of goods and the formation of human identity is the late consumer society's Achilles heel since the assent that must be established between consumer and product can be modified or even revoked by the customer at any time. The fact that consumption requires inner assent constitutes both the strength and the weakness of the consumer society: its strength because sales are thus possible beyond saturation, and its weakness because of greater dependence than ever on human expectations and demands. That is ecology's opportunity, particularly in a rich society. The wish and the will to live sustainably – without plundering nature and equitably with regard to the Third World – could provide a shared foundation out of which a new understanding develops between suppliers and consumers.

Scenario 11: Informed Eating

Almost inconceivably, 20% of total use of materials and energy is devoted to getting food to German homes. Diesel oil for tractors, animal feed for mass herding, energy for the food industry, petrol for long-distance transportation, electricity for supermarket refrigeration, power for processing: an extensive infrastructure of pipelines, motorways, processing plants, fleets of lorries, and large sales areas operate day in day out to fill people with food – conveniently, cheaply, and enormously diversely.

In the area formerly constituting the Federal Republic nutritional energy has increased by 15% since 1965, even though the physiological need has diminished because of a decline in mobility and physical work. The Germans still eat too much with excessive fat and sweetness. They buy too much meat, too little fruit and too few fresh vegetables, and consume too many sweet snacks and drinks. However, the significance of eating has changed because of an increase in available income. People do not only want to eat their fill; they are also concerned with such additional qualities as a meal's convenience, diversity, pleasure, and experiential qualities. For most customers quality is more important than price. More people than previously pay attention to taste, prefer natural foodstuffs, and are concerned about their health. Nevertheless this trend is accompanied by a constant demand for fast food and industrially produced foodstuffs. That demand is supported by the acceleration and more flexible nature of everyday life. Meal-times are no longer fixed, snacking is on the increase, and people eat quickly and alone.

A pluralization of eating-styles can be observed, following consumer behaviour in general. There is a market for natural products and nutritious diets as well as for pre-prepared meals and the classic roast pork. However, reflection on one's needs is becoming more important, particularly in the realm of food. Eating becomes a medium of self-realization – far beyond the point of satiation. People ask themselves what is good for them, think about how products are manufactured, and lovingly prepare meals.

Anyone who accords with the basic principles of high-quality eating, preferring local and seasonal vegetables and fruit, and avoiding industrially processed foodstuffs, benefits both him- or herself and nature. Fresh, seasonal, low in meat, and regional – those are the criteria for the far-sighted consumer. He or she thus makes decisions countering mass cattle-rearing, water pollution, road transportation, and waste of energy, and in addition opens up future possibilities for organic farming.

Low-impact affluence

Up to now consumers' ecological interests have mainly been felt in the spheres of health and closeness to nature. Customers demand unsprayed apples and formaldehyde-free varnishes because they are concerned about their bodily well-being. Even though there is still a considerable way to go before consumption becomes toxic-free, another guideline takes on greater importance in terms of "Factor 10": low-impact consumption. Here consumers act as citizens, seeing themselves as protagonists in an economic transition to sustainability. Some of their satisfaction and self-realization is based on pride in personal participation in this historic changeover to a more restrained way of running the economy. Their ambitions are to some extent involved in developing habits which make everyday living less material-intensive. They thus disprove orthodox economists who want to make people believe that everyone acts in strictly utilitarian fashion, following their immediate interests. Instead they feel inspired by the thought that they are part of a greater history, in a small way co-authors of an epoch-making transformation intended to make the twenty-first century more hospitable. They extend the range of their attention, asking themselves where the beautiful fur-coat comes from, who had to slave to produce their coffee, whether their wood derives from mass felling, how much energy is involved in the manufacture of a car, what heat escapes through their windows, how long their kitchen furnishings will last, or where their computers will be disposed of. If one also imagines that in future product-labelling will provide information about the material and transportation costs involved, then the alert contemporary will be able to exert considerable influence. For a new form of propriety, based on global far-sightedness rather than petit-bourgeois constraints, choosing the resource-saving, careful alternative could become a matter of course. Four criteria are of importance here: thrift, regional orientation, shared utilization, durability.

Thrift, that long-established precept in household management, takes on a new emphasis as concern about the amount of nature one uses privately, even though nature in principle constitutes a common good. That especially applies to all investment decisions such as choice of building materials, installation of heating equipment, water facilities, flooring, and means of transportation. If thought through consistently such concern leads to new housing concepts like the "Gärtnerhof" in Vienna where conservatories, solar collectors, heat exchangers, rainwater collectors, and back-gardens are integrated in a complex of detached houses and flats. All kinds of opportunities, from water-use controls to selective heating, are available for daily application, even though manufacturers often do not as yet offer really efficient products such as the car using only 3 litres of petrol per hundred km or wall-refrigerators.

Regional orientation when making purchases and for weekend recreation develops out of interest in leading a life that keeps within acceptable limits the number of kilometres travelled. That is good for the environment, the regional economy, and not infrequently the quality of goods.

Shared utilization is advocated by people who realize there is a connection between consumption of resources and individual ownership. Under-use of purchases particularly increases in times when more and more people live on their own. Organizational and technological solutions separating ownership and utilization so as to increase intensity of use would be desirable.

Scenario 12: Using instead of Owning

The calculation is simple. A product that is utilized twice as frequently during its life-time than something comparable reduces the number of goods in circulation by 50%. However, washing machines, cars, vacuum cleaners, ladders, lawn-mowers, ski equipment, etc., are usually only used for a few hours or days and then stand around uselessly for most of their lifetime.

More comprehensive utilization is hindered by the fact that many goods are designed for private use and bought for individual ownership. However, use does not have to be tied up with ownership. A customer is primarily concerned about what a product does, and not with ownership, which may involve problems as well as pleasure. Such a service can also become available through sharing, borrowing, or renting the equipment by way of a community, co-operative, or a commercial company. New production structures can grow alongside such forms of shared utilization. An increasing number of goods will then be designed for intensive commercial use, offering more advanced technology than products for private individuals.

The de-privatized car exemplifies the various possibilities of utilization. If friends or people in the same house form groups jointly owning a car, density of car-ownership declines. That is also the case with co-operative utilization by way of a car-sharing organization. Cars are always available when really needed for members in different places. A taxi or rental car system for everyday use also offers an alternative to ownership. In addition car-sharing and taxis create a market for functional, robust, and durable vehicles. Another example is provided by launderettes, which employ cheaper and more economical machines, and can also be established close to a café, day-nursery, or library. In the case of tools and other equipment, shops, workshops, and neighbourhood offices can establish hire-services. Quantities of goods in circulation are reduced while new designs further promote collective utilization.

Taking into account the durability of goods is an important attitude when buying, using, and disposing of them. Of course the consumer society still reckons with obsolescence and rapid need for replacements, but public wishes could change. More people, uniting financial prudence and ecological far-sightedness, are beginning to put emphasis on the durability of the goods with which they surround themselves. Anyone who wants to become friends with these objects does well to consider their long-term quality. Here aesthetics and ecology overlap.

Rich in time rather than goods

Time rather than money is the good that is lacking at the end of our century – at least for the broad middle class in the rich societies. People discover that spending less time on work opens up unaccustomed freedom for all kinds of life-projects, and possession of fewer goods can be accompanied by greater satisfaction. The idea that gaining time can compensate for loss of income and open up new horizons is beginning to spread.

Moreover, whatever sustainability means, it is not only about different consumption; it also calls for less consumption. For decades people took for granted that an increase in economic productivity should be largely converted into higher wages and still greater productivity, leaving only a small proportion for greater freedom from the necessity to work. Despite all their freedom to consume, people generally never had one fundamental option: the possibility of deciding how long they wanted to work. It might well be that, if they had the choice, a considerable number would prefer to work less for a lower income.[45] Ultimately the rigidity of normal working hours forces the employed into a rising spiral of income and consumption. To date it has not been possible to develop a situation where working hours are subordinate to needs rather than wants following income. However, such a situation is ecologically desirable. Disposing freely of one's time is needed today for nature's sake – not to mention the fact that fewer working hours pave the way for reducing unemployment.

But that is not the only reason. "Time-pioneers" develop their own life-styles.[46] They decide against income and goods. They want more autonomy and thus experience normal working hours as constraints. They resist the situation where an individual's daily and life rhythms are dictated by a regime determined by the needs of the world of work. Seeking more freedom for their own interests, they are ready to renounce part of their income, and deliberately take on the adventure of arranging their life so that they get by with less money. They strive to deal creatively with unavoidable problems and bottlenecks. It could be said that money and time are seen as being in competition, so they devote themselves to the art of balancing those elements.

Viewed in terms of a sustainable community, those who consciously follow the path of economic under-achievement, those who choose to live below their economic possibilities, can look forward to a great time ahead, especially in localities and neighbourhoods welcoming networks and institutions where non-commercial activities, benefiting those involved and others, find a home. Munich's "Haus der Eigenarbeit" already exists, a centre of communal workshops where people can make objects ranging from tables to amplifiers; and there are also mixed forms linking self-help and gainful employment (as with day mothers). And there is the LETS (Local Exchange and Trading) system, a modern network of reciprocity whose members can supply or demand all kinds of services utilizing an account based on the local LETS currency. The basic idea is always the same: creation of opportunities allowing people with less money and reduced purchasing power to live agreeably.

The elegance of simplicity

Beyond a certain number things become thieves of time. In a culture where each household – unlike the Navajos with only 236 objects – has an average of 10,000 things at its disposal, shortage of time must predominate. Goods both large and small have to be chosen, bought, set up, used, experienced, maintained, tidied away, dusted, repaired, stored, and disposed of. Even the most beautiful and valuable of objects unavoidably gnaw away at the most restricted of all resources: time. The number of possibilities – goods, services, events – has exploded in the affluent societies, but the day in its conservative way continues to be limited to 24 hours, so a hectic pace and stress have become characteristic of everyday existence. Shortage of time is the nemesis, the revenge, of affluence.

Satisfaction with goods does not merely derive from material convenience; there is also an inner experience. Viewed closely, satisfaction has two dimensions, material and non-material. Anyone who buys all kinds of food and prepares a multi-course meal has the material satisfaction of filling his or her stomach and also the non-material pleasure of enjoying cooking (perhaps together with others), making the meal a success, and having convivial company. That everyday experience can be generalized. Most goods achieve their full value when put to use, experienced, participated in, and made the most of. However, this inner satisfaction requires time. And that is the dilemma. Having many goods can interfere with satisfaction. The conclusion is obvious. Material and non-material satisfaction cannot be maximized simultaneously. There is a limit to possession of goods beyond which satisfaction no longer continues to grow.[47] In other words, having much obstructs living well.

It almost seems as if after its breathtaking success the affluent society is once again being driven by experiences clearly related to classical teachings about the good life. Teachers of wisdom in the East and West may have had different views about the nature of the universe, but they almost unanimously recommended adherence to the principle of simplicity in the conduct of life. That cannot just be a matter of chance. Summarizing the experience of generations, they drew the conclusion that the way towards a successful life seldom involves accumulation of possessions. Far from being any form of affliction, simplicity is advocated as one aspect of the art of life.

In this tradition the opposite to a simple life-style is not a luxurious but a fragmented existence. An excess of things obstructs everyday existence, distracts attention, dissipates energies, and weakens capacity to find a clear-cut direction. Emptiness and dross are the enemies of happiness. Anyone who wants to keep his head above the flood of goods has no choice but to be a selective consumer; and anyone who wants to remain mistress of her wishes will discover the pleasure of systematically not pursuing options for buying. Advocacy of simplicity is thus more concerned with the aesthetics of the conduct of life than with morality. Superfluity involves a danger of fragmentation of spirit. Just as in painting everything depends on an appropriate and skilful use of colours and tones, so too the art of life demands a well-chosen use of material riches. In other words there exists something akin to a subterranean relationship between austerity and hedonism. Henry David Thoreau must have known that when he wrote in his journal at Walden Pond: "A man is rich in proportion to the number of things he can afford to let alone."

5.5 Intelligent Infrastructures

Industrial countries have a lavish infrastructure, including buildings, roads, public facilities, warehouses, industrial works, bridges, railways, harbours, power stations, electricity networks, and much besides. Underground there are drainage, cable, and pipeline systems branching out in all directions. Such concentrations of materials are of great environmental significance. These materials are taken from natural deposits, processed, and transported. They give rise to waste and emissions, and they occupy land and landscapes. Sooner or later they must be dumped as demolition rubble or hazardous waste. In addition this infrastructure is much used and – with roads, power stations, and certain forms of production – by no means only for environmentally acceptable activities.

It is not exaggerated to view today's material infrastructure as expressing an economy primarily oriented towards throughput, mass production, and increasingly also global operations. In Germany a number of characteristic magnitudes have more than doubled since 1960: the length of motorways (plus 260%), the networks for gas (plus 230%) and water (plus 206%), electricity supplies (plus 398%), and transportation of goods by road (plus 159%).[48]

Infrastructure fulfils a dual role in the economic process. It is simultaneously a product preparing the way for other economic activities, and it serves end-use by customers for electricity, car-drivers, etc. It is the pivot for changing from a wasteful, throughput-based economy to one focused on services meeting needs.

Different types of infrastructure

The planning of today's infrastructure points in the wrong direction. Everywhere new airports are being constructed, roads built, cables laid, and land consumed, provoking increased use in the decades ahead. The infrastructure is being improved so as to cope with increasing international competition. This is intended both to link centres of production within a large domestic market and at the same time to serve as a turntable and launching-pad for worldwide trade. Paradoxically, European integration is supposed to be pursued by way of what are called trans-European networks furthering the movement of electricity, goods, cars, aeroplanes, ships, and information instead of the emphasis being on cultural exchange, additional qualifications, and establishment of social relations.[49]

The current lively discussion of the future reveals contradictions. On the one side there is talk of "lean" production, miniaturization, quality management, the information society, and post-materialization, while on the other vast investment is made in ever-greater mass production and throughput. On the one hand there is far-reaching agreement that the future can only be mastered by way of a well-qualified, motivated, and committed work-force, a capacity for life-long learning, culturally mediated openness and flexibility, and intact and resistant social systems, but it is those very spheres which are being dismantled and their functionality undermined. The non-material infrastructure – human capital and all levels of training – is relatively neglected.

The idea of large-scale material infrastructure as the precondition and motor for economic development derives from the period of early industrialization. Adam Smith recognized that the "Wealth of Nations" could only be achieved if specific public tasks – such as the construction of roads, canals, and harbours – were part of the state's productive responsibility. That was first implemented in the sphere of transportation. The German economist Friedrich List wrote: "The inexpensive, rapid, safe, and regular transportation of persons and goods is one of the most powerful means of achieving national affluence and civilization."[50] The first railway line in Great Britain was used to move coal. That in turn points to the connection between coal, its use in the iron and steel industry, and energy supplies. Only at the beginning of the twentieth century did a cable-bound energy industry come into being.

Today it would be fatal to base activity on the models provided by early industrialization. People may time and again maintain that investment in core infrastructure would exert a positive influence on general productivity, but this thesis can hardly be conclusively demonstrated. In fact it has frequently been empirically refuted. Other factors influencing growth of productivity – such as pricing or institutional elements – are usually neglected, so that an insufficient basis for analysis ultimately leads to wishful thinking.[51] In other words, it may be correct that investment in infrastructure basically increases affluence, but the relevant areas of infrastructure must be redefined. The guideline involved in large-scale infrastructure leads to wrong conclusions. These are the outcome of the following:

(a) Viewing nature as a storehouse. Coal, natural gas, mineral oil, important raw materials, and even water (dams) are located in widely scattered areas, extracted, transported, processed, and further refined. However, decentralized economic structures can be created, making lesser demands on the material infrastructure, with fewer – and renewable – raw materials used.

(b) An erroneous perspective. Forecasts still assume mounting demand as part of a striving for constant growth. It seems as if such growth can only be achieved through further expansion of the necessary infrastructure – but the key and lock principle is wrong. There seldom exists direct demand for kilowatt-hours or tonne-kilometres, but rather for warm and comfortable rooms, supplies that fulfil needs better, reliable mobility, etc.

Future infrastructure will be based on declining demand for energy, raw materials, and land in an "economy of avoidance".[52] Infrastructure can provide incentives for reducing consumption of nature.

Services meeting needs

Extensive material infrastructure already exists, so what is there should first be fully used. If demand increases, it can be intelligently channelled. This can be particularly well demonstrated in the case of energy utilization. If demand for energy increases, the conventional solution would be to extend power station capacity. However, it is often better to restrain mounting demand by way of energy-saving technologies. Investment should thus be directed away from mere provision of infrastructure towards eco-efficient products and services: insulation, better equipment and machines, logistics, multiple-use systems rather than additional power stations, roads, and buildings.

Customers will thereby get new possibilities of choice. They will still be able to call on the services of suppliers of utilities, but they can themselves become active producers of, for instance, heat and electricity. They may also be members of transport-pools or facilitate land-management by offering transportation or accommodation. But above all they are in demand as users. They can test every product, every form of utilization, to see whether the necessary service is provided at the least cost. If the economic context is acceptable, that pays off immediately. Support will come from advisory services. The zero-option (Do I really need this?) will become more frequent. Rarely used appliances or products will be increasingly shared among neighbours.

Four spheres will be examined more closely in what follows: reliable energy supplies with fewer power stations; safe water supplies with fewer dams and less consumption of ground-water; mobility with fewer roads; and homes and businesses with less use of land.[53] These areas are presented as prototypes for moving beyond the emphasis on more, faster, and further in today's industrial societies.

Reliable energy supplies with fewer power stations

Energy supply companies are changing into energy service companies (ESCO),[54] helping their customers to use energy efficiently. The range of ESCO activities takes in technical consultancy, financial services, customers' investment in future savings, and maintenance of buildings, equipment, and machine parks. Energy-turnover then becomes just one aspect of company activities among others. However, politicians must establish a context where saving energy pays off for an ESCO. So long as success depends on the amounts of energy used, a company harms itself by helping customers make savings.

That is why the legislative framework for the energy industry must be revised and replaced by modern legislation furthering efficient use of energy. Saving resources, protection of the climate, promotion of solar energy, and decentralization should be emphasized alongside assurance of supplies and competitiveness. At present the chief objective must be to mobilize for energy-saving the electricity supply companies' enormous capital reserves, which in Germany are today invested in waste disposal, telecommunications, and water supplies, helping establish new monopoly structures.[55] If a determined start is made on achieving savings in energy use, the need to renew power stations between 2000 and 2015 could be considerably less than predicted. More large-scale open-cast mining in the Rhineland, Lausitz, and the Central German area would be unnecessary. The need to subsidize German hard coal would decline too, and gradual elimination of nuclear energy become possible. All this would contribute towards the Federal Government's target of reducing climate-influencing CO_2 emissions by 25 to 30% by the year 2005.

The lower total energy consumption is, the easier it becomes to increase solar energy's share in production of what is needed.[56] If photovoltaic cells on roofs are used on a mass scale, the electricity industry will be transformed. The clear-cut distinction between suppliers and customers of energy will be replaced by a close-knit network of producers and consumers. Households will become "prosumers" of electricity, sometimes supplying the network, sometimes drawing on it. Reimbursement meeting the costs of the solar energy supplied is a milestone on the way towards the establishment of an integrated power network.

Only if utilization of solar technology is successfully demonstrated at home does the Federal Republic have a chance on the solar markets of the future. That is why politicians must now lay down precise targets. One conceivable proposal would involve an increase in generation of renewable energy of at least 5% annually for the foreseeable future.

Scenario 13: Integrated Resource Planning – Construction of "Negawatt Power Stations"

The least-cost planning (LCP) method was developed in the USA and has established itself in many of the individual states. This has two components. New power stations are only permitted if there is no cheaper way of meeting an anticipated shortfall between supply and demand for electricity. Low-cost investment by customers (called "NEGA watts" by Amory Lovins) is very frequently the cheapest way of closing the gap – in Europe as well as in the USA with its notoriously wasteful use of electricity. If there are still any unmet needs, these can often be supplied more cheaply by way of district heating or wind power, rather than through big new power stations. This principle of "discovery planning", involving the cheapest possible overall combination of energy-saving (through capital and know-how) and the necessary provision of energy, is applicable to the gas industry as well. Increasing thought is also being devoted to developing low-cost transportation planning (LCTP). Utilization is conceivable too in such spheres of application as water supplies and management of raw material flows.

LCP also entails a reversal of economic incentives for suppliers of energy. In today's set-up the more energy the supplier sells, the more profit he or she makes. The new suggestion is that the state should establish guidelines whereby profits rise as the amount of energy sold declines – provided that consumers' overall bill for the energy-services required (such as warm and well-lit homes and offices, and the production of goods) goes down. If the supplier of energy draws customers' attention to possibilities of saving, or personally invests in efficient appliances for lighting, ventilation, and air-conditioning, his or her tariffs will rise to a moderate extent, but customers' monthly bills will fall. "Economics of avoidance" make possible such well-founded price-rises for customers, society as a whole, and also the suppliers of energy.

LCP has mainly been successfully practised in the USA and Canada for many years now. For instance in 1993 Pacific Gas & Electric, the largest private ESCO in the USA, closed down its department for planning power stations. PG&E expects to cut anticipated growth in consumption by three-quarters through LCP programmes. The other 25% is to be bought from independent suppliers of electricity (usually wind farms and regenerative sources). Since the start of the nineties there have been pilot projects in low-cost planning in the Federal Republic and other European countries. In 1994 over 50 German ESCOs were implementing 160 LCP-oriented programmes.

A study of the area supplied by the Hanover[57] electricity works came to the conclusion that around 30% of consumption (with average costs of 6 to 8 pfennigs per kilowatt-hour saved) could be avoided or replaced by other sources of energy such as natural gas.

A projection for the Federal Republic shows that up to 18,000 MW of installed power station output could be saved through ESCO low-cost planning programmes if economy facilities were erected on this scale.

Safe water supplies with fewer dams and less extraction of ground-water

The transition to focus on services rather than sales can also be applied to the infrastructure of water supplies. Recommended usage, advisory services, and application of water-saving technologies (for shower-heads, armatures, washing machines, dishwashers) and procedures (recycling of water and more economical cooling of power stations) can bring about considerable reductions in water use. The more water is used in closed cycles, the less waste water there is and the less treatment is required, which in turn eliminates the need for capital to be tied down in plant. The basic need is to close cycles of responsibility and establish feedback mechanisms. Using savings in investment to subsidize water prices enables waterworks to make appropriate profits even if sales decline. People who sell and install integrated systems will particularly benefit from this. It will no longer be necessary to build new dams in the mountains or to extract ground-water. River valleys and wetlands with their characteristic habitats can be preserved. Water extraction and rates of renewal have to be balanced at the regional level, and agreements must be reached about shared objectives.[58] If such regional orientation is achieved in water policy, then water quality can be assured through organic farming.

Mobility with fewer roads

How can the concept of service-orientation be applied in the transportation sector? As a first step the service required can be defined as "mobility", as a person's wish to get from A to B within an acceptable time.

If that wish is taken for granted – as is usually the case in planning transportation – all that remains is to decide which means of locomotion to employ. If the distance is covered by foot or cycle, no ecological damage is done. That is why planners should strive to favour such possibilities. Convincing examples are provided by towns like Delft, Groningen, and Erlangen.[59] If powered transportation is used, then should it be rail, car, or aeroplane? The fact that trains are usually ecologically preferable to cars, lorries, or aeroplanes is generally known by now – as are demands for moving transportation off roads and onto rails, or from short-distance flights to rapid rail links. Many would also agree that it is better to construct cars that only use 3 litres of petrol per 100 kilometres than vehicles needing 10 litres. Mandatory targets and timetables should be striven for here – such as increasing the share of public transport in community x by y%; and reduction of average petrol consumption to 5 litres per 100 km in the Federal Republic – or, better still, the European Union – by the year 2010.

However, a focus on services in the transportation sector signifies more than that. It involves organization of transportation as well as choice of means. Typical examples of this are car-sharing, car rentals, agencies for arranging lifts, mobility centres, on-demand systems, commercial car pooling, electronic data processing (EDP)-backed traffic guidance systems, environmental and job tickets for local transport, etc.[60] The basic ideas behind such concepts are simple. Co-operation and co-ordination avoid expenditure. Use and ownership of means of transport are not necessarily linked; and optimization of costs and protection of the environment can go hand in hand.

An attractive sphere of action opens up here for mobility service enterprises (MSE). These MSEs will be partly public (local transportation) and partly private ventures (as with car rentals already), but some will be organized at the neighbourhood or district level. Structures with mixed commercial and self-organized elements are equally conceivable – as in car-sharing and urban car groups. The development of MSEs should be assisted by the state with tax concessions.

If the service concept is viewed more profoundly, then it can be asked: Why go from A to B? Is this journey really necessary? What specific service is required? Is it recreation, business, getting to work, going shopping, or taking youngsters to kindergarten?

For the past 40 years politicians have devoted all their efforts to opening up the country as quickly as possible, particularly through excessive road-building. The population and the economy focused on ever-larger catchment areas, and this development was encouraged by extremely low energy prices and tax concessions for road (and air) transportation. Key elements in a contemporary transportation policy for the Federal Republic today would therefore include extensive abandonment of building of more long-distance roads, gradual increases in transportation prices (inclusive of air traffic), reorganization of parking in city centres, and introduction of a kilometre rebate (irrespective of means of trans-

Scenario 14: Car-Sharing

Car-sharing initiatives offer possibilities for people for whom owning a car is too much and being without one creates problems. Members join by paying an initial contribution, thereby acquiring a right to use of a car. This is covered by a monthly charge and payment for each kilometre travelled. Members thus can choose from a range of modern, moderately powered cars and no longer have to deal with maintenance or repairs. They can also make use of cars in other cities. The environment is helped by a reduction in the number of cars, availability of land for other purposes, and a cut-back in the distance travelled. In Berlin, for instance, the number of cars belonging to members of such an initiative has declined by around three-quarters. The kilometres covered also fell by about a half.[61] That is probably the outcome of greater flexibility with people using other forms of transportation, and also of the changed cost-structure which makes the car-related expenses more apparent.

port) that must be considerably less than today's rebate for use of private cars. Acceptance of these measures would probably grow as public transport systems become more attractive. Orientation towards what is close at hand would again become more significant, and daily activities would be closer to home. Of course transitional measures would be necessary for helping particularly hard-hit groups such as commuters in rural areas. However, the traffic avalanche will be unstoppable without gentle constraints, making a settled form of existence more attractive.

Construction using less land

Land use is a great problem for environmental policy regarding infrastructure. Can the transition from sales to services also be achieved here? In principle yes, but the conditions are very difficult. Policy-makers are used to satisfying the demand for residential and business areas by making generously available separate zones for house-building and industry. However, orientation towards services entails a functional intermingling of such spheres as housing, work, shopping, leisure, and recuperation; rehabilitation of land and buildings; more close-knit construction; changed uses for real estate; neighbourly sharing of land (for courtyards or gardens); and commercial centres with joint utilization of office space, services, or technical facilities ("tele-workhouses").[62] Such a concept for land-saving services demands precise knowledge of existing real estate and businesses, and their developmental potential – in other words, a contemporary land register so as to be able to achieve optimal classification and, if appropriate, satisfaction of investors' wishes.

Of course that is more difficult than merely identifying and opening up new areas, but there is basically no alternative in view of the dramatic lack of land in densely populated areas. However, this approach will only be implementable if policy-makers make consistent use of the possibilities provided by urban and regional planning and do not rush to please every potential investor. Situating commercial zones in ecologically sensitive areas – such as water-meadows – must be made a taboo. It will also be necessary to combat land and property speculation in city centres more consistently. At the national level the target should be to gradually eliminate new use of land for housing, industry, or transportation within the next 20 years. Such new use would only be allowed if equivalent amounts of land were released.[63] To achieve that objective it is urgently necessary for cities and local authorities to establish realistic policies for preserving undeveloped areas. If the trend in recent decades continues – when an area equal to 130 football pitches was built on daily – Germany will be paved over by the year 2100.

Scenario 15: Housing in 2010

The target in the house-building and renovation programme is construction of accommodation that does justice to differing social demands, saving land and fulfilling ecological and welfare requirements. This objective is being pursued in both public and private building, inclusive of renovation of old properties. In the "Housing 2000" competition low-energy houses achieved improvements of between 65 and 83% on the targets laid down in 1982. The additional costs are relatively low (a maximum of around 50 DM per square metre) and are compensated by reductions throughout the entire period of use. A federally backed bank should launch a special credit programme to finance this venture. Such low-energy houses are already technologically possible and could become the norm within 3 to 5 years. Similar norms can be gradually implemented in old buildings too. Attention will also be paid to more flexible divisions of space. Technically possible as well are so-called "passive houses" with energy-savings of over 90%, achieved through improved insulation, glazing, and ventilation. Some aspects of renovation will be undertaken in the form of communally organized individual work.

5.6 Regeneration of Land and Agriculture

From parasitical cities...

In the European Union rural areas account for around 80% of the land where some 25% of the population live. Most people are in towns, and urbanization is particularly great in Belgium, the Netherlands, Germany, and Great Britain, where over 80% live in towns and densely populated areas. Those people make use of surrounding rural districts. Water, air, food, raw materials, waste disposal; space for recreation, settlement, and transportation; and biological diversity – all this is produced or maintained for society by the countryside with its agriculture and forestry, but little is actually paid for. Food may have to be bought but expenditure on this item has constantly sunk in relation to overall consumption in recent decades, as has the share that actually reaches farmers. For water too cities do not pay more than urban waterworks need to cover their costs. For air city-dwellers pay nothing, even though if it is regenerated at all then this is in rural areas. In addition, for recuperation in the countryside people only pay (if at all) what the commercialized tourist business can impose.

...to regionalism

Preservation of habitats and capacity for regeneration are the preconditions for sustainability. Both city and countryside belong together ecologically, economically, and socially. The ecological and economic problems facing, on the one hand, rural areas, agriculture, and forestry, and, on the other, towns and conurbations can only be jointly solved.

Understanding of mutual dependences is growing. One indication is provided by models of co-operation between waterworks and regional farmers. It is considerably cheaper for cities and local authorities to support farmers in changing over to environmentally acceptable production methods (with renunciation of synthetic chemical fertilizers and biocides) and thus reduce water pollution – rather than having to remove nitrate and pesticides when purifying drinking water.[64]

Photosynthesis offers another graphic example of mutual dependences (inclusive of human) within eco-system cycles. With the help of sunlight,

Scenario 16: Organic Farming around Munich

In 1991 Munich's public utilities decided to support conversion to organic farming in areas supplying drinking water. In fact untreated water was of comparatively high quality, but amounts of nitrate or pesticides were on the increase. Pre-emptive action was thus necessary to assure long-term quality. Contracts were concluded between the Munich authorities and every individual farm. Conditions regulating farming (including complete renunciation of synthetic mineral fertilizers and pesticides) had to be laid down so as to protect drinking water. For such water-saving ecological use of the land, farmers are paid 550 DM per hectare annually for a total of six years. During the past five years almost 100 farms covering some 1,600 hectares have switched to organic methods. That is already more than two-thirds of the land used for agriculture in the drinking water extraction zone.

Marketing organic products usually constitutes a bottleneck in expansion of ecological farming. Organic farmers from the Mangfalltal area have combined with the "Bioland" and "Naturland" ecological growers to establish a marketing organization, financially supported by Munich's public utilities. This set-up mediates contacts with dairies and cheese-makers. New sales outlets have been created by advertising, so that milk is now delivered to city kindergartens, canteens, and pubs. An essential aspect of this marketing involves making consumers aware of the direct link between organically produced food and the quality of drinking water.

Assisting this changeover is also economically worthwhile since waterworks save expenditure on purifying drinking water and investing in new technology, and farmers get fair prices for their products. The entire assistance programme puts just one pfennig onto the price of a cubic metre of water. If these costs were passed on to the consumer, the average four-person household (using about 140 litres per head daily) would have to pay an additional 2 DM annually.

plants derive biomass from the greenhouse gas carbon dioxide, taken from the atmosphere, and during this process emit oxygen. This oxygen is in turn needed by animals and human beings for breathing when they give off carbon dioxide, which plants once again absorb. Plants – or wood-production in agriculture and forestry – are (almost) the only possibility of converting solar energy, carbon dioxide, and other toxics or nutrients into usable organic substances and energy, into food and raw materials. All other sectors of production (including animal-rearing), and human beings too, use up energy and are ultimately dependent on the outcome of photosynthesis. Agriculture's and forestry's capacity for absorption and regeneration – their ability to preserve or renew soil, water, and air as the foundations of life – is thus becoming increasingly important. Recognition of that fact could lead to development of a new

Scenario 17: Wood's Five Lives

> "Wood is only a single-syllable word but it contains an entire world of stories and wonders." *Theodor Heuss*

In a sustainable economy the value of wood as a raw material will be rediscovered. If someone no longer needs a wooden object, it will be re-used instead of being thrown away. Wooden products are usually replaced when moving house or because they are no longer fashionable. Each year 11.5 million rejected items of shelving, tables, cupboards, and upholstered furniture are thrown out and end up by being burned, even though much could still be used or "done up" at little expense. The building components store in Berlin-Spandau shows that re-use is still possible on a large scale. For four years now, before houses are demolished, doors, windows, and wooden beams have been saved, cleaned up, and sold again.

The manufacture of high-class products, particularly those made from solid timber, will in future increasingly involve re-use or continued use. Maintenance, repairs, and care are then easy. Yesterday's roof beams can be tomorrow's garden posts. Rejection of chemical preservatives and increased use of protective measures (such as projecting roofs which preserve façades) make it easier to re-introduce old wood into the production cycle. If further use is impossible, the wood fibre will be employed for plywood or paper. When that is no longer viable, cellulose and lignin will be used as raw materials in the chemical industry.

Only when all the possibilities within this abundance of uses have been exhausted will wood's energy-content be released through burning. Wood will not be chemically treated in future and burning will take place in technologically advanced incinerators, so environmental problems will be greatly reduced. The natural cycle will be closed when the ashes are returned to nature – ideally to forests.[65]

balance between city and countryside, and a previously parasitic relationship could become a symbiotic one.

Cities and communities are rediscovering the countryside. In densely populated areas this is the outcome of interest in protection of water, soil, nature, and landscape, in possibilities of recreation close at hand, and in healthy food. Urban markets are in turn crucial for nearby farmers, especially for organic farmers who thus profit from many town-dwellers' increased environmental and health awareness.

Cities play a much greater part in pollution of the environment, but it is the countryside's powers of regeneration that make urban life possible, so the time has come to upgrade, and provide better financial assistance for, rural areas as compared with densely populated centres of industrial production. One possible starting-point would be a graduated tax on use of land for housing or transportation, integrated in an overall concept for ecological tax reform. This levy should be assessed in terms of whether and to what extent land use meets as many needs as possible and how sustainable it is.[66] Sealing off and building over land would attract a very high rate of tax, while intensive agriculture would only be moderately taxed. Conversely, environmentally acceptable use of land (such as organic farming or natural forestry), which creates food, oxygen, diversity of species, and recreational areas, would not be taxed at all but rather subsidized from revenue. Such a tax would not be a new source of financing state activities, but rather a long overdue financial redistribution from urban areas to the countryside.

From monoculture...

For decades now, utilization of land and forests has been developing away from original diversity towards increasing specialization. With monoculture comes monotony, and thus loss of functions. Agricultural steppes and forestry plantations, monotonous areas of green alongside roads, canalized conduits for effluent or shipping routes, and expanding areas of dense settlement can no longer serve protection of species and nature, and have lost much of their value for recuperation and recreation. Instead these areas have increasingly exerted a negative impact on nature.

This change is the inevitable consequence of misguided ideas about subsidizing agriculture. In 1991 Mac Sharry, the former EC Commissioner for Agriculture, stated:

> Income support almost exclusively in the form of price guarantees is largely proportional to volumes of production, and is thus concentrated on the largest farms with the highest degree of intensification. 50% of the area devoted to

> growing cereals, producing 60% of the total crop, thus belongs to just 6% of the producers; in the milk sector 15% of farms produce 50% of output; and in beef production 50% of herds are on 10% of farms. The outcome is that 80% of European Alignment and Guarantee Funds for Agriculture go to just 20% of producers, who operate over half the land used for agriculture. The existing system does not take sufficiently into account the financial situation of the great majority of small and medium-sized family concerns.[67]

Mounting surpluses and marketing subsidies in European agriculture, and conflict with trading partners during the Uruguay Round of the GATT negotiations in 1992, enforced reform of the common agricultural policy. This reform particularly aimed at reducing supplies of agricultural products – above all because these surpluses force down prices for producers and reduce agricultural incomes. The intention was that more farmers should profit from broader distribution of EU money, so that their incomes were stabilized and assured. Another objective was to recognize farmers' dual function in production of food and raw materials and in protection of the environment and cultivation of the landscape. This was to be achieved by way of large-scale extensification of agriculture – with appropriate financial compensation.[68]

Concrete measures of agricultural reform include considerable reduction of prices for oilseeds, protein plants, cereals, and beef, leaving areas fallow so as to relieve the market, and compensation for loss of income by direct transfer payments to farmers. With oilseeds and protein plants prices are based on the world market, so there are no longer any external tariffs or internal price supports but merely area-related compensatory payments. Support prices for cereals were gradually reduced up to 1995/6 by a total of 35%, and for beef by around 15%. As compensation for loss of income farmers receive direct payments (in accordance with the areas and numbers of animals involved) on condition that land is temporarily or permanently left fallow in crop-growing areas.[69] Cultivation of renewable raw materials is permitted on these fallow areas without loss of this payment.

These hopes of agricultural reform were not, however, fulfilled. The Commission's original objective was to preserve extensive agriculture in Europe, to slow down progressive structural change, and to extensify agriculture as a whole, but reforms were increasingly watered down under pressure from specific interest groups (big producers of cereals, agrobusiness, and companies involved in storage, importing, and exporting) which had profited from previous policy. There was a short-lived reduction of subsidies and stocks of agricultural products – partly as a result of greater use of European grain surpluses for animal feed, replacing imports and saving export subsidies – but the minuses of reform far outweighed the pluses. In the meantime the EU Commission itself is also calling for revision of this reform.[70]

However, with further reduction of protection, liberalization of the world market, and convergence of producer and world market prices, the future of agriculture will mainly lie in large farms with the most modern technology and management methods. Labour productivity – and indebtedness – will continue to rise with mounting capital input, and even more employees will lose their jobs. Negative structural change in linked processes will be accelerated too. With an increasing degree of monopolization in processing firms as well as in the agro-chemical and seed-production (genetic- and bio-technology) industries, farmers' dependence is intensified. Larger farms and the associated clearing aggravate the trend towards emptiness and monotonization of the landscape.

It remains to be seen what opportunities remain for mainly smaller farms in search of niches in unfavoured regions. Current agricultural policy threatens to bring about a "reservation agriculture" with ongoing intensive production retreating into so-called favoured areas. This will lead to increasing social, structural, and cultural processes of erosion in the countryside. Alongside mounting use of landscape for settlement, transportation, etc., this constitutes a major threat to agriculture and the rural landscape.

...back to rural diversity

Only in recent centuries was today's cultivated landscape with its diversity of species and plant-life created through human intervention – as a free by-product of what was for the most part environmentally acceptable use of land.[71] With the prices paid to producers today and enforced intensive production, with the drop in world market prices and imports of wood and food at dumping prices from non-renewable sources, most farmers and foresters are no longer able to make a living and take ecological demands into account. Society must move beyond reducing agriculture and forestry to mere productivity, since a cultivated landscape and our fundamental requirements of land, water, air, and biological diversity cannot be either imported or newly produced. The task facing agriculture and forestry now calls for preservation of the cultivated rural landscape as both a source of livelihood and a recreational area for town-dwellers. Almost all consumers are ready to pay to go to a concert or a film, but they view a Sunday walk through fields and woods as something that is free and to be taken for granted. Only if farmers and foresters receive appropriate prices for their products will they be able to work in a way that guarantees not just as many and as "cheap" consumables as possible

Scenario 18: From Plantation to Natural Wood

In a sustainable economy today's timber plantations will have been superseded. This change[72] will lead to a mixed forest with great genetic diversity. Such mixed woods with both conifers and deciduous trees will replace the monotony of fir plantations. Stands consisting of just one kind of tree will be limited to localities where only a few varieties occur naturally. Different ages of tree will be grouped together rather than completely separated. The young wood will grow under the protection of old stock. Instead of artificial reafforestation of areas stripped bare, natural rejuvenation will become the norm. Lying and standing dead wood will remain in the forest, becoming a "biotope". A balance between processes of building up and breaking down will close biochemical cycles. Woods that regulate and stabilize themselves thus come into being.

Future forestry will follow that guideline. Natural processes serve economic utilization as a model. No further use will be made of all-out deforestation, chemicals, and big machines that damage both soil and trees. The only trees harvested will be those that need to be removed for the benefit of the whole or have attained a predetermined size. Sustainable forestry will no longer be predominantly focused on timber production, but will instead ensure that the wood can fulfil its functions of protecting water supplies, preventing soil erosion, reducing noise and emissions, improving the climate, safeguarding species and ecological communities, and providing recreation for humans.

This form of management also has economic advantages – as has been demonstrated for decades by around 40 forest enterprises in Germany, following these principles. The natural forest has a higher percentage of mature trees, which clearly increases its profitability. Natural rejuvenation reduces the costs of caring for the wood, and expensive reafforestation of empty areas is not necessary. Such rejuvenation may not be completely cost-free, but expenses are considerably less than for replanting. Young saplings growing up overshadowed by older trees develop more delicate branches than in plantations, resulting in high-quality trees. The greater ecological stability of the natural forest also means that there is less risk of succumbing to disasters. The catastrophic storm damage of spring 1990 did not spare naturally managed woods, but large areas of devastation were the exception. Four out of five of the trees uprooted at that time were firs in monocultures.

The precondition for rejuvenated forests is a different attitude towards hunting. There is too much hoofed game at present, and fencing off young woods does not provide a lasting solution. Reduction of the number of animals is thus indispensable.

but also uncontaminated fresh food, clean drinking water, a diverse landscape, and assured existences for themselves.

Landscape is not possible without interventions in nature, exerting an impact on the environment and affecting the climate. Even on organically run farms nitrate gets into ground-water and every cow gives off methane whether it is in a conventional or an ecological stall. However, pollution of the environment can be drastically reduced through ecological farming methods. At the same time organic farming and natural forestry integrate various social demands. Protection of nature makes landscape and biological diversity possible as well as providing sufficient supplies of raw materials and healthy food alongside securing jobs.

In 1980 the concept of sustainability was introduced in connection with development of a global strategy for the protection of nature. This entailed a deliberate departure from the traditional concept which attempted to keep human beings out of the areas at issue. The emphasis was instead on integration of the preservation, utilization, and development of nature. The natural foundations of life and genetic diversity could not be maintained in separate, isolated eco-systems – and even less in gene-banks. Sensitive eco-systems cannot be protected so long as human influences exert a serious impact by way of airborne discharges, causing eutrophication and acidification through nitrogenous emissions. Conservationists came to accept that the previous practice of trying to seal off nature did not work in an increasingly exploited and overpopulated landscape. The long-upheld reciprocal antagonism between agriculture and protection of nature began to break down. It was replaced by a demand for extensive and environmentally acceptable farming which at the same time serves nature conservation.

From intensive linear production...

Linear, analytical thinking, concentrating on productivity, deduces a need for nutrients from the composition of plants and soils. This is followed by mandatory use of fertilizers. Linear thinking thus led to destruction of natural cycles. Animal-keeping and crop-growing are largely separated. Today it is often cheaper to buy animal feed than to produce it oneself. Immense surpluses of manure in the main centres of animal-rearing are accompanied by increasing use of artificial fertilizers in purely crop-growing regions. Both cause considerable pollution. Every 200 grams of pork cutlet on a consumer's plate involves 3.7 litres of dung elsewhere.[73]

Another example of linear thinking – or rather leaving out of account possible connections – is provided by widespread hopes of modern biological and genetic technology. Despite long-existent surpluses, plants and animals are supposed to yield ever more. Cultivated plants are intended to be resistant to specific diseases and pests – the very same pests and diseases that often only became a problem with the introduction of extensive monocultures. Developing resistant strains involves questionable attempts at compensating for mistakes made in today's intensive production. These endeavours are usually quickly overtaken by the defensive adaptability of whatever is being combated. Crops are progressively modified to meet the requirements of an increasingly concentrated and multi-national food industry.[74] Plant resources are merely viewed as storehouses of spare parts for genetic engineering. High-yield varieties from the chemistry industry's gene laboratories are intended to help establish farmers' dependence on agro-chemicals and develop new monopolistic structures.[75] Only rich countries can afford bio- and gene-technology, resistant high-yield seeds, and the necessary agro-chemicals, thus giving rise to global inequalities. Even in Germany only rich farmers can pay for such technologies – the seed or the animals that further negative structural change. In addition, the release of genetically manipulated life is highly risky. No-one knows today what changes will follow human intervention in the worldwide genetic pool, or what the nutritional impact of genetically manipulated foodstuffs will be. Sustainable agriculture and nutrition are not reconcilable with gene-technology where prudence is necessary at the individual, national, and global levels.

...to organic cycles

Ecological thinking entails cycles and involves a multiplicity of interactions and dependences. For instance, soil and plant are comprehended as a system. Plants can meet their need for nutrients from living organisms in the soil because they in turn make energy and nutrients available in the form of root mass.

Organic farming is based on largely closed operational cycles.[76] A farm integrates small-scale animal maintenance and crop-growing. That decouples agriculture from today's global flows of materials and nutrients, and at the same time prevents unhealthy concentrations in mass animal-rearing. Renunciation of synthetic chemical fertilizers and pesticides reduces consumption of resources and leads to farming allied with nature. At long last there is a renaissance of nitrogen bonding (through micro-organisms and pulses) and "turning waste into food". Biological activity and soils' stability and capacity to take in water are much improved, thereby reducing surface flow, susceptibility to erosion, and floods. Nature's powers of self-healing are revived. Unlike conventional farming where pests and diseases are usually directly combated with synthetic chemical pesticides, the capacity for self-regulation through assisting natural pest-control plays a vital part in organic farming. Protectors of nature and organic farmers are thus in general agreement about species diversity and conservation of flora and fauna.

From supplier to the processing industry...[77]

At present agriculture serves less and less as a source of directly used foodstuffs and has become increasingly downgraded to supplier of raw materials for the food industry. The degree of processing of foodstuffs has risen considerably. Farmers are paid less and less for their products,[78] while the processing industry and the wholesale trade earn more and more for what ends up in shops. The food industry, agro-chemical concerns, foreign trade in agriculture, and firms providing storage and transportation are the real winners in Europe's subsidies policy, so their resistance is mounting – in lobbies rather than publicly – to restructuring of agricultural policy and making agriculture more organic.

For politicians foodstuffs are a favoured means of restraining inflation – at the expense of farmers. The prices of many agricultural products are today no higher than in the fifties. In Germany at that time consumers spent a third of total expenditure on food; by 1970 the figure was down to 23%; and in 1991 was only 16%. In 1950 over half the earnings from foodstuffs went to farmers; in 1991 only somewhat under a fifth.[79]

An increasing percentage of crop harvests are now used in Europe to feed animals rather than human beings. These animals are fattened so as to satisfy mounting demands for meat-eating. In Germany, for instance, about half of all plant yields are used for such "refinement".[80] On average, Germans consume around twice as much (predominantly) animal protein and fat as they really need. The illnesses caused by wrong nutrition cost society over a hundred billion DM year after year.[81]

The subsidies policy to date is misguided and pursued at the expense of taxpayers. Consumers must realize that they have long met the costs of administering surpluses and dealing with the environmental damage done by intensive farming. Cheap food is only apparently a bargain because the social costs – and thus the general demands made on individuals in taxes, levies, etc. – constantly rise. Even an attempt to preserve cultivated landscape in future by paying for its care would cost society considerably more than supporting practitioners of extensive organic farming.

...to source of healthy food

What is involved in high-quality food? To date for both producers and traders the concept of quality has mainly entailed suitability: such external criteria as ease of processing plus transportability and storability. Consumers were more concerned with pleasurable aspects (appearance, aroma, taste) and the health value (positive and negative substances). A holistic evaluation of food quality must take into account the impact on society and environment of forms of production and consumption (transportation, processing, etc.). Here clearly defined and regulated organic farming and regional marketing have many advantages (as attested by numerous surveys) over conventional agriculture (also integrated farming) and large-scale centralized marketing structures.

Development of public awareness requires provision of information about the connections between product quality and the means of production – above all, clear labelling showing whether food was produced conventionally or organically, its origins (regional), composition (genetic manipulation, additives, preservatives, etc.), and specific forms of treatment (such as radiation). Only then do consumers have a chance of once again eating healthy and, above all, tasty food – beyond fast food, novel food, or food design.

From the global supermarket...

When shopping, most people still look at the wrong label – the price label rather than the place of origin (if that is indicated at all). They are angry about the increase in the number of lorries on the road and forget that Italian cheeses, kiwis from New Zealand, or Californian wine have to be brought to the supermarket on the corner (or out in the green belt). With the international division of labour customary today, food in many regions comes from all over Europe by way of wholesalers. Yet most of these goods could also be produced locally if suitable sales structures were established for these quality goods. The internationally standardized products on offer all the year round are available because of toleration of polluting transportation, health-endangering methods of preservation, and energy-intensive cultivation. A kilogram of tomatoes grown out in the open causes about 0.1 kg of CO_2 while energy-intensive production in heated greenhouses results in over 3 kg of CO_2 per kg of tomatoes.[82] Greenhouse cultivation thus leads to global warming everywhere.

If flows of imports and exports in Western industrialized states are compared, it becomes strikingly apparent that most agricultural goods are traded between countries with comparable ecologies.[83] The structure of agricultural imports and exports is also very similar. Increasingly less of today's agricultural trade – except for tropical products and Mediterranean fruits – involves local ecological advantages, but rather exploitation of dubious manipulation of costs by way of capital markets, labour conditions, and questionable subsidies. As long as international trade is subsidized by a publicly financed infrastructure and cheap fossil fuels, the enormous flows of goods and masses will continue to increase and deplete the environment.

...to the regional farmers' market

Organic farming can assure regional and national self-sufficiency in basic foodstuffs – but of course only if feeding habits at the same time become more balanced and thus healthier. Meat consumption would be reduced and replaced by more fresh fruit and vegetables or wholemeal products of regional organic farming.

Organic farming reduces animal husbandry to an environmentally acceptable level. That does not mean all consumers must become vegetarians. In fact they have an opportunity to learn to appreciate meat again, enjoying an organic Sunday roast instead of being fobbed off with the usual PSE, BSE, or hormone-treated flesh. In our eating we should pay attention to quality rather than quantity.

The creation or re-establishment of small-scale regional structures instead offers opportunities for new alliances and forms of co-operation – such as food co-ops, which are already successful in many places. Buying from farmers or at a weekly market, and revival of links between producers and consumers, awakens trust, creates mutual understanding, and answers many of contemporary consumers' questions and needs. The development of direct marketing and the preservation of local farms produces such benefits as short journeys for fresh goods, less superfluous packaging, and reduced traffic noise and emissions. Additional road-building becomes unnecessary. At the same time jobs will be created in the region, or maintained over the long term.

In a Germany and Europe "plagued" by surplus and superfluity, the question arises whether the strategy of regionalization and ecologization of agriculture and food production might not contradict the obligation to feed a growing world population. In answer it can firstly be said that the over-production resulting during the past 20 years from Western intensive agriculture has probably contributed more to hunger in the world than to its alleviation. Despite all the surpluses the number of hungry people has increased, not declined. At present around 800 million people across the world are threatened with under-nourishment and hunger. Leaving aside food aid in response to disasters, subsidized agricultural exports from Europe have superseded producers in countries of the South, thereby contributing to a decrease in self-reliance in many places.[84]

The "Green Revolution" and other measures within a false concept of

Scenario 19: A Regional Economy

This demonstrates possibilities for tourists, hoteliers, and local farmers joining forces to put to use and preserve the Rhön area. Hoteliers buy produce from regional farmers and offer typical local dishes. Menus include both recipes and accounts of their origins. Guests thus become aware that the ingredients come from nearby farms rather than a wholesale outlet for mass production. Even today almost half the produce used for gastronomy comes from the region, assuring a livelihood for many farmers.

The Rhön is an open landscape where the spread of scrub-like bushes and trees can best be prevented by sheep-herding. Re-establishment of the well-adapted Rhön sheep, previously threatened with extinction, and promotion of extensive pastoral farming can preserve this old landscape. Rhön sheep can also be marketed as a local gastronomic speciality. In addition holiday accommodation is furnished with characteristic local products, made from native woods by regional craftspeople. In the Rhön area citizens of an industrial society can become reacquainted with the charms of a long-established landscape, and see how an ecologically meaningful economic cycle works and what qualitative advantages it offers.

development aid have also created economic advantages for industrial countries rather than conquering hunger in the South. Most attempts at transferring Western-style intensive agriculture (high-yield plants, agrochemicals, etc.) to the countries of the South have failed. To assure the feeding of a rising population over the long term, the dramatic loss of fertile land must first be stopped. Wrong utilization is one of the main causes of increasing degradation and desertification of soils. However, ecological and locally appropriate use of land (i.e. agro-forestry) preserves, and even improves, natural soil fertility.

Wherever relatively low-intensity cultivation prevails – because of less favourable natural or socio-economic influences – organic farming can hold its own or even produce greater (and, above all, over the longer term more secure) yields than conventional agriculture.[85]

Through development of domestic markets organic farming seeks to improve the regional and national basis for supplying the local population. At the same time it opens up access to higher-priced markets for agricultural exports (fair trade products). In addition use of expensive mineral fertilizers and pesticides becomes unnecessary, and dependence on the predominantly Western agro-industry is reduced.

The ecologization of agriculture is accompanied by changes in what is eaten. Organic farming has thus always talked about well-informed feeding, and converted that into the basic principles of high-quality diet and the sociology of nutrition. The yields (already in short supply) of vanishing agricultural areas should not increasingly end up in animals' stomachs. As in all other spheres of life and business, the North must still work hard on its possible role as a model and first drastically reduce its hunger for meat. Initial successes are becoming apparent, backed by shock news stories about BSE or hormones and other drugs in meat.

5.7 Towards a Liveable City

The city as habitat and way of organizing social life and human activities is of great importance within sustainable development. Like the region, it offers a suitable framework for solving – in an "integrated, holistic, and sustainable way"[86] – the problems which result from our society's social, economic, and political imbalances and the associated ecological consequences. Sustainable development of society will not be possible without environmentally acceptable up-grading of local communities. Our patterns of production and consumption, our life-styles in general, are urban in character and inconceivable without the urban centre as focus of business and trade, as marketplace and cultural hub, as source of training and qualification. "Without the active integration of cities we will not be in a position to achieve the national and international objectives we have set for sustainable development."[87]

Nevertheless, signs of sustainable communal development seem almost non-existent at present. Waste management breakdown, air pollution, cars and noise; a creeping decline in quality of life in city centres and residential areas; increases in anonymity, poverty, homelessness, and criminality, in land speculation and luxury renovation; misuse of habitat and ongoing sprawl out into surrounding areas – these are the problems which often leave local authorities helpless, so that citizens feel increasingly afflicted by physical and psychological burdens, and continue to move out of cities.

"City air liberates" was the mediaeval response to serfdom and the feudal system. Today city air makes people ill. Attempts at urban ecological reconstruction, undertaken since the end of the seventies, have changed little. Today local politicians are often guided by the idea that protection of the environment and welfare programmes cost money, and so long as the economic basis for such programmes is lacking, local authorities cannot provide funds.

The economic renovation of cities has determined local authorities' political actions since the start of the nineties, if not earlier. Partly as a result of establishment of the European market, these authorities see themselves forced to demonstrate competitiveness on the European stage, to develop an autonomous image, and to deploy money cautiously. Since then their solution has been the "lean administration" as a means towards restructuring local government, breaking up hierarchies, and discovering new opportunities for reducing costs. Alongside painful cuts in welfare assistance, facilities, and services, ordinary people have come to play a greater part in co-operative activities. Citizens' hearings and forums have for some time been an everyday aspect of local politics. New, however, is discussion of guidelines, plans for city development, and concrete projects with study groups and "round tables" where the general public is expressly involved together with experts. This experience of having a say and exerting influence in turn encourages more people to take part in local affairs. This is by no means limited to traffic-calming or programmes for reduction of CO_2. Local Agenda 21, under discussion since the 1992 Rio conference, views communities as a whole, comprehending urban development as an integrated and balanced interaction of economics, ecology, and social concerns.

The city as a place worth living in does not need to remain a dream. Here we attempt to throw light on factors to be taken into account at the communal level.

What a city needs and consumes

The city has been a successful form of organization for several thousand years since it manages to integrate within a restricted area various realms of work and everyday life. As a market for the production, sale, and exchange of goods, and as a centre for commerce and trade, it makes economic development possible and provides a highly diverse range of employment. What it has to offer in the way of education and culture contributes towards political autonomy vis-à-vis region and countryside. In modern times scientific discoveries and technical inventions made cities known far beyond their immediate localities and increased their attractiveness. They were an expression and embodiment of urban consciousness and self-awareness, despite grave social differences and mounting pollution. Only recently has the urban experience become increasingly uniform with cities losing what was characteristic of them, partly because of their inhabitants' growing mobility.

For a long time, securing the foundations of urban existence – supplies of foodstuffs, water, and energy – mainly depended on local and regional products and raw materials, a situation that gave rise to relatively straightforward relations between the city and the surrounding countryside. If that relationship was disrupted, even destroyed, by over-use of agricultural resources or excessive pollution (e.g. dumping of waste), it was immediately apparent to anyone. At a very early stage cities thus developed suitable policies for safeguarding resources and dealing with any ecological threats. Their endeavours were inevitably accompanied by mistakes, serious mismanagement, and even disasters, but those could be dealt with relatively quickly (compared with today), even though there were sometimes victims.

Nowadays the consequences of urban existence are largely externalized. Direct connections with the natural foundations of local and regional life have been lost, and the dimensions involved in consumption of the environment and pollution of urban living are largely ignored by many people. Raw materials and goods come from all over the world, and negative ecological consequences, such as effluents and waste, are transported long distances, sometimes to other countries or even continents. What used to be mainly regional relations and dependences have expanded globally, and the previous city–countryside link has become a city–world market relationship. The outcome is that cities, like supermarkets, make use of "their" supplier regions scattered across the world.[88] A city with a million inhabitants on average consumes 625,000 tonnes of water, 2,000 tonnes of foodstuffs, and 9,500 tonnes of fuel daily. It produces 500,000 tonnes of effluents, 2,000 tonnes of solid waste, and 950 tonnes of air pollutants.[89]

The most economically successful cities seem to be those that can best externalize their impact on the environment and exploit distant regions. On the other hand they thereby become increasingly dependent on global economic interests. In the foreground are attractive forms of industry and trade plus a commercial culture, which improve the urban image and communal finances with earnings from festivals, sports meetings, diverse big events, and trade fairs. Ecological and welfare objectives are viewed as something tactical, but always an obstacle when the emphasis is on economic advantages. Competition for business and markets, investment and qualified staff, increasingly determines the economic and political objectives of cities and regions. Creation of the European market involves them in competition for status and spheres of influence.

However, spatial expansion and increased use of resources do not only involve meeting city needs and dealing with waste. The same process is to be found inside cities. Believing in the powers of technology and the plannability of motorized transportation of individuals, city-developers made a strict division between urban functions part of their programme.[90] This stressed the idea of healthy living in nature, which gave rise to today's space-, time-, and equanimity-consuming commuting to work as well as shopping trips to town or green-belt superstores and car-based leisure activities. The division of functions has by now gone so far that individual aspects (such as housing, work, supply network, and leisure facilities) are no longer integrated in a single policy but rather pushed around from department to department with the inevitable negative outcome. Maintenance of this zoning system and the associated extensive infrastructure is becoming increasingly expensive for cities. Urban consumption of energy and raw materials is thus constantly mounting. Demands on finances and administration become ever-greater as attempts are made to keep some of the ecological and social consequences of suburbanization under control.

Vanishing urban individuality

The urban way of life is no longer limited to the city. It thus becomes increasingly difficult to explain what distinguishes town from country. Formerly obvious architectural or natural dividing lines are now often scarcely recognizable. Farming may have taken place close to towns[91] for much of recorded history but urban limits were nevertheless clearly demarcated – unlike today when residential and commercial areas proliferate out into the surrounding area. Statistics define over 80% of the European population as "living in areas of urban settlement",[92] indicating that the city is almost everywhere. The way of life once associated with cities is no longer restricted to urban centres. It is also to be found in small towns and rural areas whose cultural, educational, and leisure opportunities are largely the same as those in cities, albeit on a smaller scale. In addition, supplying oneself with everyday requirements has become so simple everywhere that a similarly large and comparable range of products is available in both cities and countryside.

Linked with this process is a gradual transformation of what was originally urban diversity in favour of widespread uniformity as expressed in shopping malls and virtual realities. Of course cities do also retain special architectural characteristics and differing urban cultures, but a trend towards similar architectural styles and building materials is becoming increasingly apparent. Competition between cities means that each wants to follow current trends. City centres – and particularly pedestrian zones – are so uniform that it is difficult to tell them apart. Everywhere there are similar shops selling the same goods, so that local and regional specialities are correspondingly downgraded. Shopping centres are only populated during opening hours. In the evening and at night they are dead, and often have to be guarded by private security firms.

Renewing urban existence

Short distances

The ecological city is a city of short distances where the life-spheres of accommodation, work, learning, shopping, and recreation are well mixed. Closer-knit utilization of the urban area helps overall to keep down use of transportation for water, energy, materials, products, and people. Low density and a good transport system are difficult to combine. Wherever possible the functions of housing, jobs, supplies, and leisure will gradually be linked. Journeys to work and the shops will be shortened, and leisure and recreational facilities will be within easy reach either on foot or by public transport. In this "city of short distances" cars will only be used if really necessary. Streets will mainly be regarded as living-areas rather than as through-routes. It should be safe for children to play in front of their homes and to cycle to school. Even in business areas the inhabitants and people who work there will have priority over members of the public just passing through. City districts will then regain quality of life. Streets formerly made for cars will be planted with greenery, inviting people to spend time there. This process of making urban areas more compact will slowly once again give rise to city boundaries that revive distinctions between town and country, emphasizing their differing qualities.

Vital urban districts are also the best precondition for social cohesion and good neighbourliness. Anyone who likes living where he or she is and feels secure there does not always have to be rushing off on short holidays or in search of new experiences. The outcome will be a decline in compulsive mobility, fleeing this or that, and also in business traffic. For city planning and urban politics that mainly entails the necessity of providing incentives towards a settled way of life: from assistance for local clubs and associations to creation of meeting-places for children, youngsters, and old people, from community-oriented building guidelines to combating land and property speculation.

Scenario 20: The "Woonerf" or "Living Street"

In the Netherlands, Belgium, Austria, Sweden, Denmark, and Britain, there are now thousands of examples of the "Woonerf" concept. An international sign indicates streets where cars are restricted to walking speed, cannot use roads as a through-way, may have to negotiate winding narrow lanes, and cannot park without a permit – and then only in specially designated spaces. The earliest examples of "Living Streets" were carefully designed to appear as much like pedestrian zones as possible so as to condition the car driver to move more slowly. The street was paved in cobblestones from building-wall to building-wall, and kerbs were removed to emphasize the pedestrian's right to use the entire width. Plants, trees, and benches were installed in order to restrict the lane width available to vehicles, especially at the entrance to the "Living Street" where the road was narrowed by establishing trees. Later designs are often less elaborate, relying more on clear signs and inexpensive alterations, a necking of the entrance, raised ramped pedestrian crossings to slow down traffic, large plants or trees to reduce width of traffic lanes, and partial replacement of asphalt with cobblestones. The concept has now been expanded to create networks of "Living Streets" encompassing whole neighbourhoods, some with as many as 20,000 inhabitants.[93]

Closing of cycles

A parasite is a dependent organism that lives off a host's nutrients. That is also an image of today's cities.[94] They live from surrounding areas, both near and far, because they are dependent on an ongoing flow of resources from farms, forests, water supplies, oil reserves, and mineral deposits, while on the other hand they discharge gaseous, liquid, and solid waste into their surroundings.

The ecological city is not a parasite exploiting the nearby area. It is in fact embedded in the environment from which it "derives" water, good air, and foodstuffs, and which its inhabitants use as a place of recreation. Production and consumption in the ecological city will produce less waste, so the provinces will not be so abused as a "dump for the metropolis". Agriculture, forestry, food production, and water companies offer opportunities for closed regional production cycles. Links between cities and surrounding areas provide suitable forums for making co-operation possible and surmounting local egoisms. Changed consumer behaviour and increased urban awareness of health, quality, and environment promote organic farming in the region. The renaissance of farmers' markets, to be seen in many big cities today, is an initial indication of a return to regional and seasonal shopping patterns. Individual supermarket chains are also starting to offer more regional products. Ecologically produced food – without pesticides, synthetic fertilizers, or factory-farmed livestock – may be more expensive than conventional products, but in terms of the overall social balance this results in less soil erosion, reduced pollution of ground-water, and preservation of long-established landscapes – in brief, lower social costs and greater social utility.

A new urban relationship with water could be developed too.[95] This will be based on regional, decentralized, interconnected cycles, and thereby

Scenario 21: Bielefeld "Waldquelle" Settlement[96]

The new Bielefeld "Waldquelle" ("Wood Spring") settlement is next to existing residential areas. Right from the start the intention was to take ecological experience and feedback into account so that this was a socially acceptable project. The settlement is in the south-west of the town. It is meant to define the urban boundary once and for all so as to prevent further expansion. A total of 130 dwellings is to be built here: owner-occupied housing, rented accommodation, and council flats for around 400 people. Eighteen of the subsidized flats are being built by their future inhabitants, who have established a "Waldquelle Ecological Housing Building Co-operative".

The settlement will get its drinking water from two on-site groundwater wells. Consumption will be reduced by utilization of armatures and other appliances, and by use of compost-toilets. Water will be purified in the settlement's own natural plant where inappropriate use of water immediately becomes apparent. There are also plans for separation of waste products and composting of green refuse. Energy is to be supplied by a settlement unit (initially powered by gas and electricity, and then by methane) providing both current and heat. Siting the houses to face south, south-west, and south-east makes possible passive utilization of solar energy. Building materials come from local sources, avoiding long journeys, and great emphasis is put on re-usability and problem-free disposal. Two years after completion, the settlement is due to become a car-free zone with precedence for pedestrians and cyclists. Good links with the local public transport network support carless mobility. Plans for a marketplace where local organic farmers offer their produce will cut back on transportation and guarantee supplies of basic foodstuffs. A commercial area, offices, and medical facilities will create between two and three hundred new jobs. These will not be restricted to inhabitants of the Waldquelle settlement but are also intended for people living nearby in places where there are no possibilities of employment. People will thus once again live and work in the same area.

help cities towards sustainability in water supplies and dealing with effluents. Individual regional potential and structuring reflect differences in the availability of water supplies.

Changes in water-management will involve both technology and transformed attitudes. On the technical level there will be a reduction in drawing on water from far away, and effluent purification will be based on semi-natural methods. An urban region will thus first utilize its endogenous potential, particularly renewable water reserves. All inner city sources of water will be rehabilitated and safeguarded, involving saving rain water in outlying areas, decentralized treatment of household effluents, and use of recycled or rain water instead of drinking water. Decentralized cycles in houses, neighbourhoods, or districts reduce throughput and improve the quality of waste water. The potential for savings is encouraged by consumers' active participation in decisions about water use and the necessary information campaigns. People thus come to learn about the state of local and regional water supplies, thereby treating this resource more carefully.

Management of the new approach to urban water supplies builds on existing social and ecological connections. The links between the people involved – and discussion of such matters as avoidance of polluting household chemicals – are a precondition for sustainable forms of decentralized water supplies. Such cycles will gradually complement centralized provision of water, safeguarding it against crisis.

Development of existing facilities

Modern planning, commercial, and housing policies put the emphasis on development and upgrading of what is already in existence so as to limit further use of land and urban sprawl into surrounding areas. Renovation, servicing, changes in the use to which existing buildings are put, recycling of land, and increased density will become key concepts in future urban development. Revitalization, as pursued in such former industrial areas as the Ems region with its "Green Industry" concept, makes an important contribution towards local renovation. Measuring the success of regional housing or industrial policies in terms of the areas utilized is mistaken. The fact is that empty office buildings and excessively extravagant commercial facilities are highly cost-intensive and tie down capital unnecessarily. In future it will be more important to make better use of existing capacity, reacting more flexibly to potential investors' wishes. The precondition is well-founded knowledge of the character, extent, quality, and availability of existing real estate – and thus modern management and information systems. The situation is basically similar for the housing market. There too the emphasis should not recklessly entail constant expansion of the area available. First existing stocks of houses should be assessed and further developed. Above all, critical attention must be devoted to the justifiability of still filling large urban areas with detached houses. That is certainly not reconcilable with the objective of saving land.

Green areas

Local density and development of the existing housing stock make preservation of as yet unbuilt-up inner city areas possible. A city is not a city without "channels for fresh air", places where contemplation is conceivable, open areas for children, and refuges for animals and plants. In many places the presence of nature has shrunk to roadside trees and flower-tubs. The open areas that do exist are often fairly monotonous, fragmented, and constantly threatened by commercial development. To bring nature back into the city landscape gardening will have to be deployed at all levels of the built environment – streets, buildings, and public places. What is pleasant for people is also ecologically useful. Natural areas provide homes for animals, reduce air pollution, improve the water situation, and can provide both recreational opportunities and sometimes even agricultural produce.[97] It is fatally misguided to view green areas and unused land mainly as reserve stocks for later building, and thoughtlessly make them available for road construction or similar purposes – as some local politicians do today. Inner city green oases do not merely serve objectively important functions (primarily for the urban climate); they are also of exceptional importance for city-dwellers' feelings about life.

Density

As a densely populated area the city offers particular advantages in the realm of energy supplies. Decentralized block heating works, simultaneously providing both electricity and warmth, are efficient, low-cost, and relatively acceptable in environmental terms. To make an "ecology of density" possible, it will be necessary to abandon an old way of thinking whereby industrial sites should be separated from residential areas. In terms of energy policy, the opposite is the case. Anyone who wants to

Scenario 22: Planning for Proximity

De-zoning is crucial for reducing commuting distances in cities. It means creating "multi-nucleated cities" with districts accommodating both homes and working places. This is easier in a post-industrial city in which fewer people depend on jobs in large, polluting factories. Planners are also moving towards urban layouts that provide for greater built-in proximity between homes, shops, schools, and places of entertainment and leisure where civilization based on face-to-face human encounters becomes possible once again. There is a strong revival of the idea of planning cities with much greater density. A major consideration is the distances that people have to travel. In North America, Portland, Oregon, has shown how a relatively dense layout makes investment in public transport pay its way. Forty-three per cent of the city's commuters use buses and a light railway system, more than in any other North American city.[98]

utilize industrial waste heat must advocate a functional intermingling of residential and commercial areas. However, people will only accept such a situation if industries become much cleaner than they are today. Such a guideline can also mean that politicians may sometimes have to impose decisions about location in the face of considerable public protest.

Sun

The many roof-areas in a city serve as an excellent site for solar collectors and photovoltaic cells. This book takes as one starting-point a strategy which could best be described as a "pincers policy". On the one hand, rational use of energy and energy-saving are intended to ensure an absolute decline in demand, while, on the other, the share of renewable sources of energy in consumption should be increased step-by-step. If photovoltaic cells are used on a mass scale on millions of roofs, the electricity business will be transformed. The separation between suppliers and users of electricity will basically come to an end. As discussed above, households will thus become "prosumers" of electricity, sometimes feeding and sometimes drawing from the network. Fair payment for the solar electricity supplied is now established in several German Länder, and this goes some way towards the creation of local networks.

The "Conference of European Cities and Communities on the Way towards Sustainability", held at Aalborg in Denmark in May 1994, was the first such gathering. The charter approved there has in the meantime been signed by over 120 European cities, agreeing "to seek consensus on a Local Agenda 21 in our communities by the end of 1996" and to exchange the experiences gathered.[99]

5.8 International Equity and Global Solidarity

Ever since dissolution of the Second World – the Communist Bloc (some of whose former members now demonstrate characteristics of developing countries) – the Third World no longer exists and has rapidly split up into Least Developed Countries (LDCs) and Newly Developed Countries (NDCs). Categorizing them as developing countries – because of their opposition to industrialized states – obscures fundamental differences between these nations, especially as by now the concept of development involves more questions than answers. The countries of the North are industrialized, but in what sense can they be considered developed if their present way of life and production is not sustainable? It seems reasonable to discard such an overstretc.hed term that can so easily lead us astray, but since this is almost irreplaceable it is worth trying to redefine the concept and to comprehend development as "a learning-process which increases a society's viability" – as Ebenezer Mireku, the Ghanaian economist, suggests.[100] Development as the acquisition of ecological and social viability comes close to revolution. Development would then no longer refer to the relationship (and the gap) between North and South, but would become a task to be mastered by both, albeit with very different starting positions. All states would then be developing countries, and co-operation on development would involve taking concrete steps towards the common goal of viability.

The geographical terms of North and South are also becoming imprecise. It is true that poverty is concentrated in the countries of the South, but a quarter or a fifth of the population in most industrial countries must be counted among the poor too. The South is thus also to be found in the North, just as the North has established itself among the sparse upper classes in the South. All the same, for the moment it is difficult to compare the numbers and living conditions of the poor in industrialized states with the misery and starvation experienced by over a billion people in the countries of the South. Geographical demarcation thus comes closest to describing the situation. The concepts of "North" and "South" and the terms "development" and "developing country" are used in this study in full awareness of their inadequacy, and precedence is given to the geographical terms because, even though inexact, they are not discriminatory.

All international agreements, all the treaties intended to ensure joint survival and alleviation of conflict – and thus to exert a deep impact on the lives of the parties involved – will only be consented to, will only endure, if the people concerned feel they provide an approximation of justice. Such agreements must avoid or eliminate recognizable and obvious injustice.

We see a sustainable Germany's contribution to more equitable relations between North and South as follows. In general terms, industrial countries do far more harm to the poor in the South by what they lay claim to for themselves than by withholding assistance. Or, to quote a single sentence from a government statement by the prime minister of North Rhine-Westphalia: "The people of the South expect us to take less, not give them more." What is involved in taking less for ourselves is demonstrated in the following examples.

Putting our own house in order

The first part of this study showed that Germany, like other industrial countries, has greatly overdrawn its credit in the Bank of Nature – to use Tariq Banuri's memorable image. Even if the South is rushing to do the same, the North must first repay what is due to the Bank of Nature before it can credibly ask its partners and competitors in the South not to get equally in debt.

The rapidly industrializing countries of the South will certainly not be able to blame their environmental inactivity on the North's mistakes and shortcomings for much longer. In many cases the means they deploy for catching up industrially are no more sustainable than those of the North. The damage done is not merely regional but will increasingly worsen the global situation. Until recently the rule of thumb was that 20% of the world population cause 80% of the damage to climate. But if there is a continuation of the rate at which some 20 of the threshold countries (including China and India) are at present industrializing, in just a few decades the countries of the South will discharge into the atmosphere two-thirds of the trace-gases responsible for climate change.

The industrial countries must therefore take the initiative – for three reasons. First, they have already seriously damaged the environment during two centuries of industrialization (section 4.2), and for the moment they are still the worst polluters. Second, the industrial countries have at their disposal considerably more technical and financial means for the necessary changes than most of the South. Third, their life-style has become a model for countries of the South, which will in all likelihood only reconsider what they and we to date term "development" if they see us taking serious steps towards reducing pollution and limiting our own consumption.

Eliminating double standards

In their dealings with many of the poorer countries of the South, industrialized states, including Germany, apply double standards. They help them and they exploit them. One hand gives them assistance and credits, provides experts, grants, scholarships, and participates in the country's development. The other hand takes. The North gains access to cheap raw materials and hinders access to markets for processed products from those countries; it imposes a system (World Trade Organization) that favours the strong; it makes use of large areas of land in the South, tolerating soil degradation, damage to regional eco-systems, and disruption of local self-reliance; it exports toxic waste; it claims patent rights to utilization of biodiversity in tropical regions, etc.

In all such activities the industrial countries deploy their market-power against the countries of the South, many of which cannot defend themselves against such strong partners, or consent to long-term damage in order to survive, or, often enough, to make a quick profit.

More equitable relations – and thus a reduction of dangerous tension – would become a possibility if the industrialized countries renounced unfair treatment of their trading partners. For a start, that would entail the European Union removing import duties on partially processed raw materials and reducing export subsidies for its own agricultural products, plus a strictly enforced ban on exports of toxic waste and fair participation for countries of the South in the profits made from exploitation of biodiversity.

Living with transnational corporations

Transnational corporations (TNCs) have become the most important players in world trade and the motor of ever-greater globalization of economies. By now 600 companies share a third of the combined gross national product worldwide. The planet's 20 largest firms together have a greater turnover than the 80 poorest countries, and each one of them earns more than even an entire state, like Malaysia, on the point of breaking through to modernity.[101]

TNCs' economic and political power is correspondingly great, and they deploy this in many ways. They can make their profits where taxes are low. They can move production to where labour is cheap, social and ecological demands are minimal or controls lax, and where there is less protection of human rights. They can force governments to make laws in their interest and grant favourable investment conditions – through subsidies or dispensation from taxes. With their power as suppliers, they can drive national producers from the market. They can form cartels, etc.

The poorer states are, the greater their governments' hopes of investment by multinational concerns, but the less they are able to defend themselves against company demands and business practices. That is particularly the case with the poor countries of the South. TNCs' influence there is variously evaluated today. Over-exploitation, prevention of or opposition to trade unions, and severe environmental damage still feature among their practices. However, by now longer-term strategies can also be found. Exposed to international pressure, demonstrating a sense of responsibility, and interested in securing an ongoing return on capital, some TNCs pay higher wages, invest in staff training, organize health-care, and on production sites in the South also adhere to the environmental standards demanded in industrial countries.

So it is no longer justifiable to simply say that multinational companies are the bad boys of world trade. They are part of a global marketing system to which they are subject whilst driving it onwards. This system favours the rich, promotes concentrations of power, and with the World

Trade Organization (WTO), the World Bank (WB), and the International Monetary Fund (IMF) has created institutions and rules that favour the global players. They also profit from the fact that up to the present there exist no international political authorities with the power to impose sanctions, which could introduce social and environmental limits in the market. TNCs are the main actors on the world market, and that is why acceptable social and environmental behaviour must constantly be demanded of them.

By now a considerable number of agreements and codices have come into being under the auspices of the United Nations, and TNC behaviour can be measured against such standards. Healthy principles apply in these pacts and obligations, but from the start they have suffered from the fact of being merely legally non-committal declarations of intent. For the moment they can be ignored without consequences, and only determine behaviour if an alert public makes firms keep the promises they have made.

No agreement has as yet been reached on the much-discussed social clauses that lay down minimum standards (e.g. banning the employment of children and forced labour), which were supposed to become part of the WTO system. Up-and-coming Southern countries' fears are simply too great that the industrial nations want to use such measures to restrain competitors who can produce more cheaply.

The overall picture is sobering. For the moment the weakness of the United Nations and opposing interests among the countries and firms involved lead to what is in effect a regulation-free arena where the global players implement their interests almost unhindered.[102]

However, TNCs have a vulnerable aspect: their reputation among purchasers of their products. They find themselves increasingly exposed to alert and critical observation. Their business practices become the object of public discussion. Because they are powerful, they are made responsible for what they do to people and to nature. That is at present the promising starting-point for the work of non-governmental organizations (NGOs).[103]

NGOs have at their disposal three strategies for dealing with transnational corporations, and these can be combined in specific cases. First, direct conversations with firms where the latter are confronted with what has been discovered and called on to do something about it. Second, public campaigns where there are calls for boycotts of certain goods or firms, or for buying environmentally and socially acceptable products. Third, political lobby work with discussions and exertion of pressure on governments, parties, and public organizations within one's own country.

The preconditions for success involve careful research, timely legal advice, effective media presentations, and if possible also co-operation between NGOs from the countries concerned in North and South.

Campaigns in recent years have experienced both successes and disappointments. The campaign against Nestlé's baby milk, withdrawal of the big Heineken brewery from Burma, the welfare provisions that Levi Strauss imposed on clothing suppliers, and renunciation by Unilever and Nestlé of genetically manipulated soya products in Germany are classic and recent examples of at least temporary successes for NGOs. Some firms change course on their own initiative too. Hoechst is thus getting an eco-institute to evaluate three product lines. How much of this is tactics and how much genuine acceptance remains to be seen.

Discussions and campaigns will not by themselves change the economic system. They can do something about concrete need, and they attract attention and promote a public climate in which human rights and ecological standards become negotiable within world trade. But they are not a substitute for political work. Without effective international agreements neither nature nor human rights can be protected. Here too NGOs have important tasks. Actual implementation of human rights agreements, strengthening of the responsible UN agencies, evaluation of state export guarantees, and making TNCs accept independent checks of adherence to the obligations taken on — all those are short- and medium-term objectives which will be difficult to achieve without the pressures exerted by NGOs. Such organizations will increase their effectiveness the more they seek allies and join coalitions.

Creating greater equality of opportunity

Equality is a central category in this study. As stated in presentation of the concept of environmental space (section 2.2), every human being has an equal right to make use of the global commons within the bounds of sustainability.

This premise of equality is much disputed. People say there has never been equality in terms of an equal share in the global commons. That would not take into account either climatic or cultural differences. If equality were to become a criterion, it is claimed there would no longer be any development, any innovation. Diversity and mutual stimulation would vanish from world cultures. Crucial incentives would be lacking with regard to ecological renewal.

The answer to that argument is that equality is not uniformity. The objective is not uniformity but diversity among equals, not the same expectations and needs but their equal validity. The aim of human equality

Scenario 23: Fair Trade

Solidarity with the poor in the South has given rise in Europe (and North America) to organizations that sell goods on fair terms. There are two declared objectives: securing an existence for producers threatened by world market conditions, and changing the unjust structures of the international market through consciousness-raising and political work.

By now 13 organizations in 10 countries belong to the European Fair Trade Association (EFTA – whose secretariat is at Witmakersstraat 10, 6211 JB Maastricht, Netherlands). They offer coffee (1.4% of the European market), tea, cocoa and chocolate, sugar, honey, bananas, textiles, leather goods, and arts and crafts. These products are distributed in two ways: in over 3,000 World Shops largely staffed by volunteers, and through assigning franchises to what is by now a total of 30 trading chains with their supermarkets.

These franchise-holders get fair trade goods directly from producers registered with EFTA and grant them favourable conditions: a guaranteed minimum price (usually above the world market level), pre-financing, and long-term guarantees of purchases. Products traded in this way are given a seal of quality in various European countries: TransFair, Max Havelar, or FairTradeMark. Fair Trade's European turnover in 1994 was just over 200 million ecus – a modest but constantly mounting share of the world market.

With their political activities (lobbying in European centres and national campaigns) these organizations want to make the European Union ease access for products from the South (and not just raw materials) and favour fair trade. They are thus urging a European coffee agreement with price controls and a fund which – in view of over-production of coffee – supports the cultivation of other products and a ban on substitutes for cocoa-butter, etc.

Other groups work in similar fashion, assisting such ventures as carpets made without child labour, and would like to introduce an environmental label for ecologically produced goods from poor countries. Palmpool is working on behalf of ecological and social standards in coconut products, extending fair trade to industrially produced goods.

does not even involve the same quantity of material goods, but rather equality of opportunity in terms of life-chances and possibilities of development. Equality of opportunity is therefore the political form of justice for North and South today. The idea that all human beings have the same right to the global commons is thus inalienable. Maintaining otherwise would both create an irreconcilable ethical rift and also make any lasting international agreement impossible because the weaker partner would be required to recognize actual discrimination as lesser rights. No-one would accept that kind of coercion at the end of this century.

Equality of opportunity is largely absent in relations between North and South. Ecological structural change may be the prerequisite for sustainable co-existence with the South, but in itself will in no way create fair conditions for international trade. To begin with it will consolidate the industrial countries' technological advantage and thereby their economic dominance. That is precisely what the states of the South fear. Recent years have seen the revival of a distrust directed in the nineteenth century against Christian preaching from the West: they say Christ and mean cotton. The South believes that ecological change will first benefit industries in the North and will be deployed for their advantage. The North is said to want to assure its lead, which it is currently in danger of losing, by way of the necessary technologies, patents, and know-how. So is the ecological seal of quality a particularly cunning form of protectionism and control of the market? This suspicion is not completely unjustified. Ecological change is being made attractive to business by the suggestion that companies which make sustainability a major element in production and marketing will continue to be out in front of the markets of the future.

The newly negotiated World Trade Agreement also worsens opportunities for many countries in the South. Servicing of the credits once so liberally offered by the North consumes most of what they need as investment capital for development of their economies. The demand for fair conditions of trade and reasonable debt relief for poor countries has been raised for decades and has lost none of its legitimacy.

Certain other factors must be mentioned as part of the striving for more equitable and neighbourly relations. The contribution that poor countries themselves make towards their wretched situation is now becoming clearer, partly because the sharpest and most relentless criticism comes from within.[104] It is not just that industrial countries have denied those states equality of opportunity; in many of them power elites and middle classes, which have long felt part of the privileged few across the world, live at the expense of the majority of the population. The privileges of those upper classes contribute to the poverty and misery of many people in the South: economic and land policies, suppression of opposition, transfer of capital abroad, luxury in capital cities, government-decreed low prices for local products, the arms trade, and the brain drain. All efforts at establishing equality of opportunity will have to take care that the people most in need of better chances in life are not excluded, for they are the ones who must be strengthened for the struggle which will determine the future of their country.

Balancing the impact of ecological renewal

If serious ecological structural change begins in the North, this will exert considerable impact on people in the countries of the South. Here too the main issue is greater equality of opportunity – and care should be taken that the best of intentions do not produce undesirable results.

At first ecological renewal will have a beneficial impact on the South. It will become easier for countries of the South to preserve non-renewable resources and avoid over-use of renewable ones. This will enable them to call on a greater share of world consumption of energy and materials without infringing sustainability of the global eco-system. A decrease in certain kinds of exports will make it possible, and also necessary, to concentrate on the domestic market and satisfy the basic needs of the majority of their people. That in turn will contribute towards preservation of their environment and possibly lead to healthier production methods and better working conditions.

However, ecological renewal in the North will also cause problems in the countries of the South. These will arise out of saving energy and raw materials, as well as changes in everyday behaviour from reduced meat consumption by way of choice of durable products to purchases of quality goods, organic farming, and greater consciousness of the impact of long-distance transportation of goods and tourism. The export trade and foreign currency dealings will be affected – and thus already unstable national budgets, particularly in poor countries. In addition the ecological demands made of products will bring about a switch from quantity to quality, also requiring considerable changes in production methods in Southern economies which have just achieved competitiveness on the international market or are only beginning to strive for it.

A number of strategies are now under discussion for alleviating those consequences and offering better opportunities to escape from poverty. Each involves both advantages and disadvantages. All have to be assessed in terms of effectiveness, possible side-effects, and differences between what is said and what is meant. This will be done in section 7.3.

Seeking co-operation and mutual consultation

The North and the South – with great local and regional differences – must each find their own ways of achieving sustainability. This does not mean that they can dispense with co-operation and joint learning. Dependable solutions will only be found by consulting the other continents. The North needs the insights, abilities, and skills the South acquired in much more constrained circumstances plus the technology developed to suit those conditions. Renewal of industrial societies also depends on living traditions in the South and their hopes for the future. In turn the countries of the South will not be able to do without the scientific knowledge, the successes and failures, of a technological civilization.

At present "transfer of technology" is the magic slogan. The ruling classes in the South hope that future-oriented technologies will provide a crucial boost towards both an economic upturn overcoming poverty and ecological acceptability. They are mainly interested in large-scale technologies which permit rapid industrialization, economic centralization, and concentration on exports. However, that would involve transferring to ever greater numbers of people a now unsustainable Western way of life and its production methods – inclusive of ecological and social degradation.

Alternative thinkers, especially in the South, instead advocate decentralization and subsidiarity as decisive criteria for an ecologically sound way of running an economy and developing a participatory form of society. Like the North, the South will be confronted with productive disagreements about a sustainable way of life. That makes it all the more important, particularly in the case of technology-transfer, to ask: Who wants what Northern industries can supply? Who benefits from "progressive" technology? An example: Anil Agarwal has put forward suggestions for renewing Indian towns and villages with houses made of clay instead of bricks and cement, which are too expensive for most people; composting toilets instead of costly sewers and purification plants; a traffic system with bicycles and modern mass transportation instead of road-building for the 15% who can at some stage afford a car. Such proposals presuppose rethinking in India – and also in the supplier countries. For the industrial countries of the North it is initially more profitable if a country's development follows the aspirations of those who have already "made it". In fact it is innovation that will serve sustainability in both North and South.

Enlightened self-interest is not as yet very common, so this involves important tasks for all those who are working on behalf of a sustainable South – from developmental co-operation at the national level to foundations, interest groups, and lobbyists seeking to influence policy. Private capital and the associated know-how make their own way to the South. It is thus all the more important that they find enough institutions and initiatives there that base co-operation and joint consultations on responsibility and long-term self-interest.

Global solidarity – and how it can develop

Ecological renewal may begin in one country but cannot be achieved in a single state. There are more and more dangers which are a potential threat to the whole of humanity. The wind decides who will be affected by nuclear clouds after a reactor accident. Countries cannot protect themselves completely against environmental destruction originating outside national borders. Growing desertification and large-scale tree clearance in coniferous or rain forests also harm our climate. The more extensive human intervention in nature becomes, the more often our lives will be affected by what happens in distant parts of the world.

Any attempt to maintain the affluence of the industrialized countries (plus a handful of threshold states) by way of protection of the environment, letting the rest of the world fend for itself, would have little future. Trying to keep out the "new barbarians" stands little chance of success. Wishful thinking is going the rounds with scenarios promising affluent countries continuation of an ecologically modified way of life. These envisage mobile troops suppressing worldwide revolts by the poor at an early stage with electronically controlled borders keeping out streams of the deprived. It is also maintained that damage to the environment could gradually be made good – and that adaptation is cheaper than prevention anyway. However, affluence is secure only under one of three conditions. Either those in need know nothing about the existence of affluence; or they accept their need as self-inflicted or fate; or wealth is unattainable for them. None of those conditions are applicable any longer. In our interconnected world too many people already know what's what. The messages of hunger and abundance, of reforms and revolts, can potentially reach everyone. The means of resistance, from terrorism to migration, are also too easily accessible for large parts of the world's population to put up with growing misery. Determined people, such as fundamentalists or ethnic groups, have already demonstrated the capacity to create chaos, but the potential for unrest goes far beyond that. "If climatic change makes our country uninhabitable, we will march with our wet feet into your living-rooms", proclaimed Atiq Rahman from Bangladesh at the Berlin Climate Conference. A Fortress Europe would be under such pressure from outside threats and inner tension that it would be impossible to maintain social stability.

The countries of the South are also conscious of their mounting strength. That is true of both the market-power of the newly industrializing nations and of the negotiating strength of poorer countries. Without them international agreements on protection of the climate cannot be achieved, and they can threaten global repercussions if they follow the Northern example and industrialize without concern for the consequences and rob the earth of its sinks as well.

All of this signifies that political and military security, greater equity of chances of survival, sustainable economic activity, and protection of the

Scenario 24: Germany Causes a Stir at the World Bank

This is how things could be:

During the 1999 annual meeting of the World Bank's governors the German representative announces two decisions made by the Federal Government and proposes two motions. The decisions: Germany transfers a quarter of its votes to Tanzania. In addition it waives the public debt arising from financial co-operation and trade credits amounting to almost six billion DM (1994 figures) for the world's 47 poorest countries. The motions: Despite their status as preferential creditors, the International Monetary Fund (IMF) and the World Bank (WB) should seek a possibility of completely waiving the debts incurred with these two institutions by the highly indebted poorest countries, and to forgo a large part of the debts of countries with a low middle income. Furthermore the German Federal Government moves that structural adjustment programmes should be developed for industrialized countries and volunteers to be the first country for which this is done.

The German representative substantiates these measures as follows:

By transferring a share of its votes to Tanzania, one of the world's poorest countries and linked with Germany by a long history, the Federal Republic wishes to make a contribution towards democratization of international financial institutions. Domination by the industrial countries prevents partnership, thereby harming North–South co-operation.

With regard to waiving debts, the Federal Government advocates a higher level of debt remission by the IMF and WB, as it has already suggested to the Paris meeting of creditor states. In doing so it supports and expands on the ideas put forward by a World Bank working committee, which in late summer 1995 proposed establishing a fund for such a purpose and put forward ways of financing this. It is absurd that 60% of the interest-free funds the poorest countries receive from a World Bank subsidiary, the International Development Association (IDA), intended for combating poverty and protecting the natural foundations for life, should have to be used for paying back World Bank loans.

To authenticate this initiative the Federal Government has itself done what it calls on the IMF and WB to do. It has with immediate effect waived the debts of 47 countries and hopes that other industrial countries will follow suit.

With regard to structural adjustment programmes, up to now the World Bank has only prescribed them for developing countries. They always constitute a deep intervention in the economy and way of life of the country in question with serious consequences for much of the population. The World Bank has declared that such interventions are indispensable for successful development, making acceptance of these programmes a condition for credits. By now the Bank is subjecting these criteria to critical reappraisal, which should be extended by a further dimension: adjustment of Western economies and ways of life to sustainable development. That is crucial for safeguarding long-term international trade and the countries of the South will only accept change if industrial states make a start, so ecologically oriented structural adjustment programmes are equally indispensable for industrialized states. The IMF and WB should thus establish such programmes in conjunction with the World Trade Organization, and Germany volunteers to be the first country to participate.

natural foundations of life are interconnected worldwide. Anyone seeking sustainability for Germany and Europe must include the fate of the entire world in their considerations and actions – out of a sense of responsibility and self-interest.

Notes

1. Hawken, 1993, p. 35.
2. For a cultural history of the automobile, see Sachs, 1992a.
3. Canzler and Knie, 1994.
4. Zängl, 1993, p. 60.
5. For a general discussion on the manifold effects of speed, see Plowden and Hillman, 1996.
6. Zängl, 1993, p. 53.
7. Transport specialists speak of a "long-term constancy in the travel-time budget", a formula which says that a reduction in travel-time by, say, 10% will be offset by about the same amount through additional expenditure on transportation (resulting from numbers of journeys and distances).
8. Whitelegg, 1994.
9. Petersen and Schallaböck, 1995, chap. V.
10. Ibid., chap. VI.
11. Pastowski et al., 1994, pp. 21ff.
12. Schallaböck and Hesse, 1995.
13. Alt, 1995.
14. Mill, 1968.
15. Hennicke et al., 1994. For carbon emissions, see Shah and Larsen, 1992.
16. Weizsäcker, 1994b, p. 121.
17. Hohmeyer and Gärtner, 1992.
18. Moret, Ernst and Young, 1996. Other important studies are: Friends of the Earth USA, 1994, 1995, 1996; OECD, 1996; Roodman, 1996.
19. Münchener Rückversicherungs-Gesellschaft, 1993.
20. Enquete-Kommission, "Vorsorge zum Schutz der Erdatmosphäre", 1990, p. 198.
21. Details in the German text of this book: BUND/Misereor, 1996, pp. 183ff.
22. Derrick et al., 1993.

23. *Wuppertal Bulletin on Tax Reform*, several issues since 1995. European environment Agency, 1996; Weizsäcker and Jessinghaus, 1992.

24. European Environment Agency, 1996.

25. Jarass, 1993; Jarass and Obermaier, 1994.

26. See also Greenpeace and Deutsches Institut für Wirtschaftsforschung, 1994.

27. European Commission, 1994. Also see: Data Resources Institute, 1994.

28. Hawken, 1993.

29. Ayres and Simonis, 1992; Schmidt-Bleek, 1994a; Tibbs, 1992.

30. Schmidt-Bleek, 1994b.

31. Hinterberger et al., 1995. This also includes criticism of an excessively economic view of natural capital.

32. Merten et al., 1995.

33. Young and Sachs, 1994.

34. Stahel, 1994.

35. See Porter, 1989.

36. Fussler, 1996.

37. Graedel et al., 1995, pp. 286–7.

38. Inglehart, 1977.

39. Scherhorn, 1994a.

40. MacPherson, 1967; Sahlins, 1976.

41. Douglas and Isherwood, 1978, elaborate the symbolic dimension of goods.

42. Hansen and Schoenheit, 1993.

43. Schulze, 1993.

44. Dittmar, 1992, p. 105.

45. See Schor, 1995, for a very similar argument.

46. Hörning et al., 1990.

47. Scherhorn, 1994c.

48. The figures relate to changes in the former Federal Republic of Germany fron 1960 to 1992. *Sources*: Bundesverband der Gas- und Wasserwirtschaft, Deutsches Institut für Wirtschaftsforschung, Vereinigung Deutscher Elektrizitätswerke, and Wuppertal Institut.

49. European Commission White Book, 1993.

50. Quoted from: Maier-Rigaud, 1990, p. 930.

51. Holtz-Eakin, 1992; Tatom, 1991.

52. Müller and Hennicke, 1994.

53. Buildings are not always viewed as part of infrastructure, but we believe that they should be because of their length of life, the high investment costs, intensive use of energy and raw materials, and the close links with the infrastructure networks involved in heating, electricity, and mobility.

54. Greenpeace International and Stockholm Environment Institute, 1993, chap. 6; Seifried and Stark, 1994.

55. "Der Staat der Stromer", *Der Spiegel*, No. 46, 1995, pp. 76–104.

56. Lehmann and Reetz, 1995.

57. Öko-Institut and Wuppertal Institut, 1994.

58. Kluge et al., 1995.

59. See also Crowhurst, Lennard and Lennard, 1995.

60. In greater detail in Petersen and Schallaböck, 1995.

61. Petersen, 1993.

62. Loske, 1996.

63. Potential for opening up and recycling land is considerable in former industrial centres.

64. For instance a kg of Atrazin, a herbicide long banned in Germany but still present in ground-water, used to cost 20 DM. Removing a kg of Atrazin from water costs around 200,000 DM. That is why over 100 co-operation agreements have been concluded in North Rhine-Westphalia since 1989. The farmers involved get compensation from waterworks for demonstrable disadvantage or declining harvests (Umweltbundesamt, 1994b).

65. When wood is burned, the pollutants – especially heavy metals – deposited there are enriched in the ashes. Under conditions of sustainability that will no longer happen.

66. They can also be used to syphon off profits from speculation, thereby making land speculation uninteresting.

67. European Commission, 1991.

68. European Commission, 1993.

69. All farms with more than c. 16 hectares of arable land originally had to leave 15% (by now 5%) fallow, receiving compensation of at present 746 DM per hectare.

70. In its December 1995 "Strategy Paper on Preparation of Agricultural Policy for Eastwards Expansion of the EU", the European Commission for the first time conceded the necessity of far-reaching reform of the common agricultural policy. In Agra-Europe, 49/95, Documentation.

71. Many of what are by now rare biotopes originally came into existence as a result of human intervention in nature, using it for agriculture or forestry. Without an ongoing moderate level of human intervention habitats would frequently turn into steppe or bush. There are also natural landscapes which came into existence on their own and remain stable (e.g. beech woods).

72. Bode and Hohnhorst, 1994.

73. Kühbauch, 1993. On intensive agriculture in general: Young, 1991.

74. The best-known example is the "Flavr Savr" genetic tomato, which keeps for weeks – at least to a limited extent. However, substance and vitamins are lost during storage, so consumers are as good as being cheated.

75. For an overview: Edwards et al., 1990.

76. For various environmental aspects of food production, see Pimentel et al., 1989.

77. Cultivated plants are bred to be resistant to specific herbicides. The chemical industry, which has already bought up many seed producers, then sells immunized seeds together with the linked herbicide, which can be used without affecting these plants.

78. Since 1980 producer prices (real prices without VAT or compensatory payments – 1985: 100%) for animal products have fallen by around 15%, for plant products by an average of around 25%, and in some cases by more than 50% (Statistisches Bundesamt, 1994, p. 295). Today prices for many agricultural products are back at the level of the 1950s.

79. Thomas and Vögel, 1993.

80. Around 60% of the land used for agriculture in 1992/3 served the production of animal feed. Statistisches Bundesamt, 1994, p. 121.

81. These costs were estimated at 107.3 billion DM for 1990. Kohlmeier et al., 1993.

82. Kjer et al., 1994.

83. For years Germany has been the world's greatest importer of agricultural goods (1992: 69.6 billion DM). Almost two-thirds of this agricultural trade is with EU countries. Providing for the German population – with mounting net imports of foodstuffs and animal feed despite surpluses at home – makes demands on additional land abroad. Imports of animal feed serve the already excessive consumption of meat, even though domestic grain surpluses subsidized for export are at the same time dumped on the world market instead of being used for animals in Germany. If cultivated areas are in developing countries, the production of cash-crops (food, luxuries, and cattle feed for exporting to industrial countries) competes with the local population's own needs.

84. For instance in 1994 a kg of imported wheat cost a third less in Senegal than local maize. The outcome is that people's eating habits change and national food production declines. Schmidt, 1996, p. 3.

85. Yields in organic farming are usually lower than those in intensive forms of conventional production. On average agriculture in Central Europe is more intensively pursued than anywhere else in the world (Herrmann, 1996, pp. 18–20).

86. Charta der Europaïschen Städte und Gemeinden auf dem Weg zur Zukunftsbeständigkeit, 1994.

87. Ministry of the Environment Denmark, 1994.

88. Girardet, 1993; Rees and Wackernagel, 1994.

89. Haughton and Hunter, 1994, p. 11.

90. Winkler, 1995.

91. From today's standpoint, urban agriculture was in no way an exclusively negative practice. Among other things it kept numerous city-dwellers aware of ecological cycles.

92. Charta der Europaïschen Städte und Gemeinden auf dem Weg zur Zukunftsbeständigkeit, 1994.

93. Adapted from Crowhurst, Lennard and Lennard, 1995, p. 74.

94. Girardet, 1996, p. 86.

95. Schramm et al., 1994.

96. Hoffmann, 1995; Weizsäcker et al., 1997.

97. Elkin and McLaren, 1991, p. 116.

98. From Girardet, 1996, p. 146.

99. Charta der Europaïschen Städte und Gemeinden auf dem Weg zur Zukunftsbeständigkeit, 1994.

100. Mireku, 1992, p.7.

101. Korten, 1995.

102. Heerings, 1995.

103. Van den Stickele, 1995.

104. Kabou, 1993; Kothari, 1993; Soyinka, 1991.

6 Transitions

The proposed guidelines and associated scenarios offer a bold look into the future. Such visions are necessary for gaining a fresh sense of direction and for surmounting rigidity of mind and timidity of heart. They are meant to stimulate discussion of necessary structural change and open up long-term perspectives. However, neither the years immediately ahead nor the associated questions should be neglected: Where is a start to be made? What means, what strategies, provide a jumping-off point for the necessary changes? Will such changes bring about what is hoped of them? What can be done during the next two decades to bring an industrial country like Germany closer to sustainability? During this period only some of the individual paradigms will start to yield results. Their relationship with political realities, technological potential, and tangible possibilities of action must first be established.

In this section we describe transitions in energy, industry, transportation, and agriculture and forestry, presenting what can and must happen to attain first medium-term and then longer-term targets. Realistic calculations very much depend on the country concerned and are not very meaningful for other states, so in this English version of our book we only present means, strategies, and outcomes, largely renouncing statistics and absolute figures. Anyone interested in details can consult the original German text for detailed calculations and appropriate references.

The measures to be taken in individual sectors cannot be considered separately. Close connections exist between them, so that individual measures can strengthen or obstruct one another, operating contrapuntally with regard to objectives. Figure 6.1 shows reciprocal dependences between sectors and other crucial magnitudes as exemplified in agriculture.

Figure 6.1 Schematic presentation of interactions between sectors, categories of demand, and general conditions as exemplified in agriculture (*Source*: Wuppertal Institut)

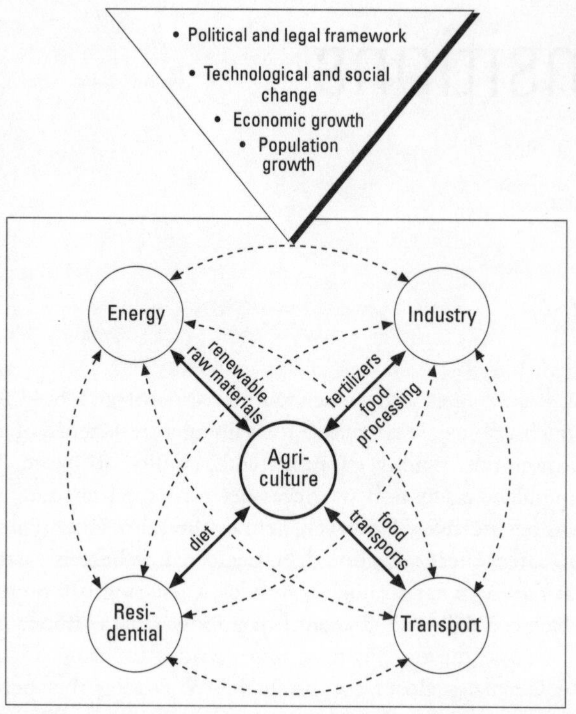

An all-embracing description of interactions and effective relationships within the overall system cannot be provided in this study, particularly because technical models for depiction of crucial structural changes are not available – and such models are necessary because of the complexity of tasks involved. So only a selective description can be offered, intended as an exemplification of the interconnections. The intention is to present a cluster of measures which – taking into account interactions and the behaviour of the overall system – leads as far as possible to achievement of the reductions hoped for.

It should be borne in mind that the best-researched sector to date is energy. For energy consumption and CO_2 emissions many highly detailed scenarios are available – but that is nowhere near the case for raw materials, water, and land use since integrated consideration of everything within the system affecting environmental indicators is not possible on the basis of today's inadequate data. The following investigations thus focus on energy with the increase in consumption and CO_2 emissions. The impact on other environmental indicators will, however, be taken into account as far as possible.

With regard to energy, studies of the German situation can build on the comprehensive findings of a commission of inquiry set up by the German federal parliament. Where they are not sufficient for achievement of a sustainable Germany we have developed our own scenarios. These also incorporate the social renewal presented in the guidelines, alongside further measures and action.

Estimates of savings resulting from social innovation are of course immeasurably more uncertain than depiction of technological possibilities in that sphere. Nevertheless an attempt has been made at an estimate. The study thus aims at provoking thought about verifiable possibilities, and invites discussion of other prospects.

6.1 Energy Supplies

The guidelines for future energy policy will be essentially determined by need to protect the climate. The requirements of future energy supplies can be derived from this with relative reliability. In conjunction with such objectives as "risk-reduction" and "sustainability", this will involve seeking a climatically tolerable and efficient energy system entailing the least possible risks for the future (see section 3.2). That can only be attained by way of a forced transition to an economy founded on savings and solar energy – thus a turning away from current trends. Four essential strategic elements can be identified:

1. Efficiency enhancement (reduction of energy input per service unit).
2. Substitution of low-carbon for high-carbon fuels.
3. Increased utilization of renewables.
4. Reduction of energy consumption through new, resource-efficient lifestyles and means of production.

1. *Increased efficiency*: Newly designed power stations – utilizing gas and steam turbines with efficiency of up to 55% – are considerably more effective than plant in operation today. Co-generation – with the waste heat from the energy generation for district heating – will produce savings of between 30 and 40%, compared with individual power stations. Such plant is between 10 and 15% more efficient than even new units for generating electricity and heat (utilizing natural gas, gas and steam turbines, and gas heating tanks). Potential profitability in using gas-steam turbines is very high, amounting in Germany to around half the present

supplies of electricity.[1] In addition this technology offers opportunities for saving energy on the supply side.

Savings potential on the demand side has by no means been exhausted either. In a study for Hanover's public utilities, the Wuppertal Institute and the Eco-Institute established what great savings could be made by employing least-cost planning (LCP) methods. If that potential is used as the basis for making a projection for the overall electricity sector, in Germany alone power stations' output can be reduced by up to 18 gigawatts within 8 to 10 years. That amounts to around 90% of current capacity for nuclear energy.[2]

With heat utilization, savings can even be considerably greater. Houses constructed for low or passive energy use make possible a reduction of between 70 and 90% in specific heat consumption.

2. *Substitution*: Over the long term, use of fossil fuels for supplying electricity and heat must be considerably reduced to a basic amount. The ratio of carbon and energy content varies in fossil fuels, so the level of this basic amount is largely determined by the mix of energy sources. It can thus be higher when low-carbon fuels are used.

3. *Increased utilization of renewable fuels*: There is great potential for renewable sources of energy, which could be employed for producing heat and electricity in an environmentally acceptable way. The main possibilities are geo-thermal energy, bio-gaseous fuels, bio-solid fuels, water, wind, and, above all, photovoltaic/solar thermal energy. In Germany it would be at least technically possible to use renewable energies to cover more than today's total electricity consumption and around three-quarters of heating requirements, thereby saving corresponding amounts of other energy. If photovoltaic systems spread rapidly and other renewable energies were applied more extensively, they could generate 25% of electricity by the year 2010 and 50% as early as 2020. According to some investigations, relinquishing nuclear energy is possible without creating additional economic problems or contravening current targets for reducing CO_2 emissions.[3]

4. *New life-styles*: These initially involve actual implementation of the measures just described. However, they can also become the motor and source of impulses for social change. There are many possibilities, including: conscious reduction of room temperatures through controlling heating and energy-saving air-conditioning; more careful purchase and use of electrical appliances, such as reduction of washing machine utilization and almost complete abandonment of machine-drying; taking a shower rather than a bath; filling up dishwashers before using them; etc.

Living-space crucially determines the need for room heating (and consumption of materials). In Germany this amounted in 1990 to 36 square metres per person, and it is estimated that will increase by 21% up to the year 2020 because of a rise in one-person households and larger living-units. The architecture of the future could make accommodation modifiable, promote granny flats, and make possible shared utilization of such infrastructure as rooms for laundry, hobbies, and watching television.

Interactions

The land use involved in renewable energies is sometimes considerably higher than in the case of established technologies, especially in built-up areas. So far as possible no additional land should be taken up by utilization of renewable energies. For photovoltaic systems that entails extensive renunciation of theoretically usable open spaces.

Renewable energies (such as photovoltaic systems) and energy-saving technologies (i.e. insulation) sometimes demand greater expenditure on materials than the current systems in terms of the amount of energy produced. On the other hand, such operations usually discharge considerably fewer toxics into the environment than conventional plants (e.g. brown-coal power stations). Production methods will improve, so it can be expected that in future more and more recycled materials will be used and consumption will also be reduced by utilization of different materials.

A switch in fuels can intensify regional and social conflicts (as when local coal-mining is abandoned), increase transport costs, and provoke a counter-development elsewhere – as when Russia exports more gas to Germany, changing at home to inefficient coal-fuelled power stations. Conflict over equity of distribution is also to be expected. All that must be taken into account in advance.

Energy consumption in setting up plant for using renewable energy sources is still high today, which is why the associated emissions are excessive too. The amortization period, i.e. the time taken for plant to produce the amount of energy needed for its construction, is still between 5 and 9 years for photovoltaic systems – but for wind-energy converters in good locations only a few months. However, there are justified hopes that expenditure of energy and materials will in future be much reduced through new production methods and cells with a transition to thin-layer cell technology, Grätzel cells, etc. It is, for instance, anticipated that the energy amortization period for thin-layer cells will be reduced to about a year.

Energy-saving technologies also involve energy consumption, but amortization periods are usually short. Surveys of use of polypropylene in insulation show that, even in unfavourable circumstances, energy amortization can be achieved in less than two years.

In addition less land is available for increasing numbers of organic farmers to cultivate energy crops. However, organic farming makes a greater contribution than biogenetic sources of energy to reduction of trace-gases affecting the climate.[4]

6.2 Industry

The degree of environmental impact caused by industrial emissions and consumption of resources is determined by a variety of factors. A great part is played by long-term and lasting changes in the structure of demand and production, plus increases in efficiency, alongside the impact of economic growth.[5] That has led in recent years to a noticeable reduction in pollution resulting from energy consumption and the well-known airborne toxics from industrial sources, but the full possibilities of making savings generated by technological progress and innovations have not been exhausted to date.[6] This trend will probably continue, but it is scarcely possible to say how land use and consumption of materials will develop. The indications are of stagnation at a high level since the way is not yet clear for large-scale dematerialization of production.

Even though economic growth's impact on consumption in recent years has been somewhat more than compensated by structural change and increases in efficiency, conscious structuring of ecological transformation remains absolutely essential. Of course a sustainable economy cannot be implemented all at once. That demands long-term strategies which must also contain immediately implementable elements providing greater protection for the environment.

A central role is played here by integrated protection of the environment, based on eco-audits. This holistic approach offers a chance of optimizing both individual components and entire processes or production units. That frequently leads to considerably lower water consumption, waste-production, and emissions.

Despite all previous successes there still exists large-scale potential for cutting back on energy consumption. Considerable possibilities exist in general applications of electricity for running machinery, which accounts for almost two-thirds of industrial consumption. The necessary investment could be found through purposeful elimination of obstacles (e.g. by industrial savings-contracting and least-cost planning programmes) in conjunction with ecological tax reform and changes in the structure of the energy industry.

Industry's self-comprehension and functioning must change so as to allow dematerialization to go beyond implementation of short-term options. Fundamentally new characteristics will develop for industrial production – in conjunction with new patterns of consumer behaviour (see section 5.3):

- The change from material to non-material satisfaction of needs will reduce the diversity and number of products.
- New forms of product utilization and manufacturers' acceptance of responsibility for a product's entire life-cycle will involve putting the emphasis on providing services rather than boosting sales.
- Emphasis on utility will allow a downsizing of equipment in many cases.
- Durability will become a major principle in construction. Through repair, reprocessing, etc., parts can be employed in the manufacture of new products or on the market for used goods.
- Modular construction will facilitate maintenance, dismantling, and adaptation to technical progress and changed demands.
- Use of raw materials will be limited so far as possible to renewables and recycled elements.

This ecological structural change will lead to powerful pressure towards adaptation, varying in intensity for individual firms. Active reorientation of business policy can result in this process becoming economically viable in many areas, provided cycles of reinvestment are taken into account. The impact on individual industries (the extraction industry or the high-tech recycling business), which will lose out greatly during such restructuring, cannot be analysed here, but such issues as the future role of the chemical industry or restructuring of the food industry following the spread of extensive organic farming need investigating.

Interactions

One important aspect involves the siting of industrial and commercial zones. Reduction of pollution will increasingly allow an intermingling of residential, work, and social functions, exerting a positive impact on urban life and leading to a reduction in traffic.

There could be individual cases of conflict between different ecological objectives. One example entails the demand for durability and recycling, on the one side, and for light-weight construction, on the other. The former opposes the use of compound materials, the latter supports it.

6.3 Transportation

Forecasts predict an increase of between 43 and 56% in use of private vehicles up to the year 2005, and even considerably more in commercial traffic.[7] A slight improvement in vehicle efficiency will nowhere near compensate for the increase in traffic.

Air traffic is also increasingly responsible for CO_2 emissions, rising from 7.2% in 1987 to a forecast of between 11 and 13% of total German discharges in transportation by 2005. It is assumed that use of jet fuel will decline by 20% by then, but this cannot in any way compensate for the anticipated 178% increase in flights.[8]

The rise in CO_2 emissions also stands here for a number of other negative side-effects of the massive expansion of transportation to be expected if the present trend continues.

The top priority must therefore be traffic prevention – and what remains must so far as possible involve low-emission or emission-free forms of transportation. Technological and organizational optimization of both individual means of transportation and the overall system is therefore the crucial element in strategies for reducing discharges of climate-changing trace-gases and making the entire set-up more environmentally acceptable. All three strategic elements are usually combined. Success – particularly with regard to traffic prevention – is very difficult to estimate in quantitative terms. Making forecasts about future leisure and business traffic is not easy.

Traffic prevention

The objective is to reduce the amount of traffic. In commercial transportation the aim is reduction of both the quantity of goods carried and the distances involved. In the private sphere the emphasis must be on limiting the length of journeys. In both cases a broad range of varying options is available. Three main directions can be distinguished:

- a traffic-reducing change in values and attitudes towards mobility;
- structural options such as development planning, restricting urban sprawl and mixing forms of land utilization; regulation of the distances covered by commercial traffic; and attractive shaping of the residential environment and improved local recreational facilities;
- potential for reduction including car-sharing, avoidance of detours, and communication and information technologies.

Improved modal split

These strategies aim at changing the proportions of different kinds of transportation so that the more environmentally acceptable predominate.

Here too a distinction must be made between carrying goods and people. A large percentage of local trips by private cars could be transferred to non-motorized forms of transport. Ten per cent of all car journeys in densely populated areas end after one kilometre and almost 40% after three kilometres. Greater utilization of local public transport can contribute towards a more environmentally benign distribution of traffic between different possibilities. In long-distance personal travel the objective is a switch from aeroplanes and individual cars to rail. There is great potential for transferring traffic, amounting to over half of personal travel. For transportation of goods the idea is to move from road to inland shipping and rail. The "local rail network" scenario presents a concept for transferring transportation of both people and goods.

Optimization

The level of savings possible through technical improvements differs considerably according to the form of transportation involved.

With cars innovative concepts are paving the way for vehicles needing only one to two litres of fuel for covering 100 km. For instance Amory Lovins' concept[9] unites the following components: ultra-light materials, improved aerodynamics, better tyres, hybrid-motors, regenerative braking, etc. In addition there are chances of savings in traditional vehicle design (see scenario 1 in chapter 5). Speed, acceleration, and vehicle weight are also crucial for economizing energy.

Technical improvements are possible in all vehicle components. Both the internal combustion and the diesel motor offer considerable potential for cutting energy consumption and toxic emissions. It is estimated that savings will be around 20% for the former and somewhat less for the latter. Those figures could probably be doubled with more extensive and innovative changes in motor construction.

New fuels are also under discussion as ways of reducing emissions. These include natural gas, alcohol-based fuels (methanol, ethanol), and plant oils (including rape, methyl and ester), which can normally be used in traditional internal combustion or diesel motors without problems. However, no clear-cut economic or ecological advantages over the usual fuels are as yet apparent. Short- and medium-term prospects for electro- and hydro-powered motors are uncertain, primarily because of the costs, and in the former case also because of the existing density of traffic. These concepts will only become attractive when their energy requirements can be massively reduced and a solar energy or solar hydrogen industry has established itself.

The greatest potential for transportation of rail passengers lies in reduction of carriage mass and air resistance, and in regaining energy from regenerative braking. Beyond that energy consumption (for heating and air-conditioning carriages) can also be cut. The empty-mass of rolling stock cannot be reduced to such an extent in goods trains, but cutting air resistance offers great potential savings. German Railways estimates that specific CO_2 emissions can be decreased by between 20 and 25% by 2005.[10]

Existing estimates predict that improvements in technical efficiency will cut fuel consumption in the air by between 20 and 25% by 2005.[11] For shipping energy consumption will be about 15% less.[12]

Interactions

It is not easy to estimate the net impact on land use of switching means of transportation since there will also be counter-effects. For instance, moving road traffic onto rail networks may reduce the amount of land used for road-building, but expansion of rail services will require additional land if existing roads cannot be converted for that purpose. However, the private car is the means of transportation requiring the greatest land use per passenger – even when full, a car's per capita land use is greater than public transport which is only 40% utilized – so a positive net outcome is to be expected over the long term. Over the short and medium term, up to the year 2010, the impact is likely to be minimal or non-existent.

6.4 Agriculture and Forestry

Present practices in agriculture and forestry cause mounting economic, ecological, and social harm. Overproduction in conventional agriculture today is based on subsidies amounting to around 800 DM per hectare, which ultimately come from tax receipts. Subsidies policy to date is misguided and pursued at the expense of the tax-payer. Consumers must therefore become aware that they have long been paying (albeit in a roundabout way) for the administration of subsidies and the environmental damage done by intensive farming. Cheap food is only supposedly a bargain; the accompanying social costs – and thus the overall burden for individuals (expenditure on food, taxes, duties, etc.) – are constantly mounting. Any future attempt at preserving the landscape through subsidies would be considerably more expensive for society than support for extensive organic farming.

The 1992 European Union reforms clearly strengthened centralized planning in the agricultural market. The decoupling of price and income policies is being extended. National and European agricultural prices are being brought into line with imaginary world market prices – in other words they are falling – and farmers' loss of income is compensated by direct financial transfers. The resultant economic, social, and ecological problems are largely left out of account or played down (and thus underfunded). It is questionable whether these agricultural reforms are sufficient for achieving the ecologically and economically necessary reduction of intense farming and the associated impact on the environment. The many problems involved demand a fundamental reorientation of policy, aiming at environmentally and climatically acceptable, resource-saving, sustainable agriculture and natural forestry, producing timber for durable products (see section 5.6).

One-sided preoccupation with production must therefore be brought to an end. Economic, ecological, and social functions and tasks should instead be regarded as being of equal importance and supported accordingly. The first step requires financial incentives for reduction of intensive utilization on the national and European levels. The EU financial set-up must be changed correspondingly. The ecologization of agriculture, directed towards reducing production of surpluses, should also be rewarded if countries act unilaterally – instead of their being punished by cuts in compensation while obligatory payments to the common fund remain unchanged. Second, transfer payments to farmers must in general be linked with ecological criteria instead of being coupled, as previously, with the amounts produced or the areas farmed. Funds for conversion to organic farming can only be made available through redistribution of existing agricultural subsidies. At present these are mainly devoted to the storage, destruction, or subsidized export of agricultural surpluses rather than going to farmers. Even in the case of extensive organic farming, at current prices total income from agriculture would remain the same if farmers received additional subsidies of 200 DM per hectare or prices for all animal and plant products rose by just 8%.

Linking subsidies and organic farming can only be a first step in this direction. Among the problems are considerable expenditure on administration and controls plus the difficulties entailed in assessing ecological achievements. In addition farmers would become even more dependent on state support and affected by the situation facing national budgets. Fundamental restructuring of the conditions underlying agricultural policy is thus necessary. Such a reorientation must be linked with reduction of subsidies and centralized control, and moves towards a market policy where prices tell the economic and ecological truth. After a transitional period reimbursement of ecological and social progress in agriculture and forestry should therefore be founded on appropriate (and thus higher) prices for food and other products.

A changed, more healthy attitude towards nutrition among the German population is the precondition for conversion to organic farming. In particular, excessive meat consumption, which in many cases threatens people's health, should be reduced to a quarter or a fifth of present levels. A healthy, balanced diet with more fruit, vegetables, grain, and pulses would replace today's over-consumption of protein and energy. Seasonally based, fresh local supplies will play an increasingly important part. Healthy nutrition thus complements organic farming and regional marketing highly advantageously. That does not need to be more expensive than today's eating patterns. Even though prices for alternative products are clearly higher than for conventional foodstuffs, ecologically conscious households spend less on food than conventional families because their consumption structure is different.

Ecological forestry would also be ideally complemented by increasing demand for natural and durable products and materials made from indigenous woods. The increase in mature timber from such forests would largely be used for production of durables (housing, furniture, etc.). In such products the carbon absorbed in trees will continue to be stored for decades or even centuries. If toxics are not used in the treatment of wood, it can be utilized several times over (see section 5.6 and scenarios 16 and 17).

If the potential for growing trees were completely developed, Germany's national requirements for timber and wood products (inclusive of paper) could be covered almost completely. Considerably more wood could also be made available through a reduction in paper use, a further increase in the recycling of paper and wood, and interlinked utilization of wood. The recycling of paper makes clear that today's possibilities are still too little exploited. At present scarcely half of German consumption is produced from old paper, but a recycling quota of 75 to 85% is technically possible.[13] That would assure complete self-sufficiency in wood, and considerably more wood for durable products would be available than hitherto. The self-sufficiency sought avoids energy-intensive transportation and reduces the ecological rucksack involved in our wood consumption.

Interactions

Organic farming's most important forms of impact on the environment are as follows:

- Organic farming reduces the harmful division into arable farming and animal husbandry, and promotes a return to linkage. The number of animals per farm and per hectare will decline. Animal feed comes from the farms themselves, making possible large-scale renunciation of bought or imported goods, reduction of energy and transportation costs, and a considerable decline in ecological rucksacks. Transportation of foodstuffs and animals would also be much reduced with regional marketing. Energy use in organic farming is about two-thirds less than in conventional operations. Renunciation of mineral nitrogenous fertilizers cuts the nitrates in surface and ground waters, and thus in drinking water and foodstuffs. Agriculture's contribution to the eutrophication of eco-systems, soil acidification, and the death of forests will decline. Complete abandonment of synthetic chemical biocides in cultivation will end the pollution of water and soils with toxics from agriculture. Comparable results are to be expected from renunciation of chemical drugs in animal husbandry.

- Agricultural emissions harming the climate will be reduced by more than a half through environmentally acceptable extensive farming.
- Species diversity in a locally structured, more variable landscape increases as a result of more diverse crop successions in differing forms of cultivation. Hedges, biotopes, and fallow areas are essential aspects of ecologically managed land, providing for growth of stability and capacity for self-regulation in (agricultural) eco-systems. Extension of the animal dung/humus cycle exerts a positive impact on soil life and structure. Erosion and degradation clearly decline. Greater stability makes it possible to work the soil with less energy-input and improves porousness with less surface loss of water, greater availability of water, more regeneration of ground-water, and less danger of floods.
- Woods managed in harmony with nature are very much more varied and attractive than today's monotonous plantations of trees of the same age. This could lead to a reduction of long-distance tourism in favour of local recreation.

Notes

1. Enquete-Kommission "Schutz der Erdatmosphäre", 1995.
2. Hennicke et al., 1994.
3. Fraunhofer-Institut für Systemtechnik und Innovationsforschung and Deutsches Institut für Wirtschaftsforschung, 1994; Greenpeace, 1994; Krause et al., 1993.
4. It has not, for instance, been proven that if rape, methyl, or ester were used as fuel, this would relieve the climate. Their production by traditional methods, utilizing fertilizers, results in emissions of large amounts of HN_2O, a 'laughing gas' which affects climate. In addition its manufacture demands energy-intensive processing and transportation.
5. For the impact on industrial energy consumption, see Schipper and Meyers,

1992, pp. 89ff. On the "ecological gratis effect" of structural change, see also Graskamp, 1992; Jänicke et al., 1992.

6. On energy consumption see Beer et al., 1994.
7. Umweltbundesamt and Statistisches Bundesamt, 1995.
8. Umweltbundesamt, 1995.
9. Lovins et al., 1983; Weizsäcker et al., 1997.
10. Deutsche Bundesbahn, 1992.
11. Umweltbundesamt, 1995b.
12. Institut für Straßen- und Verkehrswesen, 1990.
13. Friends of the Earth Europe, 1995.

7 Contexts

In this final chapter the proposals put forward in this study as being necessary, possible, and desirable are examined in terms of social fairness, economic viability, and relations with the countries of the South. The authors are well aware that each of these aspects merits a separate study and do not lay claim to completeness. Their main concern is to counter important objections to an ecological reorientation of economy and society.

7.1 Social Fairness

An ecologically sustainable society is a pluralistic society. It embraces a wealth of human possibilities, allows diverse people the freedom to live the options they choose, and by granting this freedom to everyone links it with social fairness and a sense of community. Two socially organized spheres are paramount: work and social security.

The future of work

Uncertainties about work and its future are again intensified by the currently persistent high level of unemployment. Are the political diagnoses by Hannah Arendt[1] and Ralf Dahrendorf[2] correct, namely that "work is running out in the work-society"? The phenomenon of lack of (paid) work is very much an outcome of economic organization. For almost 150 years now increasingly many of the preconditions for a labour-saving society have been established. Productivity has increased by an average factor of 20 during that period, and now people are amazed that fewer workers are wanted for producing the goods and services paying customers can afford.

Full employment belongs to the past, and the reasons are to be sought in processes of global change.

Production of goods and services is becoming globalized – and less and less dependent on the contribution made by local and national firms, technologies, capital, and labour. The outcome is that the world market – global competition and the associated revolution in rationalization of productivity – constantly intensifies the criteria of profitability and competitive capacity. Continual increases in capital investment are necessary for keeping down unit costs. Today a viable job in the industrial sector costs about half a million DM – and some industries and countries can no longer keep up. Companies do not merely move labour-intensive production to regions where wages are considerably lower (such as Eastern Europe or East Asia); they are also increasingly transferring more skilled activities (such as software development to India).

Globalization of flows of finance and capital, and the growing significance of speculation as opposed to real economic investment, result (among other things) in over 1,000 billion dollars circulating the globe daily. Electronic currency's astronomic turnovers, decoupled from productivity, destabilize money, which is linked with the real economy through central banks' policies. The harshest losses are usually suffered by innocent third parties, completely uninvolved in speculative transactions – frequently in the form of loss of jobs and thus of possibilities of survival and development.

The emphasis on automation – based on micro-electronics, computer and telecommunications technology, and new production concepts ("lean production", "re-engineering", etc.) – accelerates the rationalization process and therefore reduction of employment in many labour-intensive sectors and to a mounting degree also in services (banks, insurance companies, etc.).

There is thus an overall decline in gainful employment[3] – with high rates of joblessness as the outward sign. A general reduction in the number of hours worked frequently only generates more overtime rather than new jobs. No economic growth will bring back full employment in the traditional sense. If there is economic growth, in the industrial countries that will mainly involve "jobless growth".

Tax resource use, not work

Nature has not been a significant factor in the economic framework to date. However, increased damage to the environment is closely linked with the way work is organized. Increasing the productivity of labour has always entailed greater consumption of nature. Anyone who wants to create new paid (and payable) employment must make work cheaper, and energy and other resources more expensive. Only ecological tax reform will bring about both more employment and greater protection of the environment.

Such a reform would spark off ecological structural change linked – at least over the medium term – with an increase in jobs. A study by the German Institute of Economic Research thus comes to the conclusion that introduction of an energy tax would lead to at least half a million additional jobs after 10 years.[4] Nevertheless industrial society's structural problem would persist over the longer term. Full employment will only be possible on the basis of considerably fewer working hours and lower wages.

A re-evaluation of work is unavoidable since work has to date constituted the foundation of the democratic market economy. Other sources of meaning have to be found and invented alongside the still necessary involvement in gainful employment. Wolf Lepenies has put forward ideas worthy of consideration:

> The time of utopias is past – and our social imagination also seems exhausted. Nothing is more urgent than reflection on the nature of a future society whose core values are not those of traditional gainful employment. Lives will be characterized by alternations of periods of employment and equally long periods of leisure. Perhaps in future we will have to reward the wish to do nothing as highly as readiness to work. Having to work once seemed the nightmare of machine civilization – but in post-industrial society people will long to be allowed to work.[5]

So social imagination is needed.

Modern industrial societies should not, however, exceed a certain level of output. To assure existence they need – alongside gainful employment – a certain level of "reproductive work": looking after and training future generations, housework, health care, all possible services, information, voluntary activities, and self-help. Thus work does not simply involve gainful employment, but that will probably remain the central element for the foreseeable future. For the great majority of people it will still be the focus of social orientation.

Social fairness therefore demands that every woman and every man has at least access to a paid part-time job. That is probably the most important socio-political postulate.

Flexible working hours

The most important precondition here is more flexible structuring of working hours. The ideas and demands involved in more flexible working hours and forms of work are best expressed in the slogan "Using time as you wish". That is why social innovations and experimentation are so necessary in this sphere.[6] Expansion of part-time employment is one of the most important trends on labour markets. This mainly receives support from an alliance of interests between employers and a growing number of employees. The former achieve better utilization of capacity and the latter extension of individual options regarding use of time. Nevertheless new temporal structures do not by themselves alleviate the division of labour between man and woman if both lack motivation. They also only lead to enrichment of private life or work if people discuss and negotiate the contents of free time and the contents, conditions, and meaning of work.

Second labour market and negative income tax

More flexible working hours and forms of work, and reduction of the costs of work through ecological tax reform, are not by themselves sufficient to provide everyone with access to paid part-time work. The concept of negative income tax has long been discussed with the objective of countering the growing division of society into those with jobs and the unemployed.[7] At the heart of such a concept is a link between welfare payments and earned income. Anyone who is fit to work but has no income can claim subsistence payments. Someone who works but earns less than the socially agreed minimum income receives a state allowance. That declines as income increases, and comes to an end when earnings reach the agreed minimum level (see also the sub-section on social security below).

The negative income tax makes it worthwhile to take on low-paid work. Unlike today, additional earnings would not be clawed back by the welfare office. All additional work would lead to greater net earnings. Lower labour costs would make it possible for many firms to offer more jobs in the low-pay sector where the level of earnings (protected against abuse) would be lower than in the high-pay sector oriented towards the world market. A low labour-cost sector with acceptable incomes could thus come into being since enough work is available if it can be paid for. For millions of people who otherwise have no chance of finding employment in the high-pay sector, that would once again generate a realistic perspective. In addition this concept would ease transition to the "first labour market", oriented towards the world market. Conversely, anyone who falls out of the high-pay sector could once again find meaningful employment in the "second labour market".

Gainful employment and voluntary activities

Work and production do not merely occur in the formal economy of companies and markets, but also in the informal sector of households, voluntary involvements, etc. Alongside paid employment there exists unpaid pursuit of personal interests.

The future of work can no longer consist exclusively of gainful employment.[8] Over the long term protection of the environment and considerably less consumption of resources lead to a reduction in the volume of paid work. However, this in no way means that there will be less to do. Ways of life and means of provision will have to change towards once again according greater importance to local and regional markets, autonomous work, self-reliance, etc., employing modern means. This sphere offers such activities as growing food, repairing a wide range of products, manufacturing vital but simple utilitarian objects, rebuilding and renovating houses and flats, and neighbourhood medicine and social assistance.

Access to or the availability of workshops, tools, materials, and specialized knowledge constitutes the precondition for development of a local sphere of self-reliance. Its institutional and organizational forms can extend from an individual household by way of short-term projects, co-operatives, communal or local workshops, to small self-administered firms. These will mainly be non-profit-making organizations.

Expansion of self-reliance will reduce today's almost total dependence on taking jobs in the industrial sector to provide for survival, so that the autonomy of both urban and rural local communities can be re-established. Such expansion is not intended to split up industry into a conglomerate of small self-reliant production units but rather to establish a concurrent, effective, meaningful, and realizable alternative.

The predominance of gainful employment will be replaced by a policy involving both gainful employment and voluntary activities for men and women (rather than an either/or situation), and thus a new intermingling and evaluation of money and time, outside work and personal activities, and job and family.

Social security

The question of security is very acute and sparks off anxieties all round. Up to now organization of social security has been closely coupled with gainful employment (or the deductions from earnings). However, the system cannot function for much longer if contributions by ever fewer people at work have to provide for more and more unemployed and pensioners. If earnings also decline, many people begin to ask themselves why they should provide for others when their own difficulties are considerable. Solidarity and social morality are put to a hard test.

In the public debate some call for constraints, even a change of direction, in social security. They claim that only then can global competitiveness be maintained and improved. They want to dump ballast and call for dismantling of the welfare state. Others say that society should not economize at the expense of the old and the poor, and call for at least preservation of the status quo or even for extension of welfare provisions. Both stands reduce concern with welfare and social security to the financial dimension.

Here too social imagination is necessary. The decisive factor is that relations between state and society must change. It is no longer society and its citizens which circle, like planets, around the centralized state, but rather the other way round. Citizens and society are at the centre of things, and the state has the important task of ensuring that funds are employed to increase social capital.[9]

Increasing social capital

Social capital mainly involves those dimensions that used to socialize life and vitalize social existence: neighbourhood, social exchanges, and active communities. The task is to create once again a more closely woven civic society with self-referential spheres of exchange and solidarity no longer prescribed by a hierarchical state. This envisages self-help as a voluntary community of solidarity with neighbourhood groups and self-reliant associations providing collective services. Important legal preconditions must be established to make that possible. Voluntary communities must be recognized as legal entities with autonomous rights. In practice that could, for instance, entail recognition of a right to augment specific state services by additional provision (as in the spheres of childcare and medical services). When individuals come together to provide themselves with such additional services, the state must recognize that this "private" initiative fulfils an essentially "public" function and reward it accordingly (for instance by tax relief). That is the best possibility of promoting such collective self-service or public services in the form of local initiatives.

A more closely woven society does not mean the utopian idea of a community of small groups where individuals come together as a kind of almost self-reliant extended family. Voluntary communities are rather possibilities of practising greater social fairness and of living out more real solidarity. Institutional solidarity with all members of society is expressed for every single person through the welfare state, but the individual only practices direct solidarity and social fairness within the limited network of those closest to him or her. The various networks involved within family solidarity – whose economic importance is far greater than generally assumed – provide vital exemplification. The arising of an underground economy during crisis periods testifies to the social structure's ability to engender ways and means of coping with external upheavals. These hidden buffers may not by themselves be sufficient for defusing the crisis of the welfare state, but they are an indispensable component in a sustainable society.

The prime condition for such a development is more free time, more sovereignty over time. The less free time someone has, the greater his or her demands of the state and the more he or she consumes on the market. People can only fulfil services for one another, activate neighbourly relations, and develop forms of immediate solidarity if they have the time. Making working hours shorter and more flexible is thus an important precondition for social fairness and greater real solidarity.

Reorganizing the finances of social security

If the future of work is to be as presented here, public financing of social security must be reorganized. The crucial issue is at least partial decoupling of gainful employment and social security. That mainly involves proposals advocating integration of the tax and transferred payments system, and introduction of a basic pension or even a guaranteed basic income for all.

The present multi-part system of contribution-related and tax-financed welfare payments, and a tax system that only takes some social factors into account, are both in need of fundamental reform, for several reasons:

- Today's welfare and tax system is inconsistent with lack of provision for some and unjustified benefits for others.
- The system is becoming ever more complicated, impenetrable, and bureaucratic.
- Over the long term – mainly for demographic reasons – the present system is unfinanceable: too many recipients, too few paying contributions.
- Anyone receiving social benefits has no motivation to earn more because that usually leads to a 100% cut in welfare payments.
- An abrupt transition from employment to receiving social benefits leads to stigmatization of the persons concerned, making a return to work more difficult.
- Reform of social security also brings the advantage of compensating for the negative by-products of ecological structural change, thus ensuring implementability of the accompanying political concepts.

The general idea is that today's multi-part system of state social security should be replaced by a unique kind of basic income for all.[10] That will be financed by general tax revenue rather than by special contributions.[11] Differences in payments to recipients are determined by level of welfare benefits, availability of other income, and regulations on the right to receive benefits.

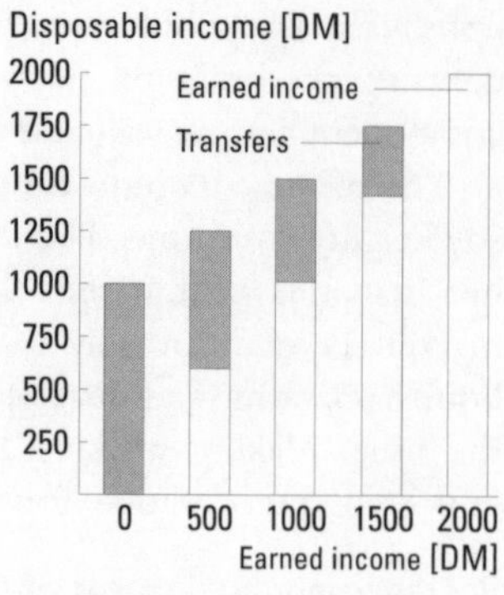

Figure 7.1 Earned income and transfer payments in a system of basic social security (*Source*: Kress, 1994)

Figure 7.1 shows a very simple case. The basic sum to which everyone without any other source of income has a right is assumed to be 1,000 DM. Fifty per cent of all earnings up to a total of 2,000 DM have to be paid to the tax or social security office, so that if someone earns 2,000 DM they keep precisely 2,000 DM (the basic income + 1,000 DM). That can be seen as involving either the basic income remaining untouched while tax is paid from the first DM onwards, or the benefit payment getting less as earnings rise (but only partly, and not 100% as is the case with many payments today).

The advantage of this kind of structuring of basic income is that an incentive for taking a job is created, even if it pays less than social benefits, as in the basically underfinanced cultural and social spheres. Simplification of procedures offers further advantages. The tangle of different legal regulations could be unravelled. Several empirical studies have shown that such a system can more easily be financed over the long term than the current pensions set-up, threatened with collapse because of the demographic situation.

Financing a negative income tax probably constitutes the greatest problem. The German Institute of Economic Research has made projections for the situation which might face Germany. These estimate that costs could range between 65 and 173 billion DM, mainly resulting from a fall in tax revenue. More than 150 billion is probably not financeable under any circumstances, but anything below that could be covered by ecological tax reform. Also of importance are the conditions regulating drawing the basic income, especially in conjunction with family benefits. Unfortunately, well-founded empirical analysis of workers' behaviour in this connection is lacking. Experiments in the USA during the seventies did not show any massive withdrawal from employment.

Preliminary and transitional stages leading to such reform are also conceivable and should be viewed positively. They are more meaningful than constant additions to the present welfare and tax system, creating an enormous patchwork of regulations.

7.2 Economic Viability

Sustainability and competitiveness

Sustainability and competitiveness[12] should not be played off against one another. Both involve assuring human well-being within a society, so they both basically involve the same objective. A sustainable economy which was not competitive would be of little use. However, it would be equally dangerous to simply carry on with the present way of managing affairs. A country's environmental space imposes restrictions on its economy, and those must be taken into account at a sufficiently early stage. In other words, an economy can only assure lasting employment and well-being for its population if the ecological context is consistently taken into account. The same is true of competitiveness. A country that is largely dependent on exchanges with others cannot provide its inhabitants with a good life if it is not competitive. If no-one wants to invest in this country, and the goods and services produced here find no customers, employment and affluence will continue to decline. That may not be a natural law because the degree of integration with other countries can diminish again, but it is an accompanying condition which must be borne in mind during current discussions about the country's sustainability. One-sided concern with economic criteria, such as gross national product, may have brought success to date, but it leads deeper into ecological crisis and deprives poor countries of developmental opportunities. Table 7.1 shows the alternatives that can arise.

Table 7.1 Sustainability and competitiveness

	Internationally competitive	**Internationally uncompetitive**
Ecologically sustainable	Scenario 1: *Sustainability*	Scenario 2: Economic crisis
Ecologically unsustainable	Scenario 3: Ecological crisis	Scenario 4: Economic and ecological crisis

Scenarios 2 to 4 are bad options because sooner or later they will lead – albeit for different reasons – to great problems. Hence a country like Germany has no alternative but to link both competitiveness and ecological sustainability.

No further rise in competitive pressures

During the decades after the second world war the global economy became increasingly integrated. That was possible because of falling transaction costs and greater mobility of capital. Transaction costs include long-distance transportation, the expenses involved in conducting business across continents, and customs duties which were reduced through GATT. The German economy thus became increasingly dependent on foreign trade.

Up to now those global trends have persisted. Capital is today almost unrestrictedly mobile. Technological innovations make international co-operation ever simpler. Falling transaction costs lead to greater specialization, and to the possibility of drawing on kiwis from New Zealand, milk products from a neighbouring state, and pocket calculators from the Far East.

We anticipate that dematerialization of industrial economies will spark off a counter-movement to this ongoing globalization. This is indicated by the following developments:

- If the full price is paid for transportation, the intensity of transportation will decline. Producers, wholesalers, and retailers will not get everyday supplies from so far away. Certain products will no longer be brought from abroad because that has become too expensive.[13]
- Preservation of resources will in general demand, and make possible, greater regionalization. Production and consumption will come closer together, which in turn involves fewer materials and less energy.
- Dematerialization favours services (particularly local services), so that part of the economy will be less subject to international competition: repairs, a kindergarten, and tool-hire cannot be imported.[14]
- If the tax burden on labour as a factor in production is lessened by neutral tax reform and utilization of the environment becomes more expensive, that favours the production of labour-intensive industrial goods, which in the past were manufactured abroad where labour costs were less.

It is difficult to determine whether these developments – facing increasing globalization of the world economy – will lead to a net decline in foreign trade. Whether technological developments will further reduce the costs of international business, making centrally produced mass goods even cheaper, is unforeseeable. However we expect that overall international pressure on a sustainable economy will not increase and might even decline.

At any rate fixation on cost-differences between countries is completely misguided. What really counts with regard to competitiveness is an economy's capacity not to be left behind in the international race for innovation. Social and technological innovations will play a large part in achievement of economic development based on considerably less use of raw materials and energy, so that ecological structural change is only attainable in a functioning market economy.[15]

Innovative powers, not today's economic structure

Dematerialization is not possible without a transformation of economic structures. Structural changes will lead to contraction of certain parts of the economy while others will grow. This is always the case in a dynamic economy. Economic structures and processes, individual preferences and the technologies employed, would also change dramatically without any "ecological structural transformation" – as they also changed dramatically during the past 50 years. Ecological structural change certainly also favours different sectors of the economy. The targets for reduction put forward in this study will lead to a decline in the manufacturing sector. The production of automobiles and drills will be reduced in favour of enterprises that increase their share of the market with transportation services (such as car hire) and leasing machines and tools.

In political discussions people frequently express anxiety that environmental policy will undermine powers of innovation and economic dynamism, especially if industry is expected to pay for its consumption of the environment. This worry would only be justified if structural change were prescribed in detail by the state, if future economic structure were predetermined and regulated by bureaucrats. However, that is neither necessary nor meaningful. If households and firms are left to decide about how old and no longer viable branches of the economy should gradually be replaced by new ones, there are very good chances that structural change will occur without any reduction of dynamism. One great advantage of a resource-efficient strategy becomes apparent here. It influences the capacity for innovation in a direction that makes possible social sustainability alongside drastic reduction of consumption of raw materials, energy, and land.[16] The most important task to be dealt with centrally – at the national or, better still, European level – involves determining clear-cut targets for reducing consumption with a specific timetable. In its characteristic process of evolutionary self-organization the market economy in an open and free society will then time and again "re-invent" the accompanying conditions for its further development.

Environmental policy as we know it today is essentially based on regulations and prohibitions that restrict freedom of action. The "current state of technology" is often taken as a criterion of what is possible. Entrepreneurs are then only left with few possibilities of behaving in an enterprising way. Their economic efforts are thus directed towards fulfilling tasks at the lowest possible cost. These costs can easily be passed on to customers, so there is little incentive for any innovative seeking of potential for avoiding environmental pressure in the first place. At best environmental improvement will get stuck with the desired goal and scarcely move any further.

But what we need is ecological innovation, not strict adherence to increasingly inadequate regulations. Politics cannot foresee what is required in the future. Only on the market (with an abundant supply of creative inventions) does it become apparent which innovations are worthwhile for a firm, for consumers, and thus for the general public – and which not. Politicians' task is to establish the "ecological crash-barriers" in such a way that innovations are favoured and unecological behaviour is at a disadvantage without slowing down overall dynamism. This entails furthering specific types of innovation rather than specific technologies, which at a certain moment the state views as being promising and environmentally acceptable. Also from an economic point of view, dematerialization is a better way of trying to achieve sustainability than regulation of ever more single flows and materials.

Decoupling growth from resource use

The traditional way of looking at things assumes that economic growth (increases in output) is accompanied by accelerated structural change, and that more environmentally friendly innovations will flourish better in a climate of growth than in an economic context where growth is not to be expected. But empirical data show that economic growth to date has gone hand in hand with increased pollution.[17] Economic growth is usually characterized as an increase in gross national product. GNP expresses the value of all the goods and services produced in a year. Leaving aside structural changes, real economic growth (i.e. after taking account of inflation) entails greater production of goods and services. This increase in production was long associated with greater utilization of materials, energy, and land, and also with a considerable increase in industrial pollutants such as waste, effluents, and airborne emissions.

To achieve sustainable development structural and technological changes must lead to a decoupling of environmental consumption and GNP.[18] In previous discussion of economic growth and impact on the environment, great hopes have been put in "qualitative growth" – allowing growth to continue despite mounting environmental problems.

There are three reasons why that hope must be viewed with caution:

- Decoupling merely means that environmental impact increases to a lesser degree than GNP. If gross national product increases to such an extent that, despite decoupling, energy consumption and flows of materials proliferate or remain at a high level, this only signifies a gaining of time but not a development towards sustainability. Economic growth can thus be consumed by the outcome of structural change.
- Even an absolute decline in environmental impact fails to achieve sustainability if that impact is greater than the eco-system's buffering capacity, which is already the case today.
- There are limits to dematerialization. It will never be possible to produce goods and services without using materials and energy. That state of affairs cannot be avoided through recycling either.

There thus exist definitive limits to decoupling. Where these lie cannot be precisely determined. However, their existence should underline the need for caution about all-too-optimistic assumptions regarding "qualitative growth".

A revolution in efficiency (accelerated intra-sectoral structural change) is certainly of central significance for an ecologically and economically sustainable Germany. However, it is improbable that such changes are sufficient – while economic growth continues – to achieve a reduction in material flows to the degree thought necessary in this study. If dematerialization by a factor of 10 is already an enormous social and economic challenge, the task of reducing material flows to a sustainable level in a growth situation is even more difficult to solve. Any growth must be balanced by a corresponding and greater improvement in resource-efficiency – over the long term.

A stop to growth?

Current debates arouse the impression that any loss of growth must lead directly to crisis. This study maintains that observing environmental limits instead opens up great positive potential for life and economy, and certainly does not have to bring social development to a standstill.

The simple demand for a stop to growth is, however, inappropriate. First, such a stop would not per se bring about any positive ecological consequences. Without movement towards dematerialization of the economy environmental impact would merely remain on a high level. Second, simply demanding renunciation of growth would be as problematic as calls for continued growth. Reality in no way responds to such demands. Just like nature, society and economy are not a machine where minor interventions are sufficient to bring about a specific impact (such as reduction of pollution).

From the ecological point of view it is neither meaningful nor possible – because of the limited opportunities for regulation – to begin by cutting back the gross national product. Reduction of flows of materials will rather lead over the long term to restriction of economic growth. Such a restriction of growth – we again stress: as a result of reduction in the flow of materials – is reconcilable with a market economy. In its first annual report, the German Committee on Global Environmental Issues emphasizes the market economy's dynamism, but also states that, "contrary to some views, it is reconcilable – if ecological conditions enforce this – with the idea of zero growth".[19]

We do not know – and cannot know – whether over the long run the logic of the market economy is irreconcilable with sustainability, or whether it must (and can) be outgrown. However, we do know with relative certainty what is necessary to achieve sustainability. When it becomes apparent at some future date that a reduction in consumption of energy and raw materials is not reconcilable with the dynamics of the market economy system, other ways of managing the economy will have to be considered. Only in that case would society be faced with a choice between either fundamentally changing the market economy system or renouncing the ecological adaptation demanded by sustainability.

Problems of going it alone

We have argued that the problem of (international) competitiveness is less dramatic than is often maintained in public discussion today – and certainly different. Nevertheless the problems that would arise if Germany or just a few industrial countries were to take the lead in essential restructuring are of relevance, and it is worth considering how such problems might be resolved. What would be the situation with regard to imports from countries of the South which could not be expected to change so quickly? Do we have to protect our economy with new tariffs and bans on imports so that greater demands for environmentally acceptable production and consumption do not one-sidedly harm German producers? In other words, will not higher demands at home lead to displacement of production to other countries so that pollution will only be transferred from a rich industrial state to poorer countries? Will not eco-dumping – with cheaper imports from states with lower environmental standards and taxes – destroy national environmental policy? (See also section 7.3)

A preliminary view helps characterize the range of themes at issue. Only part of what we consume can (also) be produced in other countries. And only a part of what we produce can (also) be sold abroad. The question of eco-dumping and displacement of economic activities abroad only refers to those spheres. Whether competition from other countries represents a danger for an ecological transformation in Germany initially very much depends on the measures involved.[20] Discussion is well under way and must be taken further. The following should be borne in mind:

- Regulations and prohibitions within existing environmental policies already apply to imported products. Such measures should be part of a new eco-policy for Germany, but they must also relate to production processes, particularly consumption of materials and energy. World Trade Organization regulations will have to be changed.
- New tax policies constitute one of the key demands in this study. If they make utilization of the environment more expensive while secondary labour costs are simultaneously reduced, that gives rise to problems in foreign trade. Material- and energy-intensive products could return to the domestic market again after previously having become too expensive. Firms could also transfer investment to more favourable countries.

However, such undesirable consequences of a dematerialization strategy for Germany are more likely to occur in isolation. The following considerations support that view:

- The most important progress in resource-productivity must occur in spheres that are not part of international trade: housing and leisure activities.[21] Even if there are some internationally tradable products (such as furniture) involved in housing, most of the consumption of energy and materials in these spheres – for local transportation, entertainment, etc. – relates to the national market.
- Far-reaching aspects of ecological structural change will be achieved by way of a general change in social guidelines rather than through direct prohibitions or tax regulations. If households show an interest in environmentally acceptable production processes and the way the environment is used in consumer goods, then eco-dumping will not be a problem since many products will simply no longer be bought. An impact will also be exerted on investment decisions. That will

particularly be the case if suitable eco-labelling provides clearer information about products' utilization of the environment.

- Even in other spheres great distortions of the market are not necessary. Economists – using theoretical models, empirical data, and various scenarios – have endeavoured to calculate the impact of eco-taxes on international displacement, but their findings to date do not support the worries of employers' associations and some trade unions.[22]

Nevertheless a need for action may develop if Germany (initially[23]) stands alone:

- If prices for certain goods and resources rise (as compared with other countries), thought will have to be given to action at borders. However, at present a tariff on the materials and energy contained in imported goods is not yet reconcilable with European Union and World Trade Organization law. The Federal Government will have to take steps to ensure that compensatory measures at frontiers are allowed to cover the use of energy and materials in production processes. The countries of the South will have to be integrated in such measures step by step.
- Better international eco-labelling, revealing the amounts of materials and energy used in goods, will often make state measures unnecessary. The Federal Republic can also speak out in international bodies, urging declaration of the environmental consumption involved in production and transportation.
- There is no economic rationale for assisting industries particularly affected by ecological tax changes. Those are industries which are no longer sustainable. Relieving them of, for instance, taxes on energy (using the arguments of international competition) would be just as meaningless as subsidizing dying branches of industry that have long slowed down structural change.

7.3 Adjusting the Balance between North and South

By now the UNCTAD category of the world's poorest countries (LDCs, Least Developed Countries) amounts to 47 states. In 1981 there were only 31.[24] These countries with a total population of almost 500 million in 1992 only contributed 0.4% to world trade (figure 7.3). If the next category is added, a total of 130 states account for just 3.6% of world exports.[25] That means that two-thirds of all the countries in the world are of virtually no significance for the global market. They exert almost no influence on what happens there, but are highly dependent on that market for their imports and exports. Many of the poorest countries have little

Figure 7.2 Distribution of economic activity between North and South, 1991 (% of global total) (*Source*: UNDP, 1994)

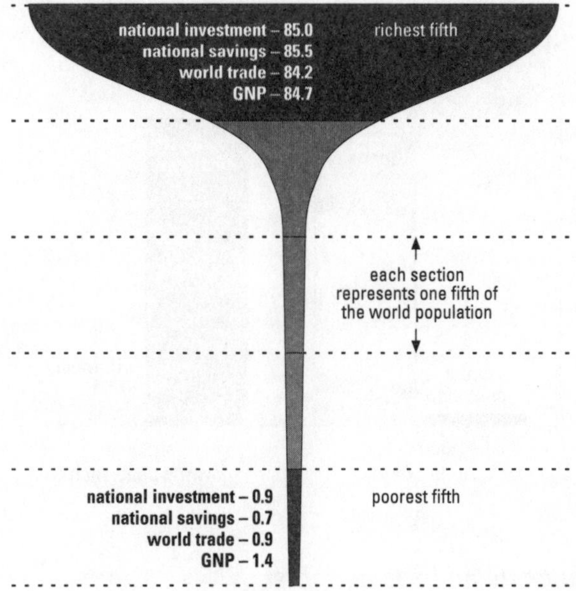

more to offer than raw materials and agricultural produce, and foreign exchange earnings are often dependent on exporting one, two, or three products, which increases dependency to an even greater extent.

A marginal position in the world economy and high indebtedness go hand in hand. According to the World Bank, in 1995 33 of the 60 low-income countries had high debts. They are also termed severely indebted low-income countries (SILICs). All of them belong in the category of those countries that have no influence on the movements of the world market.

In the meantime the financial stability of the poor countries is under even greater threat. International trade in goods is losing out to markets for capital and electronic services. On the one hand the financially weak countries are hard hit by foreign exchange fluctuations due to speculation on the derivatives market, and on the other their economies lack the capital for participation in the symbolic economy of communications networks and data banks with investments of billions. Once again they are forced to the margins.

Figure 7.3 The 47 poorest countries and Germany in the world market
Almost 500 million people in the poorest countries only contributed 0.4% to world trade in 1992. (*Source*: UNCTAD, 1994b)

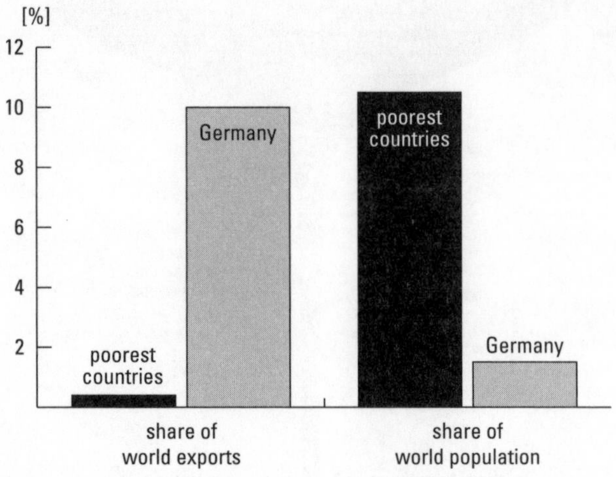

Ecological costs and social rights

The North's over-use of the global commons and the transferring of ecological costs to the South were discussed in section 4.2. An important dimension – in terms of the South's view of the North – should be added here. The recipients and users of raw materials and agricultural produce from the South do not usually pay their share of the ecological and social costs of cultivating and extracting these goods in the producer countries. The selling price of pineapples from the Philippines, bauxite from Jamaica, and roses from Colombia does not include any contribution towards protection of the environment, health insurance, or social security for workers. The impoverishment, contamination, desertification, and erosion of soils; the uprooting of much of the rural population and their migration to cities, driven by need; the violent expulsion and not infrequently decimation of indigenous populations – none of that has prevented the small class of those who benefit in the countries concerned from implementing this destructive means of production; and nor has it stopped many more people in the industrial countries from enjoying buying and using these products. To the degree that such consequences are measurable at all in monetary terms, they have almost never been reflected in prices. In their imports the countries of the South pay for all the protection of the environment that industrial countries include in the prices of their goods. On the other hand, poor countries' sales of raw materials and agricultural produce include no charge for the burden producers incur by exporting these goods.[26]

GATT agreements

According to official declarations the new World Trade Organization (WTO) is supposed to particularly benefit the developing countries.[27] In place of the market dictates of the mighty or uncertain agreements that can be abrogated at any time, there will now be an abiding set of regulations governing the rights and duties of all concerned, and liberalization of markets will provide the countries of the South with better access. That will be the case for the stronger. However, whether opportunities really exist is determined by those who can take advantage of them. The main beneficiaries of the WTO thus continue to be the industrialized states, what are known as threshold countries, and multinational companies. A study by the World Bank and the OECD anticipates an annual boost of US$195 billion when the GATT agreements are put into effect with over a half (105 billion) going to industrial countries.[28] These have also obtained additional advantages for themselves by means of limits on quantities, special terms, and delays in the removal of import restrictions and export subsidies. The all-important agricultural policies contain a clause about postponing discussion of controversial issues until the year 2004.

Among the consequences for the countries of the South are expectations of a rise in world prices for agricultural produce when subsidies are reduced. A number of developing countries will profit from that, others certainly not. The many countries of the South dependent on food imports will be further hit by higher prices – and even more so if they export such classic colonial goods as coffee or cocoa where price rises are scarcely to be anticipated. The general reduction of customs duties will also be accompanied by an end to existing forms of preferential treatment (the General Preference System and the Lomé Conventions), which assured poorer countries a degree of stability for export earnings. The WTO has certainly recognized these adverse effects and stated that there will be compensation for the poorest and the net food-importing developing countries. However, that is not a binding declaration or worth any more than industrial countries volunteering to make available 0.7% of their gross national product for development co-operation.

Impact of ecological renewal

If Germany becomes sustainable, that will very much affect trading partners in the South – in both desirable and undesirable ways (section 5.8).

If consumption of raw materials and energy is reduced, if eating patterns and agriculture are changed, and if the transportation of goods and the wish for mobility are harmonized with protection of nature, quite a few Southern countries will lose a considerable proportion of current foreign exchange earnings. Nevertheless it is not possible to predict how quickly such losses will occur and how great they will be. Initially, rapidly expanding markets in Asia and Latin America will probably absorb what is no longer exported to Germany, and these states may also provide replacement tourists. However, that only postpones the problem. Even the new customer countries will have to make their economies sustainable, probably sooner than they today realize. The South will not be spared the changes on which the North must now make a start.

The loss of earnings awaiting the poor countries of the South is thus a sign of unavoidable change. They will surely be able to produce goods (from natural fibres to hydraulic oils) ecologically; they will discover new market niches; and they will have to find access for processed goods in the markets of the North. However, sustainability – and particularly for the countries of the South – demands greater thought about the place of foreign trade in national economies, the development of local and regional economies, self-sufficiency in foodstuffs, and the role a subsistence economy plays in national development plans. Transition can only be successful if these countries can reduce their current dependence on export-oriented production which harms both nature and society. That depends on their own efforts, accompanied by international agreements and financial support.

World trade, subsistence economy, and what lies between

In their efforts to overcome poverty and dependence the poor countries of the South are faced by conflicting objectives. For what should they strive? Standard economic thinking views the greatest possible integration in the world market as the best, even the only, way for a country which wants to develop economically and socially. But that is questionable. Which of these countries can pay to catch up with industrialization without becoming oppressively dependent on international financiers? Who benefits in those countries from what is extolled here? Is the volume of world trade unlimited? Is there room for everyone struggling to enter a sustainable market? What happens if globalization of flows of raw materials and transportation declines again because such flows are not compatible with protection of the global commons?[29] It is clearly apparent that in many parts of the South orientation towards national economies or regional economic communities is more conducive to the well-being of the great majority of the population than harsh competition on the world market.

In the face of such evidence, those in favour of an alternative form of development in the South advocate a clear-cut choice in favour of self-reliance. Mohamed Suliman[30] from Sudan argues that for his country the most positive aspect of ecological structural change in the industrialized countries would be the anticipated reduction of trade with the North. That would force the producers of exportable agricultural goods to rediscover the national market and work to satisfy the basic needs of their own people. That could increase the reliability of national food supplies and alleviate the massive damage which has been done to the soil. Where this is linked with land reform, subsistence farming could be revived – as could, at the same time, a well-tried way of life including barter and mutual help. In turn that could slow down migration to the towns and induce some people to return to their villages. Anil Agarwal and Sunita Narain likewise advocate the revival of village republics in India as holistic, local, self-reliant eco-systems.[31]

Of course alternative thinkers are also aware that only production for export brings in the foreign exchange indispensable for machines, equipment, and fuel, and that a market will remain in the industrialized countries for what can only be grown in the tropics or extracted from the ground there.

So how much world trade should there be? How much of the economy should be dependent on foreign exchange? What share of the market should be regional and local? How much commercialization should there be? How much decentralization? Answers will (and must) be different from country to country, but in future such questions increasingly have to be raised and fought out – contrary to all current trends.

Equalizing opportunities

During the next few decades the countries of the earth will be faced with immense – and correspondingly expensive – shared tasks: protection of the global commons and creation of a balance of opportunities and burdens, shared between North and South.

A large number of strategies and methods intended to make such objectives financially feasible have entered international discussions in recent years. The most important will be mentioned in this section. They entail very different approaches, so it is important to be aware of the advantages and disadvantages, and to be cautious about possible hidden drawbacks.[32]

Producer cartels

Prices for raw materials on world markets have fallen in recent decades, whereas prices for processed industrial products have risen. For that reason countries in the South dependent on farming and raw material extraction for export have time and again tried to unite and force through price increases by reducing the amounts produced.[33] The best-known cartel is the Organization of Petroleum Exporting Countries (OPEC). Twice – in 1973/4 and in 1979/80 – it managed to implement drastic oil price increases, but each time only for a short period. Similar attempts have been made for coffee, cocoa, wheat, sugar, rubber, tin, etc., sometimes in the form of producer–consumer agreements. Those that did take off were short-lived, and few are still effective. In summer 1995 a coffee-producer cartel, re-established two years earlier, failed again. This is the outcome of an imbalance in market-power between suppliers and buyers, and of irreconcilable interests among the suppliers themselves.

Compensation payments by the industrial countries

These can be justified on the grounds that industrial countries lay claim – and always have – to considerably more than their fair share of the global commons – especially the atmosphere, the seas and all they contain, and biological diversity.

Compensatory payments serve a dual purpose: compensation of the South for utilization rights not previously taken up, and promotion of ecologically sound development.

Montreal Protocol

The 1987 Montreal Protocol on substances causing depletion of the ozone layer (tightened in 1990 and 1992) regulates gradual reduction and actual termination by the year 2000 of production and use of chlorofluorocarbons (CFCs) and other toxic materials. The signatory states have set up a multilateral fund so that the industrialized countries can meet developing countries' incremental costs, arising out of relinquishing use of CFCs and halons or conversion of production methods. Even though this programme is entirely financed by Northern countries, the fund's executive committee consists of equal numbers of representatives of developing and industrial countries, and a two-thirds majority can decide on how the money is used if majorities from both groups agree.

The fund is reasonably well provided for with 510 million dollars covering the years 1994 to 1996. Initially there was a lot of controversy over its use,[34] but overall it is a successful model for dealing with the global commons in a spirit of partnership. The real test is yet to come. Uncertainty prevails about whether the USA will overcome reluctance to pay its dues, and whether – once a 10-year grace period runs out when they were exempted from protocol requirements – the developing countries will really fulfil their treaty obligation to preserve the ozone layer.[35]

Climate Change Convention

The seventh principle in the 1992 Rio Declaration on Environment and Development states that the industrial countries acknowledge their responsibility within the international pursuit of sustainable development in view of the pressures their societies place on the global environment and of the technologies and financial resources they command. To fulfil this responsibility, in article 4 of the Climate Change Convention the developed countries accept a series of obligations towards the developing countries: bearing the costs of the emission inventories required, paying for the additional costs incurred in the climate-protection measures agreed, providing financial support to help reduce and prevent the impact of climatic change on countries and regions particularly affected, and also making environmentally sound technologies available for that purpose.

The first follow-up conference held by signatory countries took place at Berlin in March 1995. That demonstrated how difficult it is to direct diverse and often opposing interests (sometimes contradictory within themselves) towards a shared objective even when all have recognized its urgency. The main areas of tension between industrialized and developing countries are as follows:

- In the Convention the industrialized states promised to lead the way in protecting the climate, making an immediate start on the necessary measures and reporting back as a basis for discussions in Berlin. Only 15 out of 24 countries fulfilled that obligation, and their reports show how inadequate such measures are with regard to the dangers invoked in the Convention. However, so long as the industrial countries do not take climate protection seriously, there is little chance that developing countries will give precedence to protection of the world's climate over trying to catch up economically. In the Berlin mandate for a working group charged with drawing up a protocol on climate, developing countries successfully avoided introduction of any new obligations.
- For the moment there is no consensus about what is covered under additional costs incurred by implementation of protection of the climate in developing countries.
- The Global Environmental Facility (GEF), administered by the World Bank, has been entrusted with handling financial implementation of the Convention. In Agenda 21 the Rio Conference strongly urged the

GEF to guarantee balanced and equitable representation of developing countries' interests (section 33.14 of the Agenda). That guarantee has not even been fulfilled in the draft for revision of the Facility.

Convention on Biological Diversity

This Convention, also passed at Rio in 1992, is intended to serve protection of the earth's biological resources and their equitable and sustainable utilization, thus safeguarding them from neglect and exploitation.

This too entails a financial obligation whereby the industrialized states meet the developing countries' "agreed full incremental costs", so as to pay for the measures agreed in the Convention and also so that the developing countries might benefit from the Convention (article 20.2). This applies in particular to the poorest and most endangered states.

The Convention assures the countries of the South an "equitable and fair sharing of the benefits arising out of the utilization of genetic resources" (article 1). Patent rights should be "supportive of" and "not run counter to" the objectives of the agreement (article 16.5).

There are in fact considerable areas of conflict between this Convention and the commercial aspects of intellectual property rights as established in the GATT Uruguay Round. The industrial countries' disproportionate financial power and legal dexterity could in effect undermine the rights of the poor.[36] Patent rights provide a striking example. The habitats of probably 90% of all species are to be found in the world's tropical and sub-tropical regions. The GATT agreement allows large companies to patent the biological material they take from the South and then further develop it. No form of protection – and thus franchise fee – is as yet envisaged for the collective intellectual property involved, for instance, in centuries-long cultivation of food plants or in the wisdom of traditional medicine and its curative herbs.

Ecological tax reform

Ecological tax reform, one of the most important strategies for desirable structural change in the North, also involves a North–South dimension. This is a source of conflict. At dispute is who should ultimately pay taxes and who will benefit from the revenues. Such taxes will after all be paid in industrialized countries and are intended to create great incentives for reducing consumption of energy and raw materials. To make them more acceptable and politically feasible, they are meant to be used to reduce other levies, especially taxes on earned income, rather than to provide additional revenue for governments.

Using the eco-tax for that purpose arouses opposition among advocates of the South. They object that the North already dominates trade with its market-power, so that the countries producing raw materials and energy only get a price just a little above production costs. Above all, this tax does not in any way take the ecological costs of production into account. If the industrialized countries now decide to put an ecological tax on fuels and raw materials with the declared aim of reducing demand, then the additional revenue should not just be for their benefit. All the more so since reduced consumption will probably make producer prices fall rather than rise. It is argued that the countries that export energy and raw materials, which are usually on very tight national budgets, will have to try to compensate for the decline in earnings by selling more elsewhere, leading in turn to mutual undercutting because of the great competition. The outcome – it is maintained – would then be that the North buys fewer raw materials at lower prices and the exporting countries in the South will be forced into even greater dependence and self-exploitation. They will pay for the costs of ecological change in the North where industrialized countries can also develop economical forms of technology for extending their dominance of world markets. So this once again involves a transfer of capital from the South to the North – this time under the guise of protection of the environment.[37]

1. It is beyond dispute that the poor countries of the South, dependent on exporting energy and raw materials, must not suffer loss of income from the fact that production and consumption in the North become more ecological in orientation with reduced imports of fuels and raw materials. At present it is still uncertain whether expanding industries in Asia and Latin America will take over the share of the market lost in the traditional industrialized states. Even if that should be the case, the countries of the South will certainly not achieve sustainability in this way. Sustainability is only attainable if dependence on over-exploitation of natural resources and on environmentally destructive agriculture is eliminated. The poor countries need special help there.

2. The conflict over whether ecological tax reform should provide additional revenue or not, and whether the producer countries should receive a share, can be resolved. If an eco-tax is a strategy of change with good prospects for success (as we believe is the case), then it is highly important that the tax be actually introduced and can take effect. If being revenue-neutral helps an eco-tax overcome the resistance which does exist in industrial countries, that is crucial – even from a global perspective – since there is no alternative to worldwide conservation of energy and raw materials. It is very important for the global ecological movement – says Mohamed Suliman – that this reform can be successfully introduced in a significant industrial region without leading

to disaster.[38] Suliman thus recommends introducing such a tax step by step, allowing developing countries a share of the eco-tax revenue at a later stage.

Greater equality of opportunity for the countries of the South with responsibility shared by the industrial countries – both objectives are incontestable. However, neither must be linked with ecological tax reform if its implementation is thereby endangered. Those objectives can (and should) be linked at a later stage when the eco-tax is established, but they can also be promoted (as the following paragraphs show) by way of compensation payments or a compensation fund.

3. The responsibility shared by the industrialized countries does not change the fact that many of the exporting countries (and particularly the very rich oil states) have to date invested too little in a sustainable future and the well-being of the majority of their populations. If sustainability partly involves satisfying the basic needs of the poor and combating the causes of their misery, then governments should not simply be recipients of compensation payments and other such funds. A different approach is needed towards the unholy alliance which developed and still exists between privileged classes in the South and the trading interests of the North. Institutions where those immediately involved and affected have a seat and a vote (represented, for instance, through independent non-governmental organizations), implementing clearly defined objectives and subject to inspection, are most likely to keep abuses to a minimum.

CO_2 permits

The Intergovernmental Panel on Climate Change (IPCC) thinks a 60% reduction in carbon dioxide emissions (compared with today's total) necessary in order to prevent further increases in atmospheric concentrations. At the same time the countries of the South – with increasing populations and developmental needs – will need to discharge a considerably higher percentage of global CO_2 emissions than previously. A system of internationally tradable permits (CO_2 certificates) is intended to transform a source of conflict into a productive relationship. This is in the meantime viewed as a promising way of limiting the threat of global warming at the international level, and of bringing about greater equity between North and South.[39]

CO_2 certificates are conceived as follows. First of all a global maximum CO_2 level is determined on the basis of the available data, and that is set as a standard. Then permits covering a specific period will be issued to each country – either free of charge or at fixed prices – in accordance with criteria discussed below.[40] Industrialized countries will receive considerably fewer permits than would cover the amount of CO_2 they are at present emitting, and most of the countries of the South considerably more. The one group can buy what the other does not use. That initiates international trading, which will be arranged and regulated by a clearing-house or kind of stock exchange. The turnover will be considerable, probably exceeding the total amount of current development aid.

Its advocates believe that the problems involved in fact-finding, control, and implementation are in part complicated but solvable. All the countries involved will have to be basically interested in making the system work, so national self-control, international ostracism of offenders, and a watchful public should ensure success.

Tradable CO_2 permits offer advantages to all those involved. For the South those benefits are obvious. The countries of the South will receive considerable funds furthering development. There will be a great incentive to protect the environment as much as possible so as to continue to have surplus permits. The recipients of development aid, of charity from donor countries, will become trading partners with equality of rights. Anil Agarwal thus asks whether this kind of exchange might replace the inequity of the system of development aid and project assistance that for the past 40 years has mainly served Western exporters and elites in the South.[41]

CO_2 certificates also offer advantages to the North. Because of its past and present over-use of the atmosphere the North will have to pay a considerable price for protecting climate anyway. That pressure to pay now becomes an incentive to pursue ecological structural change – such as tax reform – as quickly as possible. The North will also be able to market to the countries of the South the insights it gains and the technological innovations resulting from this transformation.

The means of distribution will probably constitute the most tricky problem. To arrive at quotas for initial permits a large range of criteria have been suggested, including countries' current emissions, their gross national product, their land area, the reductions already achieved, etc. Each of those criteria favours specific countries and puts others at a disadvantage. In our opinion, a fair criterion – the only one reflecting the equal right all people have to the global commons – would involve the size of a country's population at the time this agreement comes into effect.[42]

However, there are also serious objections to a system of tradable permits.[43] The agreement on CO_2 certificates is concluded between governments and they also receive the money. In the light of past experience it is by no means certain that the money will be used for overcoming poverty and dependence in the population at large, reaching the people meant to enjoy the global rights justly belonging to each individual. It is not unlikely that governments will mainly use the revenue from CO_2 certificates to finance modernization, copying the Northern example of ecologically and sociologically unenlightened progress, which only favours the middle and upper classes in these countries. The CO_2 certificate system offers no protection against this kind of use or abuse, but it does not prevent proper utilization either. It succeeds in part of what is necessary. In one important area this frees the South from its beggar's role and provides substantial means for the development of these countries. Equitable use of these certificates must be assured in different ways.

International funds

Sustainable development of the countries of the South is almost as important for the North as for the states directly concerned – because of the global consequences. However, the necessary funds are very scarce in the South. In the North ecological structural change is part of modernization of economies and serves competitiveness, thus providing powerful impetus towards transformation and release of financial potential. This thrust is almost completely lacking in the countries of the South. Ecologically and socially acceptable ways of life and means of production are thus only attainable there as part of joint international efforts. Without such assistance from the international community, poor countries will not be able either to put a stop to over-exploitation of their raw materials, or deal with the environmental damage that has already been done, or provide the unspoiled natural habitats the North desires.

Beyond the conventions referred to above,[44] CO_2 certificates, and debt relief, there will thus have to be one or several large funds. A number of suggestions about financing such funds have been put forward, but these still require careful scrutiny. The difficulties involved in establishing and managing such a worldwide fund, using the money purposefully and then checking up on that use, are immense. However, an attempt at institutionalizing international solidarity in this way is probably inescapable.

Among the possibilities are a global trade tax, a global income tax,[45] and what is known as the Tobin tax. The latter, suggested by James Tobin in 1978, puts a unified levy on all international financial deals involving an immediate exchange of currency. This should be collected by the governments involved and transferred to a fund administered by the IMF or the World Bank. The levy was originally directed against currency speculation which undermined the stability of exchange rates, but today such a tax would also serve another purpose: financing the great international tasks involved in environmental and development policies. It could thus increase the opportunities open to poor countries, particularly as they are especially hard hit by the rise and fall of exchange rates.

Debt relief

The great majority of the world's states are indebted, in the North and in the South. In 1994 the public debt in Germany amounted to 1.81 billion DM (about the same as state revenue that year) – and the figure for the USA in 1993 was 4.02 billion dollars. No matter how much such public debts may burden national economies, and how much worldwide indebtedness threatens the international financial system, this does not result in an acute crisis so long as the public purse services and repays loans on schedule.

That is just what has become impossible for many countries in the South. Since the start of the eighties there has been a debt crisis specific to the developing countries. General consensus exists about causes, but there is disagreement about extent, consequences, and possible solutions.[46]

According to the World Bank, in 1994 the foreign debts of all those states classified as developing countries amounted to 1.72 billion US dollars,[47] which was an increase of 7% compared with the previous year.

A number of threshold countries (such as South Korea, Malaysia, and Taiwan) have been very reliable in servicing and repaying their debts. Such countries continue to seek and find mainly private capital to finance economic advancement. Neither they nor their creditors are worried about these debts becoming excessive. But other countries have followed Mexico in declaring themselves insolvent, and have entirely or partially stopped payments or postponed them until later. Concerted international action, such as the Baker plan or the Brady initiative, aims at providing long-term relief for these and other indebted countries, reducing their old debts by means of rescheduling programmes and granting new credits. Whether efforts of this kind are successful for long much depends on what happens to interest rates.

However, the main source of concern must be a group of highly indebted Southern countries, which need more radical assistance to achieve sustainability.[48] They are almost crushed by their obligations – with serious social consequences. In order to service their debts and remain creditworthy, and also to maintain the privileges enjoyed by a small group of beneficiaries, most of them carry exploitation of raw materials to extremes, promote agro-industry for exports of cash crops, and simply accept the fact that this destroys habitats, drives out local populations, and depletes and contaminates the soil. The basic needs of the great majority of the population remain unfulfilled. The struggle against mass poverty does not take place.

In hardly any case has this strategy hindered further indebtedness. So changing the terms of debts, even when accompanied by partial debt release, is not the answer since – despite the temporary breathing space – it increases the long-term burden. Of course indebtedness is not the only cause of impoverishment, but it creates some problems and intensifies others. Resolving the debt crisis is thus not sufficient for getting the poor countries on their feet but it is a necessary prerequisite.

The poorest countries (SILICs – severely indebted low-income countries) should be accorded complete but not unconditional debt cancellation unless they are persistently guilty of serious infringements of human rights. The reasoning is as follows:

1. The release from debt must be complete since otherwise the entire economy will remain directed towards exporting products that can provide the foreign currency for servicing debts and maintaining creditworthiness – with the social and ecological consequences mentioned above. A social order and an economy which provide the general population with better chances of survival can only be established if the indebted country can choose how much it wishes to become involved in the world market, and if social movements seeking alternatives in those states do not run up against a wall of debts.
2. Debt release can be complete if public creditors are able to take a political decision to that effect (this applies to three-quarters of all credits for Africa). For more than a decade now, private banks in Germany have been able to write off such claims as depreciation – and what has been written off can no longer be demanded back from the poor. Nevertheless, fugitive funds that have been taken out of the countries in question must, wherever possible, not be included in debt relief.
3. Debt relief should in general be linked with specific social and ecological conditions. Involvement of social movements and non-profit-making, independent NGOs in individual countries in the distribution and administration of funds is therefore essential. Otherwise there is a danger that the amounts waived will be used to enrich the upper class, buy arms, or finance undertakings promising quick profits but actually prolonging social misery and the destruction of nature.

Highly indebted countries with a growing middle class (where there are often also many people existing below the poverty-line – India, Brazil, etc.) require partial, graded debt relief subject to certain conditions plus debt rescheduling with long contract periods and low stable interest rates to give these states more security in their planning.

The European Union and the countries of the South

Relations between the European Union (EU) and the countries of the South are determined by two differing, un-coordinated, and thus opposing tendencies.[49]

On the one hand the EU supports the countries of the South, particularly those with which it is linked through the colonial past. The ACP (African, Caribbean, and Pacific) states involved in the Lomé Conventions are guaranteed duty-free exports (with a few exceptions) to the EU without having to accept any obligation to liberalization in return. The General Preference System (GPS) provides the same guarantee for the poorest countries of the South and those most endangered by the cultivation of drugs, while other states are granted graduated tariffs. The ACP countries also receive partial protection against great fluctuations in their export earnings up to the year 2000 by way of two compensatory set-ups. In addition EU organizations concerned with co-operation and development make great efforts to improve self-sufficiency in poor countries in order to reduce the food imports that swallow up foreign currency. The EU also provides funds for the opening up of regional markets to alleviate the tough demands of the world market for countries only just starting to develop economically. The motivation involved is by no means purely altruistic, but the poor countries of the South do benefit directly.

What the EU gives with one hand, it takes away with the other. It simultaneously protects its own markets and European trade interests with measures that harm the countries supposed to be supported through development co-operation. That mainly occurs by way of restrictions on imports and subsidies for exports. This EU protectionism is primarily directed against countries in the South that have gained a degree of economic strength. For decades the North has contributed towards promotion of such development in its own image, but when those efforts bear fruit the countries concerned are viewed as competitors which should not gain easy access to European markets. However, those are not the only states hit by such restrictions. Also affected are the poor countries of the South, which are far from being serious competition.

With regard to import restrictions, the EU codification of tariffs is extensive with countless regulations about specific goods, grading, special conditions, and exceptions. Of course the underlying principle is clear. Raw materials that are important for European industry, including agro-industry, are welcome imports and thus duty-free. On the other hand, restrictions on amounts and tariffs complicate or prevent access to the European market for processed products. The poor countries of the South are particularly affected.[50]

Export subsidies place poor countries at a disadvantage in a different way. The EU uses such subsidies for disposing of its great agricultural surpluses on the world market. Meat and grain are the main exports to the developing countries. For instance in 1993/4 subsidies reduced the price of wheat exported to sub-Saharan Africa from 181 to 80 US dollars per tonne.[51] Locally grown grain cannot compete with such prices. The best-known example of export dumping is the sale of EU beef to coastal regions in West Africa, which ruined cattle-raising nomads in the Sahel zone.

A number of Southern governments welcome these cheap imports because they help save foreign exchange and offer inexpensive basic food for urban populations. Other countries, like Mali, have levied a tax on such imports and use the proceeds to supplement the national budget. On the whole, however, these subsidized exports harm the countries of the South. Local varieties of grain, such as millet and sorghum, are neglected, eating habits change, and the ability and motivation for self-sufficiency are lost and replaced by long-term dependence on imports which have to be paid for with foreign exchange.

The demands to be made of EU trading policy are thus:

- complete opening of EU markets to all raw materials *and* processed products from the countries of the South;
- no subsidies for agricultural products exported to poor countries, but instead support for the development of self-sufficiency in food;
- famine relief from EU stocks only if food cannot be bought at regional markets.

Stricter standards

Ecologizing ways of life and production can thus no longer be delayed even for the poor countries of the South – both for the sake of those countries themselves and because the demands of trading partners on the international market are changing. Managing economies at the expense of people and nature (section 4.2) has already led to severe local and regional damage. Eco-dumping may bring short-term profits; the absence of environmental protection regulations or their non-enforcement may attract investors – but such over-exploitation remains a sell-out of the future.

Rightly comprehended, even the trading interests of the countries of the South speak in favour of ecologically sound products and means of production. Anyone who wishes to export processed products alongside raw materials must adapt to a changed market in the industrial countries. The ecological demands made of imported products are rising, and these are expressed in many ways. Bans or limits on harmful substances are laid down by law (e.g. pentachlorophenol – PCP – in Germany), and seals of quality are intended to guarantee that products are environmentally and socially sound, not only in themselves but also in the production methods involved (carpets not made by child labour and tropical timber only from sustainable forestry). Information campaigns run by consumer organizations and groups interested in development policies promote certain goods or forms of production, and call for boycotts of others (Action Coco), while some large mail order companies make high demands of their suppliers and publicize these.

All that demands considerable adjustment on the part of producers in the South. The weaker their economies, the more these countries experience the bans, limits, conditions, and regulations set by the North as new trade barriers. Even where there is growing insight that this does not (only) involve an ecological diktat which the South must accept because of the North's market power but that it also entails protecting the local environment, the necessary adjustments may easily demand too much. There is justified concern that ecological renewal will burden Southern economies with demands that are too high too soon so that they will be strangulated by good intentions. The crucial questions are thus: Who is to set the standards? Who decides on the length of the transition period? Who assesses the motivation involved so that protection of the environment or health are not given as reasons where fending off competition is the real concern?

Finding sustainable answers to such questions calls for joint action among producers and buyers, exporting countries and importing countries, on a variety of levels and with incorporation of all those affected and involved in both South and North. Complete information must be available at a sufficiently early stage. With regard to government regulations, poor countries need a longer transition period and step-by-step changes. They also need financial assistance to achieve objectives for which they have scarcely any money of their own. This is one of the most important spheres of application for international funds.

However, most important of all is that ecological standards should also apply to those companies operating with capital from the North, which so often go unchecked or have special dispensations. Sustainability involves industrialized states taking on responsibility for what companies from their countries do in the South.[52] The EU already carries out obligatory environmental impact assessments and the Commission now wishes these to be made tougher.[53] Such assessments are also planned for large-scale bilateral and multilateral undertakings in the South. They must be extended to include social factors, consider the people concerned and their rights, and not simply make national administrations the ultimate authority. The people must have access to international arbitration to resolve their unfulfilled needs.

Learning together

Joint learning must today prove itself in a sphere where change is particularly sought: the development and transfer of sustainable technologies. The hope is that these will overcome poverty, assure food supplies, provide economic development, and protect nature. The predominant idea is that whatever is devised for attainment of sustainability in industrialized countries will also be suitable, with certain alterations and simplifications, for advancement of the countries of the South.

That may be true for a few already considerably industrialized countries, most of all, perhaps, for China. An entirely different principle, frequently confirmed by experience, applies to the poor countries of the South: useful technologies cannot be developed *for* partners in the South, only together *with* them. These must be technologies that allow users self-determination and responsibility for the consequences of their actions, create as little dependence as possible on foreign know-how and money, and in a joint learning-process establish a connection between traditional knowledge and Western science and technology. Such possibilities are exemplified by improved mills, methane installations, building with local materials, and solar heating systems. This process reflects the insight that technologies involve training, organization, and networking as well as machines and systems; that they create or break down social systems, change habits and values; that technologies are life-forms which do more harm than good if they cannot be rooted in local cultures.

The outcome of these integrated efforts does not only benefit users in the South; partners in the North are also enriched. It is of course wrong to think that adapted technologies are to some extent "village technologies" – simple, small-scale equipment for backward Third World countries. The term "appropriate technology" shows more clearly what is meant. These are technologies that are right, suitable, fitting for their purpose.[54] The North will learn that technology appropriate to the objective of sustainability must entail a combination of small-, medium-, and large-scale technology. Processes that used to flourish in Europe but were lost as a result of industrialization will return again by way of the South. The most striking example is provided by building technology. Other areas in which the North is learning from the South include biological pest control, use of medicinal plants, furniture design, water recycling systems,[55] and credit programmes in the slums of Northern cities modelled on the Grameen Bank in Bangladesh – just to mention a few examples.

Institutionalized forms of joint learning include links between local communities and NGOs in the North and South. There are several such communal partnerships between North and South, and two can be mentioned here.

"Towns & Development" wants to translate into action the insight that the industrialized countries need to be developed too – just like Third World states. That is to be achieved by way of twinning, arousing mutual awareness and promoting exchanges of experience with regard to health, education, technology, and transportation – and also carrying out projects in partner towns in the South (but why not also in the other direction: not just, for instance, Bremen's backing for development projects in Poona, but also Poona activities in Bremen?).

The "Climate Alliance"[56] is a group with a very specific target. Its efforts to integrate the social and political aspects of ecological sustainability are exemplary. A total of 423 European cities and 16 regional administrations[57] have agreed to reduce CO_2 emissions by 50% by the year 2010, to eliminate the production and use of CFCs, and avoid use of tropical timber in public works unless sustainable cultivation is guaranteed. At the same time they have established links with the Indian peoples of the Amazon Basin, providing political and financial support in the struggle for self-determination, land rights, and efforts to preserve the rain forest.[58] Campaigns will later extend to indigenous peoples from other regions. The reciprocity involved in this alliance has to date received expression in joint efforts towards protection of the climate, advocacy of partners in the South, and in the organization's administrative structures – but not as yet in any recognizable form of counselling of Northern partners by the South.

In conclusion – the term "development co-operation between North and South" has taken the place of "development aid", which could never rid itself of a condescending undertone. However, a change of words cannot by itself change a way of thinking. The flow is still (with exceptions) from North to South, with the North appearing as the more developed, the donor and teacher, and the South as the follower, the recipient, the learner.

From the perspective of sustainability that way of seeing things is completely unjustified. Both North and South still have to become sustainable. Both bring different abilities to this difficult process, and both have to relinquish or at least correct long-cherished guidelines. Lasting results will only be achieved if they learn together and from each other.

Notes

1. Arendt, 1958.
2. Dahrendorf, 1982/3.
3. For a comprehensive view: Fox, 1994; Giarini and Liedtke, 1996; Rifkin, 1995.
4. Bach et al., 1995.
5. Lepenies, 1995.
6. A still largely unexploited potential exists in the sphere of flexible forms of work and working hours. For Germany, for instance, the recently published McKinsey study of the labour market shows that with part-time work, job-sharing, and sabbaticals, 1.4 million new jobs, or 1.9 million new part-time jobs, could be created today without any additional costs for employers. Examples show that part-time work is worthwhile. For firms it brings constantly better results, avoidance of welfare costs, and retention of qualified staff. Employees can dispose over their time more freely and have greater job-security. State budgets are relieved and the social situation is improved. See also Sanne, 1992.
7. Wohlgenannt and Büchele, 1990.
8. Robertson, 1990.
9. Putnam, 1995.
10. For further reading, see: Kress, 1994; Theobald, 1967; Walter, 1989.
11. Apart from income tax there is the possibility of an energy (and raw materials) tax where revenue can be used for financing a basic wage. Employers' and employees' contributions to social insurance would then lapse.
12. For a critical view, see Krugman, 1994.
13. Krugman, 1991, uses models and data to show that, in a world where capital is mobile, transaction costs in trade really do play a decisive part in the strength of international competitive pressure.
14. More recent technological developments, especially in telecommunications, will free some services from the need for a fixed location. It is not yet clear whether these developments require more or less net materials and energy per service unit.
15. Only an economy capable of creating something new will over the long term avoid being economically steamrollered by others. The fact that this "new" element must also be ecologically acceptable goes without saying, and that is also becoming increasingly clear to those involved in other countries' economies. People in South Korea have already recognized that the competitive position achieved can be endangered over the long term by the country's ecological problems as well as by "backwardness" in the realm of public infrastructures. In these countries further successes can no longer be achieved by simply undercutting competitors' costs.
16. Hinterberger et al., 1996.
17. Cf. Bruyn and Opschoor, 1994; Jänicke et al., 1992.
18. Cf. Arrow et al., 1995.
19. Wissenschaftlicher Beirat für Globale Umweltveränderungen, 1993, pp. 138f.
20. For a general view, see Daly and Goodland, 1994.
21. See the section on "Consumption of Raw Materials" in this study. Just under half the total energy consumption is accounted for by housing and leisure activities. Similar findings apply to material input in the "Energy Consumption" section (both in chapter 5).

22. For a good summary of the relevant literature, see Klepper, 1994.

23. Other sections have shown that over the long term all industrial countries have no choice but to make the changeover to reduction of use of energy and raw materials. For Germany to go it alone would therefore only be a transitional state of affairs. It should therefore be called "leading the way".

24. UNCTAD, 1994b. On the problems involved in planning, see Khushi, 1992.

25. UNCTAD, 1994b. In 1992 total world exports amounted to US$3,662 billion. These 130 countries only accounted for US$133 billion. Almost the whole of world trade thus takes place between the industrial nations and 20 or so threshold countries and the oil states.

26. According to an estimate presented to the World Commission on Environment and Development, the industrial countries would have to pay US$14 billion more each year for their imports of raw materials if environmental standards in the source countries were the same as in the USA. Quoted from Knox, 1991.

27. See also Buntzel, 1994, 1995; FAO, 1995; Page and Davenport, 1994; Suliman, 1995.

28. Goldin et al., 1992.

29. Cf. also the discussion between Bhagwati and Daly, 1994.

30. See note 32.

31. Agarwal and Narain, 1993.

32. Two research institutes for alternative development in the South – the Institute for African Alternatives (Mohamed Suliman) and the Centre for Science and Environment (Ravi Sharma, New Delhi) – made particularly valuable contributions to these proposals and plans. They have been incorporated in this chapter, citing the authors' names.

33. Cf. Egger et al., 1992; Massarrat, 1993.

34. Wood, 1992.

35. On the development and practical application of the Montreal Convention, see Gehring, 1994; Greene, 1993.

36. World Wide Fund for Nature, 1995.

37. Massarrat, 1993.

38. "It is to our advantage that your project is politically successful, not just politically correct." Suliman, 1995.

39. UNCTAD, 1992, 1994a, 1995. The use of internationally tradable permits is discussed in terms of CO_2 certificates because discussions are furthest advanced there.

40. The suggestion that permits should be auctioned would result in destruction of attempts at achieving a balance between North and South.

41. Agarwal, 1994.

42. See also Ravi Sharma (1995), who would, however, also incorporate population projections far into the next millennium. He would also like to see retrospective attention devoted to over-use by industrial nations during past centuries. Such an expansion would probably lead to never-ending disputes and block the way to agreement.

43. Well summarized in Sharan and Sharan-Meili, 1994, pp. 32ff.

44. To the operative areas of the Global Environment Facility (GEF) belongs protection of international waters and the ozone layer – as well as greenhouse gases and biodiversity.

45. UNDP, 1994, p. 91.

46. On the overall complex and differing assessments, see: Eberlei and Fues,

1995; George, 1987 and 1992.

47. Estimated value (without Eastern Europe), World Bank, 1994. In fact that does not even amount to 40% of the USA's debts.

48. That mainly involves the 32 countries (without Nigeria) which the World Bank calls severely indebted low-income countries (SILICs), but also takes in 15 countries in the lower half of the next category (SILMICs). In 1993 the former had an average income of less than US$695 per head, while the latter figure was between US$696 and US$1720. The World Bank calls countries highly indebted if debt-servicing exceeds 80% of the GNP or 220% of annual exports. World Bank, 1995a, pp. 250ff.

49. Cf. Walter, 1994; Wiemann, 1994.

50. Escalating customs duties as raw materials are increasingly processed can be well illustrated in the case of cotton products. Raw cotton can be imported into the EU duty-free, but for cotton-thread (for commercial use) from the ACP countries 4.9% duty is imposed, for cotton fabric 8.3%, and for T-shirts 10.6%. Textile duties run until the year 2005. Similar "cascade duties" apply to coffee products. Raw coffee from ACP countries is duty-free; for decaffeinated raw coffee the EU duty is 8.5%; for roasted coffee 11.5%; for decaffeinated roasted coffee 12.5%; and for instant coffee 13%. Exceptions are made for 54 particularly poor areas affected by the cultivation of drugs, and also for five Central American states. Additional examples are provided by shoes, processed wood, etc.

51. Walter, 1994, p. 61.

52. In Germany the state-backed Hermes organizations provide an effective means of checking whether support is being given to the export of goods that hinder autonomous development in importing countries, initiate capital-intensive enterprises with high ongoing costs, directly or indirectly infringe human rights, or are ecologically harmful.

53. COM (93) 575, 16.3.1994.

54. Gate, 1993.

55. For thousands of years now the Chinese have been using recycling cycles. A garden pond serves as a toilet and for absorption of household waste. Hyacinths in the pond purify the water, fish eat the hyacinths, are themselves eaten – and the cycle begins anew.

56. Klima-Bündnis, 1993, 1994.

57. As of June 1995.

58. From an application by the Confederation of Indian Nations in the Ecuadoran Amazon Area: "The amount of leaked oil polluting rivers and land in the Amazon area has long exceeded what was involved in the *Exxon Valdez* catastrophe."

Bibliography

Adams, F. et al. (1986), "The Benefits of Pollution Control. The Case of Ozone and US Agriculture", *American Journal of Agricultural Economics*, 68, pp. 886–94.

Agarwal, A. (1994), "Forderungen des Südens an die Industrieländer des Nordens", in M. Henze and G. Kaiser (eds), *Ökologie-Dialog. Umweltmanager und Umweltschützer im Gespräch*. Düsseldorf et al., pp. 27–35.

Agarwal, A. and Narain, S. (1991), *Global Warming in an Unequal World. A Case of Environmental Colonialism*. New Delhi.

Agarwal, A. and Narain, S. (1993), "Towards Green Villages", in W. Sachs (ed.), *Global Ecology. A New Arena of Political Conflict*. London, pp. 242–56.

Alt, F. (1995), "Kostenlos – Erneuerbare Energien reichen", *Frankfurter Allgemeine Zeitung*, 9.5.

Apel, D. et al. (1995), *Möglichkeiten zur Steuerung des Flächenverbrauchs und der Verkehrsentwicklung. Zwischenbericht*. Berlin.

Arendt, H. (1958), *The Human Condition*. Chicago.

Arrow, K. et al. (1995), "Economic Growth, Carrying Capacity, and the Environment", *Science*, 268, pp. 520–1.

Ayres, R.U. and Simonis, U.E. (eds) (1992), *Industrial Metabolism*. Tokyo and New York.

Bach, W. (1993), *Mögliche Energiesparmaßnahmen und CO_2-Reduktion für die Bundesrepublik Deutschland*. Münster.

Bach, W. et al. (1995), *Wirtschaftliche Auswirkungen einer ökologischen Steuerreform*. DIW-Sonderheft No. 153. Berlin.

Barbier, E.B. (1989), *Economics, Natural-Resource Scarcity and Development. Conventional and Alternative Views*. London.

Beer, J.G. de et al. (1994), *ICARUS-3. The Potential of Energy Efficiency Improvements in the Netherlands up to 2000 and 2010*. Paper No. 94013. Utrecht, University of Utrecht, Department of Science, Technology and Society.

Behrensmeier, R. and Bringezu, S. (1995a), *Zur Methodik der volkswirtschaftlichen Material-Intensitäts-Analyse. Ein quantitativer Vergleich des Umweltverbrauchs der bundesdeutschen Produktionssektoren*. Wuppertal Paper No. 34. Wuppertal: WIKUE.

Behrensmeier, R. and Bringezu, S. (1995b), *Zur Methodik der volkswirtschaftlichen Material-Intensitäts-Analyse. Der bundesdeutsche Umweltverbrauch nach Bedarfsfeldern*.

Wuppertal Paper. Wuppertal: WIKUE.

Bergen-Report (1990), *Sustainable Development, Science and Policy.* A Conference organized by the Norwegian Research Council for Science and Humanities in Liaison with the European Science Foundation, and in Cooperation with the Regional Conference on the Report of the World Commission on Environment and Development in ECE Region. Bergen, 8–16 May 1990. Oslo.

Bhagwati, J. and Daly H.E. (1993), "Debate: Does Free Trade Harm the Environment", *Scientific American*, November, pp. 17–29.

Bhagwati, J. and Daly H.E. (1994), *Spektrum der Wissenschaft/Scientific American*, 1, pp. 33–46.

Bleischwitz, R. and Schütz, H. (1993), *Unser trügerische Wohlstand.* Wuppertal: WIKUE.

Bode, W. and Hohnhorst, M. von (1994), *Waldwende. Vom Försterwald zum Naturwald.* Munich.

BP (British Petroleum) (ed.) (1994), *BP Statistical Review of World Energy. June 1994.* London.

Bringezu, S. and Schütz, H. (1995), "Wie mißt man die ökologische Zukunftsfähigkeit einer Volkswirtschaft? Ein Beitrag der Stoffstrombilanzierung am Beispiel der Bundesrepublik Deutschland", in S. Bringezu (ed.), *Neue Ansätze der Umweltstatistik. Ein Wuppertaler Werkstattgespräch. Wuppertal Texte.* Berlin et al.

Brown-Weiss, E. (1990), "In Fairness to Future Generations", *Environment*, 32(3).

Bruyn, S.M. de and Opschoor, J.B. (1994), *Is the Economy Ecologising? De- or Relinking Economic Development with the Environment.* Amsterdam: Tinbergen Institute.

BUND/Misereor (eds) (1996), *Zukunfstfähiges Deutschland. Ein Beitag zu einer global nachhaltigen Entwicklung.* Basle et al.

Buntzel, R. (1994), "GATT-Ergebnisse nach Marrakesch", *BUKO Agrar-Info*, 32.

Buntzel, R. (1995), "Vom neuen Welthandelssystem haben die Armen wenig zu erwarten", *Frankfurter Rundschau*, 11.1.

Burdick, B. (1994), *Klimaänderung und Landbau. Die Agrarwirtschaft als Täter und Opfer.* Heidelberg.

Busch-Lüty, C. (1994), "Sustainability. Elemente einer am Leitbild der Nachhaltigkeit orientierten ökologischen Ökonomie", in B. Biervert and Held, M. (eds), *Das Naturverständnis in der Ökonomik.* Frankfurt. et al.

Canzler, W. and Knie, A. (1994), *Das Ende des Automobils.* Heidelberg.

Charta der Europäischen Städte and Gemeinden auf dem Weg zur Zukunftsbeständigkeit (Charta von Aalborg) (1994), *Die Kampagne europäischer zukunftsbeständiger Städte und Gemeinden.* Brussels.

Cobb, C. and Cobb, J. (eds) (1994), *The Green National Product. A Proposed Index of Sustainable Economic Welfare.* New York.

Costanza, Robert (ed.) (1991), *Ecological Economics. The Science and Management of Sustainability.* New York.

Crowhurst Lennard, S.H. and Lennard, H.L. (1995), *Livable Cities Observed. A Source Book of Images and Ideas.* Carmel, CA.

Crucible Group (1994), *People, Plants, and Patents. The Impact of Intellectual Property on Biodiversity, Conservation, Trade, and Rural Society.* Ottawa: IDRC.

Dahrendorf, R. (1982/3), "Wenn der Arbeitsgesellschaft die Arbeit ausgeht", in J. Matthes (ed.), *Krise der Arbeitsgesellschaft? Verhandlungen des 21. Deutschen Soziologentages in Bamberg.* Frankfurt. et al., pp. 25f.

Daly, H. (1990), "Towards Some Operational Principles of Sustainable Development", *Ecological Economics*, 2, pp. 1–6.

Daly, H. and Cobb, J. (1989), *For the Common Good. Redirecting the Economy toward*

Community, the Environment, and a Sustainable Future. Boston.

Daly, H. and Goodland, R. (1994), "An Ecological-Economic Assessment of Deregulation of International Commerce under GATT", *Ecological Economics* (special issue on trade and the environment), 9, pp. 73–84.

Data Resources Institute (DRI) (1994), *Potential Benefits of Integration of Environmental and Economic Policies.* London.

D'Aveni, R. (1994), *Hypercompetition.* New York.

Derrick, A. et al. (1993), *Photovoltaics. A Market Overview.* London.

Deutsche Bundesbahn (ed.) (1992), *Stellungnahme zur Verkehrsanhörung der Enquete-Kommission "Schutz der Erdatmosphäre". CO_2-Minderung im Verkehr durch Aktivierung besserer Technik und Organisation (Verkehr II).* Kommissionsdrucksache 12/8–e.

Dieren, W. van (ed.) (1995), *Taking Nature into Account. A Report to the Club of Rome.* New York.

Dittmar, H. (1992), *The Social Psychology of Material Possessions. To Have Is To Be.* Hemel Hempstead.

Douglas, M. and Isherwood, B. (1978), *The World of Goods. Towards an Anthropology of Consumption.* New York.

Dutch Advisory Council for Research on Nature and Environment (ed.) (1994a), *Towards Environmental Performance Indicators Based on the Notion of Environmental Space.* Rijswijk.

Dutch Advisory Council for Research on Nature and Environment (ed.) (1994b), *Sustainable Resource Management and Resource Use. Policy Questions and Research Needs.* Rijswijk.

Eberlei, W. and Fues, T. (1995), *Schuldenreport 1995. Plädoyer für ein Sofortprogramm.* Bonn: WEED.

Edwards, C.A. et al. (1990), *Sustainable Agricultural Systems.* Delray Beach, FL.

Egger, U. et al. (1992), *Internationale Agrarmärkte.* Zurich.

Ekins, P.P. (1992), "Sustainability First", in P. P. Ekins and M. Max-Neef (eds), *Real-Life Economics.* London.

Elkin, T. and McLaren, D. (1991), *Reviving the City. Towards Sustainable Urban Development.* London.

Enquete-Kommission "Schutz der Erdatmosphäre" (ed.) (1992), *Klimaänderung gefährdet globale Entwicklung. Zukunft sichern – jetzt handeln.* Karlsruhe (published in English: Enquete Commission "Protecting the Earth's Atmosphere" of the German Bundestag, *Climate Change. A Threat to Global Development.* Bonn 1992).

Enquete-Kommission "Schutz der Erdatmosphäre" (ed.) (1994a), *Schutz der grünen Erde. Klimaschutz durch umweltgerechte Landwirtschaft und Erhalt der Wälder.* Bonn.

Enquete-Kommission "Schutz der Erdatmosphäre" (ed.) (1994b), *Mobilität und Klima. Wege zu einer klimaverträglichen Verkehrspolitik.* Bonn.

Enquete-Kommission "Schutz der Erdatmosphäre" (ed.) (1994c), *Landwirtschaft. Studienprogramm.* Vol. 1. Parts I and II. Bonn.

Enquete-Kommission "Schutz der Erdatmosphäre" (ed.) (1994d), *Verkehr. Studienprogramm.* Vol. 4. Bonn.

Enquete-Kommission "Schutz der Erdatmosphäre" (ed.) (1995), *Mehr Zukunft für die Erde. Nachhaltige Energiepolitik für dauerhaften Klimaschutz.* Bonn.

Enquete-Kommission "Schutz des Menschen und der Umwelt" (ed.) (1996), *Die Industriegesellschaft gestalten. Perspektiven für einen nachhaltigen Umgang mit Stoff- und Materialströmen.* Bonn.

Enquete-Kommission "Vorsorge zum Schutz der Erdatmospäre" (ed.) (1990), *Schutz der Erde. Eine Bestandsaufnahme mit Vorschlägen zu einer neuen Energiepolitik.* Vols 1 and 2. Bonn (published in English: Enquete Commission "Protecting the Earth's Atmosphere" of the German Bundestag, *Protecting the Earth. A Status Report with Recommendations for a New Energy Policy*, Vols 1 and 2, Bonn 1991).

European Commission (1991), *EG-KOM 100/91*.

European Commission (1993), *Berichte und Informationen*, No. 13, 5.5; Europäische Kommission, Vertretung in der Bundesrepublik Deutschland (ed.).

European Commission (1994), *European Economy, Annual Economic Report 1994*. Luxemburg.

European Environment Agency (1996), *Environmental Taxes. Implementation and Environmental Effectiveness*. Copenhagen.

FAO (Food and Agricultural Organization) (ed.) (1995), *Impact of the Uruguay-Round on Agriculture*. Committee on Commodity Problems. Rome.

Flitner, M. (1993), "Biologische Vielfalt nach UNCED – Erhaltung durch wen, Erhaltung für wen?", in S. Jutzi and B. Becker (eds), *Der Tropenlandwirt*. Beiheft No. 49.

Fox, M. (1994), *The Reinvention of Work. A New Vision of Livelihood for Our Time*. San Francisco.

Fraunhofer-Institut für Systemtechnik und Innovationsforschung (ISI) and Deutsches Institut für Wirtschaftsforschung (DIW) (1994), *Gesamtwirtschaftliche Auswirkungen von Emissionsminderungsstrategien. Studie im Autrag der Enquete-Kommission "Schutz der Erdatmosphäre"*. Karlsruhe et al.

Friends of the Earth Europe (ed.) (1995), *Towards Sustainable Europe*. Brussels.

Friends of the Earth Netherlands (Milieudefensie) (ed.) (1993), *Action Plan Sustainable Netherlands*. Amsterdam.

Friends of the Earth USA (1994), *The Green Solution to Red Ink*. Washington, DC.

Friends of the Earth USA (1995), *Green Scissors*. Washington, DC.

Friends of the Earth USA (1996), *Roads to Ruin*. Washington, DC.

Fussler, C. (1996), *Driving Eco-Innovation*. London.

GATE (ed.), *Appropriate Technology in Postmodern Times*. Braunschweig.

Gehring, T. (1994), *Dynamic International Regimes. Institutions for International Environmental Governance*. Frankfurt.

George, S. (1987), *A Fate Worse Than Debt*. London.

George, S. (1992), *The Debt Boomerang*. London.

Gethmann, C.F. and Mittelstraß, J. (1992), "Maße für die Umwelt", *Gaia*, 1, pp. 16–25.

Gettkant, A. (1995), "Suche nach dem grünen Diamanten", in J. Wolters (ed.), *Leben und leben lassen. Biodiversität – Ökonomie, Natur- und Kulturschutz im Widerstreit*. Giessen, p. 116.

Giarini, O. and Liedtke, P.M. (1996), *The Employment Dilemma and the Future of Work. A Report to the Club of Rome*. Geneva.

Girardet, H. (1993), *The Gaia Atlas of Cities. New Directions for Sustainable Urban Living*. London.

Girardet, H. (1996), *The Gaia Atlas of Cities. New Directions for Sustainable Urban Living (featuring Habitat II)*. London.

Goldin, I. et al. (1992), *Trade Liberalisation. What's at Stake?* Paris: OECD.

Graedel, T., Graedel, E. and Allenby, B. (1995), *Industrial Ecology*. Englewood Cliffs, NJ.

Graskamp, R. (1992), *Umweltschutz, Strukturwandel und Wirtschaftswachstum*. Untersuchungen des Rheinisch-Westfälischen Instituts für Wirtschaftsforschung No. 4. Essen.

Greene, O. (1993), "Limiting Ozone Depletion. The 1992 Review Process and the

Development of the Montreal Protocol", in J.B. Poole (ed.), *Verification 1993*. London et al.

Greenpeace (ed.) (1994), *Was kostet der Atomausstieg?* Hamburg.

Greenpeace (ed.) and Deutsches Institut für Wirtschaftsforschung (DIW) (1994), *Ökosteuer – Sackgasse oder Königsweg? Wirtschaftliche Auswirkungen einer ökologischen Steuerreform*. Berlin.

Greenpeace International and Stockholm Environment Institute (1993), *Towards a Fossil Free Energy Future. The Next Energy Transition*. Boston.

Grubb, M. (1989), *The Greenhouse Effect. Negotiating Targets*. London: Royal Institute of International Affairs, pp. 36ff.

Grübler, A. (1993), "Emissions Reduction at the Global Level", in International Institute for Applied System Analysis (IIASA), *Energy*, 18(5), pp. 539–81.

Guehenno, J.-M. (1994), *Das Ende der Demokratie*. Munich.

Haas, G. and Köpke, U./Institut für Organischen Landbau an der Universität Bonn (1994), "Vergleich der Klimarelevanz ökologischer und konventioneller Landbewirtschaftung", in Enquete-Kommission "Schutz der Erdatmosphäre" (ed.), *Landwirtschaft. Studienprogramm*, Vol. 1. Parts I and II. Bonn.

Hansen, U. and Schoenheit, I. (1993), "Was belohnen die Konsumenten?", *Absatzwirtschaft*, 12.

Harborth, H.-J. (1991), *Dauerhafte Entwicklung statt globaler Selbstzerstörung*. Berlin.

Haughton, G. and Hunter, C. (1994), *Sustainable Cities*. London.

Hawken, P. (1993), *The Ecology of Commerce*. New York.

Heerings, H. and Zeldenrust, I. (1995), *Elusive Saviours*. Utrecht.

Heins, V. (1993), " 'Survival of the Fattest?' – Genetische Ressourcen und globale Biopolitik", *Peripherie*, 51–2, pp. 69–85.

Hennicke, P. (ed.) (1986), *Die Energiewende ist möglich*. Frankfurt.

Hennicke, P. et al. (1994), *Nutzen und Kosten von Energiesparmaßnahmen. Vorschläge für neue Förderinstrumente. Studie des Wuppertal Instituts im Auftrag der Deutschen Ausgleichsbank*. Wuppertal: WIKUE (unpublished).

Herrmann, G. (1996), "Ökolandbau und Welternährung – Strategie oder Utopie?", *Ökologie und Landbau*, 2, pp. 18–20.

Hinterberger, F. et al. (1995), *What is "Natural Capital"?* Wuppertal Paper 29. Wuppertal.

Hinterberger, F. et al. (1996), *Ökologische Wirtschaftspolitik: Zwischen Ökodiktatur und Umweltkatastrophe*. Basle et al.

Hoffmann, A./Clearing House for Applied Futures (1995), "Bielefeld Waldquelle – Europe's Most Sustainable City Planning Project?", *INEM Bulletin*, 4(1), 1995, p. 12.

Hoffmann-Kroll, R. and Wirthmann, A. (1993), "Wandel der Bodennutzung und Bodenbedeckung", *Wirtschaft und Statistik*, 10, pp. 70–780.

Hohmeyer, O. and Gärtner, M. (1992), *The Costs of Climate Change: A Rough Estimate of Orders of Magnitude*. Karlsruhe.

Holtz-Eakin, D. (1992), *Public Sector Capital and the Productivity Puzzle*. National Bureau of Economic Research WP No. 4122.

Hörning, K. H. et al. (1990), *Zeitpioniere. Flexible Arbeitszeiten – neuer Lebensstil*. Frankfurt.

Hüttler, W. and Payer, H (1994), *Wasser und Wirtschaftswachstum. Schriftenreihe Soziale Ökologie*. Vol. 38. Vienna: Interuniversitäres Institut für interdisziplinäre Forschung und Fortbildung (IFF).

Inglehart, R. (1977), *The Silent Revolution*. London.

Institut für Straßen- und Verkehrswesen (ISV) (ed.) (1990a), "Maßnahmenprogramm zur Technologieentwicklung im Verkehrsbereich. Trendszenario", in Enquete-Kommission "Vorsorge zum Schutz der Erdatmosphäre" (ed.), *Schutz der Erde. Eine Bestandsaufnahme mit Vorschlägen zu einer neuen Energiepolitik*. Vol. 2. Bonn, pp. 429–86.

Intergovernmental Panel on Climate Change (IPCC) (ed.) (1994), *Climate Change 1994. Radiative Forcing of Climate Change*. Cambridge.

International Panel on Climate Change (IPCC) (1996), *IPCC Second Scientific Assessment of Climate Change*. Cambridge et al.

Jänicke, M. (1993), *Ökologisch tragfähige Entwicklung, Kriterien und Steuerungsansätze ökologischer Ressourcenpolitik*. FFU-Report 93–7. Berlin.

Jänicke, M. (1995), "Tragfähige Entwicklung. Anforderungen an die Umweltberichterstattung aus Sicht der Politikanalyse", in S. Bringezu (ed.), *Neue Ansätze der Umweltstatistik*. Wuppertal Texte. Basle.

Jänicke, M. et al. (1992), *Umweltentlastung durch industrielen Strukturwandel? Eine explorative Studie über 32 Industrieländer (1970–1990)*. Berlin FFU an der Freien Universität Berlin.

Jarass, L. (1993), Annex 1 (to L. Jarass and G. Obermaier, *More Jobs, Less Pollution*, 1994). *Data on Energy Taxes and Prices*. Wiesbaden.

Jarass, L. and Obermaier, G. (1994), *More Jobs, Less Pollution. A Tax Policy for an Improved Use of Production Factors*. Wiesbaden.

Kabou, A. (1993), *Weder ohnmächtig noch arm*. Basle.

Kaiser, K. et al. (1991), *Internationale Klimapolitik*. Bonn.

Keeling, C.D. (1994), "Global Historical CO_2–Emissions", in T. A. Boden et al. (eds), *Trends '93. A Compendium on Global Change*. Oak Ridge, CA.

Khushi, M. Khan (ed.) (1992), *Die ärmsten Länder in der Weltwirtschaft*. Hamburg.

Kjer, I. et al. (1994), "Landwirtschaft und Ernährung. Teil A. Quantitative Analysen und Fallstudien", in Enquete-Kommission "Schutz der Erdatmosphäre" (ed.), *Landwirtschaft. Studienprogramm*. Vol. 1. Parts I and II. Bonn.

Klemmer, P. et al. (1993), "Globale Umweltveränderungen und institutioneller Rahmen", *Zeitschrift für angewandte Umweltforschung*, Special Issue No. 4, p. 72.

Klepper, G. (1994), *Trade Implications of Environmental Taxes*. Kiel Working Paper No. 628. Kiel.

Klima-Bündnis (ed.) (1993), *Klima – lokal geschützt! Aktivität europäischer Kommunen*. Munich.

Klima-Bündnis/Alianza del Clima (eds) (1994), *Amazonasindianer am Main. Die Klima-Bündnis-Stadt Frankfurt und ihre Partnerschaft mit den Aguaruna- und Huambisa-Indianern Perus*. Frankfurt.

Kluge, T. et al. (1995), *Wasserwende. Wie die Wasserkrise in Deutschland bewältigt werden kann*. Munich.

Kneese, A.V. et al. (1970), *Economics and Environment. A Material Balance Approach*. Baltimore et al.

Knox, H.L.M. (1994), *World Development*, 9, pp. 933–43.

Kohlmeier, L. et al. (1993), *Ernährungsbedingte Krankheiten und ihre Kosten*. Baden-Baden.

Korten, D.C. (1995), *When Corporations Rule the World*. Hartford, CT.

Kothari, R. (1993), *Growing Amnesia*. New Delhi.

Krause, F. et al. (1993), *Energy Policy in the Greenhouse. Cutting Carbon Emissions. Burden or Benefit?* El Cerrito: IPSEP.

Kress, U. (1994), "Die negative Einkommenssteuer. Arbeitsmarktwirkungen und sozialpolitische Bedeutung. Ein Literaturbericht", *MittAB*, 3, pp. 246–54.

Krugman, P. (1991), *Geography and Trade.* Cambridge, MA.

Krugman, P. (1994), "Competitiveness, A Dangerous Obsession", *Foreign Affairs*, 73(2), March–April, pp. 28–44.

Kühbauch, W. (1993), "Intensität der Landnutzung im Wandel der Zeiten", in *Geowissenschaften*, 11(4), pp. 121–9.

Kuhn, M. et al. (1994), "Umweltökonomische Trends 1960 bis 1990", *Wirtschaft und Statistik*, 8, pp. 658–77.

Kumar, P. (1993), "Biotechnology and Biodiversity. A Dialectic Relationship", *Journal of Scientific and Industrial Research*, 52, pp. 523–32.

Lehmann, H. and Reetz, T. (1995), *Zukunftsenergien. Strategien einer neuen Energiepolitik.* Basle and Berlin.

Lepenies, W. (1995), "Notizen zu Ernst Jüngers Säkulum", *Neue Zürcher Zeitung*, 71.

Linz, M. (1994), "Der aufgeklärte Eigennutz", in H. Däubler-Gmelin (ed.), *Gegenrede. Aufklärung-kritik Öffentlichkeit.* Baden-Baden.

Loske, R. (1992), "Harmonisierung als Fluchtpunkt. Beim Klimaschutz versteckt sich die EG hinter dem Nichtstun anderer", *IÖW-Informationsdienst*, 5, p. 4.

Loske, R. (1996), "Die Dichte als Chance. Ein Essay zu den Konturen zukunftsfähiger Stadtentwicklung", *Raumforschung und Raumordnung*, 54(2/3), pp. 98–102, Cologne.

Lovins, A. et al. (1983), *WirtschaftlichtserEnergeeinsatz. Lösung des CO_2–Problems.* Karlsruhe.

Lunde, L. (1991), "North–South and Global Warming. Conflict or Cooperation?", *Bulletin of Peace Proposals*, 22(2).

McNeely, J. A. (ed.) (1990), *Conserving the World's Biological Diversity.* Washington, DC: World Bank.

MacPherson, C. B. (1967), "The Maximization of Democracy", in P. Laslett and W. G. Runciman (eds), *Philosophy, Politics, and Society.* Oxford.

Maier-Rigaud, G. (1990), "Die Rolle der EG im Verkehrssektor", in Enquete-Kommission "Vorsorge zum Schutz der Erdatmosphäre" (ed.), *Schutz der Erde. Eine Bestandsaufnahme mit Vorschlägen zu einer neuen Energiepolitik.* Vol. 1. Bonn, pp. 921–950.

Marland, G. et al. (1994), "Global, Regional and National CO_2-Emissions", in T. A. Boden et al. (eds), *Trends '93. A Compendium on Global Change.* Oak Ridge, CA.

Massarrat, M. (1993), *Endlichkeit der Natur und Überfluß in der Marktökonomie.* Marburg.

Mayer-Tasch, P.C. (1987), *Die verseuchte Landkarte. Das grenzenlose Versagen der internationalen Umweltpolitik.* Munich.

Meadows, D. (1972), *The Limits to Growth.* New York.

Meadows, D. et al. (1992), *Beyond the Limits.* Vermont.

Merten, T. et al. (1995), *Materialintensitätsanalysen von Grund-, Werk- und Baustoffen (1). Die Werkstoffe Beton und Stahl.* Wuppertal Paper No. 27. Wuppertal: WIKUE.

Mill, J.S. (1984), *Principles of Political Economy.*

Ministerium für Wohnungswesen, Raumordnung and Umwelt der Niederlande (ed.) (1994), *Zweites Nationales Maßnahmenprogramm für die Umweltpolitik.* The Hague.

Ministry of the Environment Denmark (ed.) (1994), *A National Policy on the Urban Environment and Planning.* Copenhagen.

Mireku, E. (1992), "Strukturreformen für die Schweiz", *Beilage zu I3W aktuell*, 9.

Moll, P. (1991), *From Scarcity to Sustainability. Future Studies and the Environment: The Role of the Club of Rome.* Frankfurt.

Moret, Ernst and Young (1996), *European Commission Tax Provisions with Potential Impact on Environmental Protection*. Brussels, September.

Müller, M. and Hennicke, P. (1994), *Wohlstand durch Vermeiden. Mit der Ökologie aus der Krise*. Darmstadt.

Münchener Rückversicherungs-Gesellschaft (ed.) (1993), *Immer mehr und teurere Naturkatastrophen – Volkswirtschaftliche Schäden erstmals bei 100 Mrd. DM, davon 40 Mrd. versichert*. Munich, 19.4.

Niang-Diop, I. (1994), "Impacts of Climate Change in Coastal Communities. The Senegal Example". Paper presented to the IPCC Workshop on "The Climate Change Issue, Equity and Social Aspects", Nairobi.

Nitsch, J. (1995), "Erneuerbare Energiequellen in Deutschland – Technische und ökonomische Bewertung sowie strukturelle Effekte bei ihrer Einführung". Manuscript. Stuttgart.

OECD (1993), *OECD Environmental Performance Reviews*. Paris.

OECD (1996), *Subsidies and Environment: Exploring the Linkages*. Paris.

Öko-Institut and Wuppertal Institut (ed.) (1994), *Least-Cost Planning. Fallstudie Hannover der Stadtwerke Hannover AG*. Supplementary Vol. I. Freiburg et al.

Opschoor, J.B. (1992), *Environment, Economics and Sustainable Development*. Groningen.

Opschoor, J.B. (1994), *Economic Incentives and Environmental Policies*. Dordrecht.

Opschoor, J. and Costanza, R. (1995), "Indicators of Sustainability", in K. Gundlach et al. (eds), *Global Environmental Change and Sustainable Development in Europe*.

Österreichische Bundesregierung (ed.) (1995), *NUP – Nationaler Umweltplan*. Vienna.

Page, S. and Davenport, M. (1994), *World Trade Reform. Do Developing Countries Gain or Lose?* London: Overseas Development Institute.

Pastowski, A. et al. (1994), "Potentiale an Verkehrsvermeidung durch Raumstruktur", in Enquete-Kommission "Schutz der Erdatmosphäre" (ed.), *Verkehr. Studienprogramm*. Vol. 4. Bonn.

Pearce, D.W. et al. (1989), *Blueprint for a Green Economy. Report for the UK Department of the Environment*. London.

Pearce, D.W. and Turner, R.K. (1990), *Economics of Natural Resources and the Environment*. Baltimore.

Pearce, D.W. and Warford, J.J. (1993), *World without End: Economics, Environment, and Sustainable Development*. New York.

Petersen, M. (1993), *Ökonomische Analyse des Car-Sharing*. Berlin Technische Universität.

Petersen, R. and Schallaböck, K.O. (1995), *Mobilität für morgen. Chancen einer zukunftsfähigen Verkehrspolitik*. Basle and Berlin.

Pfriem, R. (1995), *Unternehmenspolitik in sozialökologischer Perspektive*. Marburg.

Pimentel, D. et al. (1989), *Food and Natural Resources*. San Diego et al.

Plowden, S. and Hillmann, M. (1996), *Speed Control and Transport Policy*. London: PSI.

Porter, M.E. (1989), *The Competitive Advantage of Nations*. New York et al.

Putnam, R.D. (1995), "Bowling Alone. America's Declining Social Capital", *Journal of Democracy*.

Rees, W. and Wackernagel, M. (1994), "Ecological Footprints and Appropriated Carrying Capacity. Measuring the Natural Capital Requirements of the Human Economy", in A.-M. Jansson et al. (1994), *Investing in Natural Capital. The Ecological Economic Approach to Sustainability*. Washington, DC et al., pp. 362–92.

Reid, W.V. et al. (1993), "A New Lease on Life", in W.V. Reid (ed.), *Biodiversity Prospecting. Using Genetic Resources for Sustainable Development*. Washington, DC: WRI.

Rifkin, J. (1995), *The End of Work*. New York.

Robertson, J. (1990), *Future Wealth: A New Economics for the 21st Century*. London.

Roodman, D.M. (1996), *Paying the Piper. Subsidies, Politics, and the Environment*. World Watch Paper No. 133. December. Washington, DC.

Sachs, W. (1992a), *For Love of the Automobile. Looking Back into the History of Our Desires*. Berkeley.

Sachs, W. (ed.) (1992b), *The Development Dictionary. A Guide to Knowledge as Power*. London.

Sachs, W. (ed.) (1993), *Global Ecology. A New Arena of Political Conflict*. London.

Sachs, W. (1997), "Sustainable Development", in M. Redclift and G. Woodgate (eds), *The Handbook of Environmental Sociology*. London.

Sachverständigenrat für Umweltfragen (SRU) (ed.) (1994), *Umweltgutachten 1994. Für eine dauerhaft-umweltgerechte Entwicklung*. Stuttgart.

Sahlins, M. (1976), *Culture and Practical Reason*. Chicago.

Sanne, C. (1992), "How Much Work?", *Futures*, Jan.–Feb., pp. 23–6.

Schallaböck, K.O. and Hesse, M. (1995), *Konzept für eine Neue Bahn. Schlußbericht*. Wuppertal: WIKUE.

Scherhorn, G. (1994a), "Die Unersättlichkeit der Bedürfnisse und der kalte Stern der Knappheit", in B. Biervert and M. Held (eds), *Das Naturverständnis in der Ökonomik*. Frankfurt et al.

Scherhorn, G. (1994b), "Konsumentenverhalten und Wertewandel", in M. Henze and G. Kaiser (eds), *Ökologie – Dialog*. Düsseldorf, pp. 196–221.

Scherhorn, G. (1994c), *Güterwohlstand versus Zeitwohlstand. Über die Unvereinbarkeit des materiellen und immateriellen Produktivitätsbegriffs. Fachtagung Zeit in der Ökonomik*. Ev. Akademie Tutzing.

Schipper, L. and Meyers, S. (1992), *Energy Efficiency and Human Activity. Past Trends and Future Prospects*. Cambridge.

Schlesinger, W.H. (1991), *Biogeochemistry. An Analysis of Global Change*. San Diego et al.

Schmidt, G. (1996), "Kann man die Welt ernähren?", *Ökologie und Landbau*, 2, p. 3.

Schmidt-Bleek, F. (1994a), *Wieviel Umwelt braucht der Mensch? MIPS – Das Maß für ökologisches Wirtschaften*. Berlin.

Schmidt-Bleek, F. (ed.) (1994b), *Carnoules Declaration. Factor 10 Club*. Wuppertal: WIKUE.

Schor, J. (1995), "Can the North Stop Consumption Growth? Escaping the Cycle of Work and Spend", in V. Bhaskar and A. Glyn (eds), *The North, the South, and the Environment*. London, pp. 68–84.

Schramm, E. et al. (1994), *Abschlußbericht Teilprojekt Modellanalyse für das BMBF-Forschung Wasserkreislauf und urban-ökologische Entwicklung*. Frankfurt.

Schulze, G. (1993a), "Soziologie des Wohlstands", in E.U. Huster (ed.), *Reichtum in Deutschland*. Frankfurt, pp. 182–209.

Seifried, D. and Stark, N. (1994), *Energiedienstleistungen. Strategien und Marktansätze für eine ökologische Energieversorgung*. Freiburg: Öko-Institut.

Shah and Larsen (1992), *Carbon Taxes, the Greenhouse Effect and Developing Countries*. Washington, DC.

Sharan, H. and Sharan-Meili, A. (1994), *Joint Implementation for Global Sustainability. Principles and Criteria*. Seuzach: DASAG Energy Engineering Ltd.

Sharma, R. (1995), *Evaluation of "Zukunftsfähiges Deutschland"*. New Delhi.

Shiva, V. (1993), "Patenting Life Forms. Why Ecologists Should Worry about the Dunkel Draft", *Third World Resurgence*, 35, pp. 2–4.

South Centre (1991), *Environment and Development. Towards a Common Strategy for the South in the UNCED Negotiations and Beyond.* Genf.

Soyinka, W. (1991), "So nicht, meine Herren Präsidenten", *Die Tageszeitung*, 5.6.

Stahel, W.R. (1994), "Innovation braucht Nachhaltigkeit", in K. Backhaus and H. Bonus (eds), *Die Beschleunigungsfalle oder der Triumph der Schildkröte.* Stuttgart.

Statistisches Bundesamt (StaBu) (ed.) (1994), *Statistisches Jahrbuch für die Bundesrepublik Deutschland 1994.* Wiesbaden.

Statistisches Bundesamt (StaBu) (ed.) (various years), *Fachserie 4. Produzierendes Gewerbe. Reihe 3.1. Produktion im produzierenden Gewerbe.* Wiesbaden.

Statistisches Bundesamt (StaBu) (ed.) (various years), *Fachserie 4. Produzierendes Gewerbe. Reihe 4.1.1. Beschäftigte, Umsatz und Energieversorgung der Betriebe im Bergbau und im Verarbeitenden Gewerbe.* Wiesbaden.

Statistisches Bundesamt (StaBu) (ed.) (various years), *Fachserie 4. Produzierendes Gewerbe. Reihe 8.1. Eisen und Stahl.* Wiesbaden.

Statistisches Jahrbuch der Stahlindustrie (ed.) (various years), *Wirtschaftsvereinigung Stahl und Verband der Deutschen Eisenhüttenleute.* Düsseldorf.

Stüben, H. (1992), "Sinkt der Ozonwert, wächst die Gefahr", *Kieler Nachrichten*, 4.7.

Suliman, M. (1995), *Evaluation of the "Zukunftsfähiges Deutschland" Study.* London.

Tatom, J. (1991), "Public Capital and Private Sector Performance", *The Federal Reserve Bank of St Louis Review*, 73, pp. 3–15.

Teufel, D. et al. (1994), *Entwicklung der CO_2-Emissionen der BRD seit 1987.* UPI-Bericht No. 33. Heidelberg: UPI.

Theobald, R. (1967), *The Guaranteed Income.* New York.

Thomas, F. and Vögel, R. (1993), *Gute Argumente – Ökologische Landwirtschaft.* Munich.

Tibbs, H.B.C. (1992), "Industrial Ecology. An Environmental Agenda for Industry", *Whole Earth Review*, pp. 4ff.

Tobin, J. (1994), "Eine Steuer auf internationale Devisentransaktionen", in UNDP, *Human Development Report* 1994. New York et al., p. 81.

Turner, T. (1995), *The Conserver Society. Alternatives for Sustainability.* London.

Umweltbundesamt (UBA) (ed.) (1993), *Stellungnahme zur Verkehrsanhörung der Enquete-Kommission "Schutz des Menschen und der Umwelt". Mobilität – Darstellung, Bewertung und Optimierung von Stoffströmen.* Kommissionsdrucksache 12/10a. Berlin.

Umweltbundesamt (UBA) (ed.) (1994a), *Daten zur Altpapieraufbereitung.* UBA-Texte No. 19. Berlin.

Umweltbundesamt (UBA) (ed.) (1994b), *Stoffliche Belastung der Gewässer durch die Landwirtschaft und Maßnahmen zu ihrer Verringerung.* UBA-Berichte No. 2. Berlin.

Umweltbundesamt (UBA) (ed.) (1995a), *Nachhaltige Entwicklung erfordert langfristige Umweltqualitätsziele.* Presse-Information No. 28. Berlin.

Umweltbundesamt (UBA) (ed.) (1995b), "CO_2-Minderungsszenario für den Verkehr". Paper dated 29 March.

Umweltbundesamt (UBA) and Statistisches Bundesamt (StaBU) (eds) (1995), *Umweltdaten Deutschland 1995.* Berlin.

UNCTAD (United Nations Conference on Trade and Development) (ed.) (1992), *Combating Global Warming. Study on a Global System of Tradeable Carbon Emission Entitlements.* New York.

UNCTAD (United Nations Conference on Trade and Development) (ed.) (1994a), *Combating Global Warming. Possible Rules, Regulations and Administrative Arrangements for a Global Market in CO_2 Emission Entitlements.* New York.

UNCTAD (United Nations Conference on Trade and Development) (ed.) (1994b), *Handbook of International Trade and Development Statistics 1993.* Genf.

UNCTAD (United Nations Conference on Trade and Development) (ed.) (1995), *Controlling Carbon Dioxide Emissions. The Tradable Permit System.* Genf.

UNDP (United Nations Development Programme) (ed.) (1994), *Human Development Report 1994.* New York et al.

United Nations Economic and Social Council (ECOSOC) (ed.) (1995), *General Discussion of Progress in the Implementation of Agenda 21, Focussing the Cross-Sectoral Components of Agenda 21 and Critical Elements of Sustainability.* Draft decision submitted to the chairman. April.

Vanden Stichele, M. and Pennartz, P. (eds) (1996), *Making It Our Business – European NGO Campaigns on Transnational Corporations.* London: Catholic Institute for International Relations.

Walter, B. (1994), *Die Auswirkungen der EU-Agrarexportsubventionen am Beispiel der Getreideexporte nach Afrika. epd-Entwicklungspolitik Materialien I.* Frankfurt.

Walter, T. (1989), *Basic Income. Freedom from Poverty, Freedom to Work.* London.

Walz, R. (1995), *Synopse aktueller Konzepte von nationalen Umweltindikatoren. Zweiter Zwischenbericht zum Forschungsvorhaben zur Weiterentwicklung von Indikatorensystemen für die Umweltberichterstattung.* Karlsruhe: FhG ISI.

Weber, C. and Fahl, U. (1993), "Energieverbrauch und Bedürfnisbefriedigung. Eine Analyse mit Hilfe der energetischen Input–Output-Rechnung", in *Energiewirtschaftliche Tagesfragen*, 9, pp. 605–12.

Weizsäcker, E.U. von (1994a), *Earth Politics.* London.

Weizsäcker, E.U. von (ed.) (1994b), *Umweltstandort Deutschland. Argumente gegen die ökologische Phantasielosigkeit.* Berlin.

Weizsäcker, E.U. von and Jessinghaus, J. (1992), *Ecological Tax Reform.* London.

Weizsäcker, E.U. von et al. (1997), *Factor Four. Doubling Wealth – Halving Resource Use.* London.

Weterings, R. and Opschoor, J.B. (1992), *Ecocapacity as a Challenge to Technical Development.* No. 74a. Rijswijk: Advisory Council for Research on Nature and Environment (RMNO).

Whitelegg, J. (1993), *Transport for a Sustainable Future. The Case for Europe.* London.

Wiemann, J. (1994), *Entwicklungspolitik nach der Uruguay-Runde.* Berlin: Deutsches Institut für Entwicklungspolitik.

Winkler, B. (1995), "Die Praxis der Stadterneuerung und Stadtentwicklung in Europa". Lecture to the 1. Xantener Stadtkongress 8.-10.3., Europäische Schule für Städteplanung. Xanten.

Wissenschaftlicher Beirat für Globale Umweltveränderungen der Bundesregierung (WBGU) (ed.) (1993), *Welt im Wandel. Grundstruktur globaler Mensch-Umwelt-Beziehungen.* Bonn.

Wissenschaftlicher Beirat für Globale Umweltveränderungen der Bundesregierung (WBGU) (ed.) (1994), *Welt im Wandel. Die Gefährdung der Böden.* Bremerhaven.

Wohlgenannt, L. and Büchele, H. (1990), *Den öko-sozialen Umbau beginnen. Grundeinkommen.* Vienna.

Wood, A. (1992), "The Interim Multilateral Fund for Implementation of the Montreal Protocol", in D. Reed (ed.), *The Global Environment Facility. Sharing Responsibility for the Biosphere.* Vol. 2. Washington, DC: WWF.

World Bank (ed.) (1992), *World Development Report.* New York.

World Bank (ed.) (1994), *World Debt Tables 1994–95.* Vol. I. Washington, DC.

World Bank (ed.) (1995a), *World Tables 1995.* Baltimore.

World Bank (ed.) (1995b), *World Development Report 1995. Workers in an Integrating World.* Oxford.

World Commission on Environment and Development (WCED) (1987), *Our Common Future.* Greven.

World Energy Council (ed.) (1992), "Energy for Tomorrow's World – the Realities, the Real Options and the Agenda for Achievement"; Draft Summary Global Report. London.

World Resources Institute (WRI) (ed.) (1992), *World Resources 1992/93.* New York et al.

World Resources Institute (WRI) (ed.) (1994), *World Resources 1994/95.* New York et al.

World Wide Fund for Nature (WWF) (eds) (1995), The UN Biodiversity Convention and the WTO TRIPS Agreement, Gland.

Young, J. and Sachs, A. (1994) *The Next Efficiency Revolution, Creating a Sustainable Materials Economy.* Worldwatch Paper No. 121. Washington, DC.

Young, M.D. (ed.) (1991), *Towards Sustainable Agricultural Development.* London.

Zängl, W. (1993), *ICE – Die Geisterbahn.* Munich.

Index

Zed Titles on Sustainable Development in the North

Too often sustainable development is regarded as an issue primarily of relevance to developing countries. In a range of titles, Zed Books has sought to combat this notion and to contribute to the debate – at the level of shifts in paradigm as well as changes in policy – on the necessity of transforming our present economic and industrial model in order to create systems and institutions in genuine long-term harmony with the environment in the North as well as the South.

Ecological Economics

A Practical Programme for Global Reform

Group of Green Economists

In this book the Group of Green Economists – who are associated with the German Greens, but draw on the thinking of various environmental, women's and human-rights movements – argue that there are practical alternatives to the vast inequalities and social and environmental dislocation caused by two centuries of market-led industrialization and European colonial rule. These alternatives are based on the principles of ecological balance, democracy, social equality, feminism, non-violence and respect for cultural identity and diversity.

In policy terms, this means an ecological and social reshaping of industrial society and a policy towards the Third World that abandons the cul-de-sac of 'development' and instead considers the world economy as a whole.

With these ideas in mind, the authors propose basic principles for a global ecological economy, and produce striking suggestions for restructuring international trade, reorganizing the global financial system, controlling transnational corporations and building both an all-European economic order that transcends the EC and a global economy relevant to the needs of all humanity.

'A most valuable contribution to the debate.' Sara Parkin

'*Ecological Economics* is one of the finest attempts to develop a comprehensive concept of world economics based on ecology and solidarity.' Acharya Shambhushivananda, *New Renaissance*

'This manifesto should appeal to economists, politicians and others interested in another approach to development at home and abroad.' *Nature and Resources*, UNESCO

ISBN 1 85649 069 6 Hb
1 85649 070 X Pb

Economists and the Environment

What the Top Economists Say About the Environment

Carla Ravaioli

Economics has without doubt proved to be the most influential branch of social science in the twentieth century. As we approach the millennium, the destabilization of the environment is widely perceived to be the most serious threat to human existence. But how are economic development and environmental disequilibrium connected? What does economics have to say on one of the most urgent and fundamental questions of our times?

In this extraordinary book some of the world's most eminent economists from a range of different intellectual positions engage in conversation with Carla Ravaioli. The results are always compelling, sometimes illuminating, more often profoundly disturbing.

In the second part of the book, Paul Ekins provides an overview of the state of resource and environmental economics, and spells out the paradigmatic shift the discipline must effect if it is to be of use in fashioning a radical new kind of environmentally sustainable and humane economic system.

'This book poses a challenge to the social responsibility of professional economists, and a scientific and political challenge to their competence.' James F. Becker, former Professor of Economics at New York University

Carla Ravaioli is a writer, feminist and former Italian senator whose previous books have dealt mainly with social issues. **Paul Ekins** is the author of *The Living Economy: A New Economics in the Making.*

Economists interviewed include (among others):

Abel Gezevic Agambegian, Elmar Altvater, Gary B. Becker, Mercedes Bresso, Herman E. Daly, Milton Friedman, John K. Galbraith, Nicholas Georgescu-Roegen, Frank H. Hahn, Volkmar Hartje, Albert O. Hirschman, Wassily Leontief, Juan Martinez-Alier, James E. Meade, James O'Connor, David W. Pearce, Paul A. Samuelson, Stanislav Sergeevic Shatalin, Herbert A. Simon, Robert M. Solow, Immanuel Wallerstein.

ISBN 1 85649 277 X Hb
1 85649 278 8 Pb

The Conserver Society

Alternatives for Sustainability

Ted Trainer

Over the past twenty years many writers have explained why the way of life we take for granted in the rich countries is unsustainable, and why it is impossible for all people in the world to adopt such a resource-intensive way of living. Ted Trainer moves the agenda on to the new forms a sustainable society might take. He shows that practical and attractive alternatives exist and that, although the transition to an ecologically sustainable and just world must involve huge changes, it could yield a higher quality of life than most people, North or South, currently experience.

Ted Trainer describes the many viable alternatives already in existence regarding housing, food production, energy, the design of settlements, the development of a new economy, and the shift to new values. He argues that the essential principles of sustainability must be more materially simple living standards and small-scale, self-sufficient local economies. He discusses actual examples of alternative communities, and offers a strategy for people to begin moving their own communities in that direction.

As people around the world begin to grapple with how to implement Agenda 21 in the wake of the Earth Summit, this book provides not only a source of inspiration but also a demonstration that new ways of doing things can work.

'The scale and scope of the environmental crisis is now widely understood. The difficult challenge is doing something about it that goes beyond recycling and taking the bus. Ted Trainer's book provides us with a vision of where we are heading and a concrete strategy that each of us can start to work on. Now we don't have the excuse of saying "What can I do?"' Dr David Suzuki

'The book is refreshing in its principled stance and zestful practicality.' Piers H.G. Stephens, *Environmental Politics*

ISBN 1 85649 275 3 Hb
1 85649 276 1 Pb

Silenced Rivers

The Ecology and Politics of Large Dams

Patrick McCully

'Patrick McCully's *Silenced Rivers* could not come at a better time. It's all here. The power and the glory, the money and the lies, the fear, the broken dreams, the inescapable geological, financial and ecological realities. And, from California to India to Nepal to China, the grassroots resistance.... You need a good book on dams. Here it is.' Tom Athanasiou, author of *Divided Planet: The Ecology of Rich and Poor*

'Superlative ... enormously instructive information for those seeking to learn about the astonishing array of impacts caused by damming rivers and what is being done to look at alternatives and to resist the powerful dam-building lobby. McCully's book should be required reading for all politicians and a prime text for engineering schools.' Brent Blackwelder, President, Friends of the Earth USA

'The most thorough and devastating critique of the global dam-building industry that I know. It shows convincingly how the conquest of nature is an outmoded and dangerous idea.' Donald Worster, Hall Distinguished Professor of American History, University of Kansas

'The best-researched, best-written account ever of what we have done to our rivers. McCully lays it all out – the tragedy, the waste, the vainglory, and the profits. And he provides hardheaded evidence that there are much more sensible ways of dealing with these bountiful and beautiful aspects of creation.' Catherine Caufield, author of *In the Rainforest*

'McCully graphically enumerates what errors have been perpetrated; now it is up to dam proponents to learn from this warning and strive for sustainability.' Robert Goodland, Environment Department, World Bank

Patrick McCully has captured the legacy of man's bad judgement on the control of rivers and the resulting loss of ecosystem diversity, environmental health and biodiversity. This book should be required reading for all those who think that control of rivers is the solution to man's problems.' Dave Wegner, US Department of the Interior, Glen Canyon Environmental Studies

ISBN 1 85649 435 7 Hb
1 85649 436 5 Pb

The Eco Principle

Ecology and Economics in Symbiosis

Arthur Lyon Dahl
Foreword by Elizabeth Dowdeswell

The really important books are those that provide ideas for a fundamental recasting of our thinking and institutions. This is such a book.

At a time when most societies have lost all sense of control and direction, this book not only explains why present economic and political systems are not working, but integrates economic, environmental, social and spiritual dimensions into a new paradigm for understanding and changing them. Instead of our usual thinking in terms of mechanical analogies and essentially static entities, the author introduces the notion of Ecos. This, he argues, provides a more accurate portrayal of the real world as a complex 'nested' structure of interacting, dynamic and constantly changing systems. He then applies this analytical approach based on the time-proven organic systems of the natural world to our understanding of human institutions. He shows how these are not immutable, but shaped by our values and understanding. This opens the way to a more integrated view of the solutions required for the economic, environmental and social problems we face.

'A beautifully written and well reasoned book with conclusions that are thought-provoking.' Carl Djerassi, Professor of Chemistry, Stanford University

'There is nothing more exciting than to read the minds of those ... thinking beyond the cutting edge of issues before society.' Lawrence Arturo, Director, Office of Environment, Baha'i International Community

'I really like the way [this book] brings together Economics and Ecology and moves towards ideas for a new paradigm.' Dorothy Marcic, Fulbright Scholar, Czech Management Centre

'It is rare to find an approach that is ... equally appropriate to the industrialized and developing countries.' Elizabeth Dowdeswell, Executive Director, UNEP

ISBN 1 85649 433 0 Hb
1 85649 434 9 Pb

Other Titles of Related Interest from Zed

From the Ground Up
Rethinking Industrial Agriculture
Peter Goering, Helena Norberg Hodge and John Page
1 85649 223 0 Hb 1 85649 224 9 Pb

World of Waste
Dilemmas of Industrial Development
K.A. Gourlay
0 86232 988 4 Hb 0 86232 989 4 Pb

In the Wake of the Affluent Society
An Exploration of Post-Development
Serge Latouche
1 85649 171 4 Hb 1 85649 172 2 Pb

Responding to Global Warming
The Technology, Economics and Politics of Sustainable Energy
Peter Read
1 85649 161 7 Hb 1 85649 162 5 Pb

State of the World's Mountains
A Global Report
Peter Stone (ed.)
1 85649 115 3 Hb 1 85649 116 1 Pb

Earth Politics
Ernst von Weizsacker
1 85649 173 0 Hb 1 85649 174 9 Pb

Ecological Tax Reform
A Policy Proposal for Sustainable Development
Ernst von Weizsacker and Jesinghaus
1 85649 095 5 Hb 1 85649 096 3 Pb

In the Servitude of Power
Energy and Civilization through the Ages
J. Debeir, Jean-Paul Deléage and Daniel Hémery
0 86232 942 6 Hb 0 86232 943 4 Pb